D0871956

Never Enough

Never Enough

CAPITALISM AND THE PROGRESSIVE SPIRIT

Neil Gilbert

OXFORD
UNIVERSITY PRESS

Oxford University Press is a department of the University of Oxford. It furthers
the University's objective of excellence in research, scholarship, and education
by publishing worldwide. Oxford is a registered trade mark of Oxford University
Press in the UK and certain other countries.

Published in the United States of America by Oxford University Press
198 Madison Avenue, New York, NY 10016, United States of America.

© Oxford University Press 2017

All rights reserved. No part of this publication may be reproduced, stored in
a retrieval system, or transmitted, in any form or by any means, without the
prior permission in writing of Oxford University Press, or as expressly permitted
by law, by license, or under terms agreed with the appropriate reproduction
rights organization. Inquiries concerning reproduction outside the scope of the
above should be sent to the Rights Department, Oxford University Press, at the
address above.

You must not circulate this work in any other form
and you must impose this same condition on any acquirer.

Library of Congress Cataloging-in-Publication Data
Names: Gilbert, Neil, author.
Title: Never enough : capitalism and the progressive spirit / Neil Gilbert.
Description: Oxford; New York : Oxford University Press, [2017] |
Includes bibliographical references and index. | Description based on print version
record and CIP data provided by publisher; resource not viewed.
Identifiers: LCCN 2016019254 (print) | LCCN 2016011765 (ebook) |
ISBN 9780199361342 (e-book) | ISBN 9780199361335 (alk. paper)
Subjects: LCSH: Welfare state—United States. | Capitalism—Social aspects—United States. |
Equality—United States. | Distributive justice—United States. | Social justice—United States.
Classification: LCC HV91 (print) | LCC HV91 .G453 2017 (ebook) | DDC 361.6/50973—dc23
LC record available at https://lccn.loc.gov/2016019254

9 8 7 6 5 4 3 2 1

Printed by Sheridan Books, Inc., United States of America

For Evan, Jesse, Nathaniel, and Nicole

CONTENTS

ACKNOWLEDGMENTS

Writing this book was at once a solitary affair between the author and his keyboard as well as an activity nurtured by the intellectual companionship of many people. I am particularly grateful to Skip Battle, Douglas Besharov, Richard De Neufville, Bekki Gilbert, and Richard Scheffler, whose wisdom and good counsel have benefited me over the decades. Through countless conversations their critical observations have honed my thinking about the social and economic issues examined in these pages.

While working on this book, I had the good fortune to participate in a three-year project on *The Social Contract Revisited: The Modern Welfare State*, which was sponsored by the Foundation for Law, Justice and Society in association with the Center for Socio-Legal Studies at the University of Oxford. Our biannual workshops encouraged thoughtful exchange among scholars from different disciplines and embraced a wide range of political perspectives on social policy issues. One lively meeting included a law professor who had resigned from the Clinton Administration in protest against the 1996 welfare reform and a political scientist whose work provided much of the intellectual drive behind that legislation. These learned gatherings offered a congenial atmosphere for the give and take of academic discourse, thanks to the good offices of Amir Paz Fuchs, Denis Galligan, John Adams, Judy Niner, and Phil Dines.

The Organization for Economic Cooperation and Development's 2009 conference on Measuring Poverty, Income Inequality, and Social Exclusion— Lessons from Europe provided a venue in which to test out some of my initial thoughts about contemporary measures of material deprivation. I wish to thank the editors of the *American Interest* for permission to incorporate a revised and expanded version of my reflections on "What Poverty Means," which appeared in the August 2012 issue of that magazine. I am also indebted to the National Research Foundation of Korea for support in the early stages of research for this book and to Zach Morris for his comments on several chapters. Although stretching the deadlines may have tried his patience, throughout the process Dana Bliss at Oxford University Press was a continuous source of encouragement and sound editorial advice, delivered with a gentle touch.

In challenging widespread assumptions about social conditions in America, *Never Enough* is likely to raise some hackles. Thus, I am obliged to say that although this work has profited from the guidance and critical contributions of the fine people and organizations mentioned earlier, none of them bear any responsibility for my interpretation of the evidence. Indeed, I expect that few of them would fully agree with all that follows.

I owe a long-standing debt to the family members who established the Milton and Gertrude Chernin Chair in Social Services and Social Welfare at the University of California, Berkeley, which afforded me the time and resources to pursue this project. Finally, I want to express my heartfelt appreciation to my wife, Bekki, and our children, Nathaniel and Nicole, whose unfailing warmth and good humor were a constant source of comfort.

Never Enough

Introduction

1

The Progressive Spirit

In 2009 a group of scholars met at Oxford University to consider the effects of the recession on modern welfare states. Chairing one of the sessions, my job was to summarize and comment on several of the papers prepared for this learned gathering. In such instances it is customary to offer a few complimentary remarks followed by a mild critique, usually disguised as questions, intended to spark the conversation. One of the papers expressed deep concern that since the 1990s inequality had increased in the welfare states of prosperous nations—those that qualified for membership in the Organization for Economic Co-operation and Development (OECD). I asked whether, in wealthy countries such as these, increasing inequality was necessarily a matter of grave consequence—or indeed of any concern to the average citizen.

In that company it was, perhaps, a bit provocative. But intellectual discourse is enlivened by the clash of competing ideas. This one seemed worth exploring. Although a few of the people around the table were much wealthier than the rest of us, the overall level of well-being in our microcosmic society made that economic inequality almost irrelevant. If the floor is high enough, why worry about the ceiling? The stock answer would likely refer to the oft-cited studies which show that people tend to place more importance on their financial position relative to others than on their absolute standard of living and that inequality produces troubling social consequences. Indeed, I expected to hear a recitation of the empirical findings frequently invoked to extol the many benefits of equality, including health, happiness, and reduced stress. And I was prepared to respond.

Instead, the discussion opened (and closed) with an expression of disbelief from one my distinguished colleagues: "Neil, how can you say that about inequality? It's, it's its," he stammered struggling for the right word, "BASIC." A gentle scholar, he did not want to condemn me too harshly for desecrating the hallowed grounds of progressive thought. The silence that followed signified a firm consensus that the subject of economic inequality bore no further contemplation. It started me wondering about the topic for this book and places that progressive thought dared not go.

Six months later I participated in a symposium on "What Is Living and What Is Dead in Social Democracy?" organized by Tony Judt. The title was drawn from a piece that he had recently published in the *New York Review of Books*.[1] It was an impassioned appeal to revive the waning influence of social democracy by one of the foremost public intellectuals of the late twentieth century. Though other publications followed, this plea was in a way Judt's swan song. Suffering the final stages of ALS (Lou Gehrig's disease), he arrived at the conference table in a motorized wheelchair, physically immobilized and on a breathing machine—and joined the conversation as if nothing else mattered beyond the quest for fresh ideas to rejuvenate the ailing system of social democracy. Eyeing the future, he argued for the need to engage the next generation of progressive scholars, while staring down a fatal illness. The force of Judt's intellectual spirit remains firmly etched in my mind and also, I would expect, in those of the other participants.[2]

According to Judt, the very success of the progressive agenda in the twentieth century has dampened present-day support for social democracy. The welfare state has become such an integral part of the institutional landscape of modern capitalist democracies that the core progressive assumptions about its duties are embedded across the political spectrum in advanced industrial societies—though they may vary in scope and method of implementation. The result, as Judt acknowledged, is that progressive social democratic parties are left with nothing distinctive to offer.[3]

This state of affairs was anticipated in Daniel Bell's classic analysis of the "end of ideology," which detected a rough consensus among intellectuals in the Western world concerning "the acceptance of the Welfare State, the desirability of decentralized power, a system of mixed economy and of political pluralism."[4] In this context it would be difficult to mobilize labor for social change. Although the working class had not achieved utopia, Bell argued, "their expectations were less than that of intellectuals and their gains correspondingly larger." Foreseeing the malaise that Judt wished to alleviate, Bell observed that the middle way between socialism and capitalism was for the middle-aged and held little appeal as a unifying cause for the next generation of reform-oriented progressives.[5] The prognosis was correct, but a bit premature.

Although the welfare state was accepted (if not entirely embraced) in 1960 by most serious thinkers on the Left and the Right, considerable work remained to be done by progressive reformers in bringing it to maturity. As with Bell's end of ideology, Gunnar Myrdal observed the convergence of political attitudes accelerating the expansion of the welfare state. The agreement among political parties was such that he noticed "they sometimes even compete in propagating new and constantly more sweeping redistributional reforms;" and when conservative parties came to power, they rarely sought to retract earlier advances.[6]

Published in 1960, both Myrdal and Bell's analyses appeared well before the immense growth spurt, which over the next two decades would double the size of welfare state expenditures relative to GDP in nineteen wealthy OECD nations. When Judt's distress about the declining enthusiasm for social democracy was voiced in 2009, social spending (including education) by these more fully developed welfare states averaged almost 30 percent of their GDPs compared to the 13 percent in 1960.[7] With shrinking room for continued expansion, aging populations, growing competition from around the globe, heavy obligations to finance existing social welfare benefits, and new demands from single-parent and two-earner families, the mature welfare state entered the twenty-first century under considerable fiscal duress.

Did social democracy have something new to offer? The symposium was organized to address Judt's concern about the current state of social democracy and its future directions. As to where things now stand, a lively discussion conveyed much dissatisfaction with the ascendancy of economic liberalism and increasing public resistance to government spending. One of social democracy's greatest achievements, the modern welfare state, was seen as abandoning the progressive ideal of universal benefits delivered by public agencies to protect labor from the uncertainties of the market. This was true. Although social welfare expenditures continued to rise, the welfare state was indeed moving on a new course. Forsaking the progressive formula, since the 1990s a wave of welfare reforms had advanced the private delivery of aid to those most in need with the objectives promoting labor force participation and individual responsibility.[8]

Scholarly efforts to express these changes spawned the Schumpeterian Workfare State, the Hollow State, the Contract State, the Enabling State, the Social Investment State, the Active State, the Third Way, and the Post-Modern Welfare State.[9] Habitually striving for social discovery, academics are sometimes too quick to paste new labels on old ideas. But in this case the various bids to rebrand the welfare state signify more than academic claims to naming rights. They reflect the numerous welfare reforms introduced to check the mounting costs of social benefits and to adapt to the competitive demands of markets in the global economy of the twenty-first century.[10] These measures were also triggered by worldwide concerns that modern welfare states were undermining the work ethic. The United States had its notorious image of the Cadillac-driving "welfare queen";[11] Denmark had "Carina," the pseudonym for a single mother collecting a hefty $2,700 a month on welfare;[12] the Netherlands had the "Dutch Disease," an exceptionally high dependency ratio attributed to the generosity of its social benefits;[13] and even in Sweden, in the early 1990s Prime Minister Bildt declared that benefit levels had become so high as to reduce the incentives to work.[14]

Throughout the twentieth century, the welfare state served in many ways as an institutional counterforce to capitalism. In the twenty-first century while continuing to provide a substantial safety net it has evolved into an institutional support of capitalism, which seeks to enhance productivity and personal responsibility. Once offering a cushion of financial aid to those in need, the social safety net guywires have tightened to form a trampoline that quickly bounces welfare recipients back into paid employment. Whether the shift toward market-oriented welfare has gone too far or not far enough depends largely on how one views the appropriate relationship between the state and the market as well as the level of economic well-being and communal security that should be assured by the state.

When Judt's symposium turned to explore alternative futures, the conversation was driven by critical appraisals of contemporary welfare reforms. This concentrated the participants' aspirations for the future of social democracy on the established progressive agenda of expanding universal public benefits along the lines of the Scandinavian welfare state model.[15] However, universal pensions, health care, education, disability insurance, unemployment insurance, and an array of children and family benefits are already routinely available in most advanced welfare states. The social reforms being argued by policymakers on the ground involve questions about increasing the standard age of retirement by a few years, extending or reducing the length of unemployment compensation, means-testing various social benefits, outsourcing social services to private providers, and the like. These are not trivial matters. But they fail to forge a distinctive vision of social democracy that would inspire the next generation of progressives. Most are incremental reforms that rely upon numbers crunching, model building, and cost–benefit evaluations, which have a certain technical appeal to social science policy analysts, especially economists—hardly grist for the mill of a progressive social movement.

Though one might expect the 2008 recession would have stimulated public support for the progressive-oriented welfare state, it was not to be, as evidenced in the United States by the results of the 2010 midterm election.[16] The conservative landslide was less a rejection of the US welfare state than recognition of the need to limit its reach. Similarly, in Europe the conservative victories in Germany, England, Sweden, and elsewhere confirmed Judt's assessment that social democrats had little that was new to offer. By 2015, Republicans controlled both houses of Congress, conservative Prime Minister David Cameron won a majority in Britain, Chancellor Angela Merkel continued to reign in Germany, Erna Solberg was the conservative prime minister of Norway, and France's socialist President Francois Hollande's approval rating stood at a dismal 20 percent.

Unlike public support for government spending in the early 1930s, the 2008 recession generated no strong political demand for expanding the welfare state in part because of public concerns that the cost of government spending was approaching unsustainable levels. But even more to the point, the safety nets already in place had automatically stretched to cushion the recession's impact. In nineteen of the major OECD countries, the level of public spending on social programs expanded on average by more than 10 percent between 2007 and 2009.[17]

Progressive Spirit Gone Adrift

I recall the issues raised in these academic gatherings because they crystallized my increasing intellectual discomfort with the conventional progressive attitude and highlight some of the reasons for this book, which seeks to explain the progressive spirit and why it has gone adrift in the twenty-first century.

But first a few words about the term "progressive," a colloquial vessel into which different identities may be poured. Historically it brings to mind the political activists and their supporters who advanced the minimum wage, women's right to vote, the abolition of child labor, and other worthy causes during the late nineteenth and early twentieth century—a period known as the Progressive Era. By the 1960s the designation for political activists promoting social reforms in the United States had morphed into "liberals." The 1960s liberal creed is not to be confused with the ideology of classical liberalism, which favored limited government intervention. Within a few decades, the 1960s liberal brand was tarnished in part by cultural identification with pot-smoking, free-loving, sandal-clad hippies. Additionally, it suffered from the political realignment of the Reagan Revolution, which cast government not as the solution to the difficulties of that era, but as the problem. In recent times there has been a linguistic shift as those who used to be identified as liberals have adopted the progressive label. Although one may draw nuanced distinctions between progressives and liberals, they hold in common a high regard for the role of government as an instrument to curb the destructive forces and rectify the distributional shortcomings of capitalism.

There is much to recommend the progressive spirit. From the dawn of the Industrial Revolution through the twentieth century, progressives have sought to improve society by advancing human rights, economic security, and environmental protection. During the twentieth century they achieved a notable record on all of these fronts. Progressives stood at the head of movements to protect the environment and promote the rights of women, children and ethnic, racial, and sexual minorities. But the focal point of their resolve concentrated on material well-being.[18] On this front, their most impressive accomplishment was the unprecedented level of social protection granted to average citizens through the creation of the welfare state.

Over the course of the twentieth century there was an increasing need to cushion the insecurities that emanate from what Joseph Schumpeter described as capitalism's compulsion to incessantly revolutionize "the economic structure from within, incessantly destroying the old, incessantly creating the new."[19] In response to the risk and insecurity generated by this process of "creative destruction," the modern welfare state evolved as a social mechanism to harness the productive forces of capitalism for the common good, securing a modicum of material well-being amidst the uncertainties of the bourgeoning capitalist economy.

Views differ, of course, about how much of the economy should be devoted to the welfare state and exactly where the money should go. When it comes to maintaining the material well-being of average citizens, conservatives clearly favor the invisible hand of the market over the collective measures of the welfare state. Granting this preference, we should not exaggerate the difference between conservative and progressive positions on the appropriate functions of the state. Thomas Carlyle's depiction of "anarchy plus the constable" is sometimes cast as the nineteenth century's classical "liberal" (a school of thought now identified with conservatives) view on the role of the state. This extreme doctrine, however, did not represent the intellectual stance of mainstream liberals. The functions of the state delineated by Adam Smith, for example, included erecting and maintaining public works and public institutions to perform crucial services that would not be profitable in the private market.[20] Similarly, the government cabinet in Jeremy Bentham's utopian system included ministers of health, education, and indigence relief.[21]

While penning a forceful defense of the liberal doctrine, Friedrich Hayek argued that the state should provide a guaranteed minimum income. He found no reason why a society that had reached England's level of wealth should not guarantee a basic measure of security "to all without endangering general freedom."[22] That was in 1944 when the level of wealth he referred to was quite low by current standards; one estimate put the mean income in 1944 at approximately 300 pounds.[23] Recognizing that the precise standard was difficult to stipulate, he allowed it should provide sufficient food, shelter, and clothing to maintain one's health and capacity to work. His main concern was that this economic security should not obstruct the functioning of market competition.

In 1962, Milton Friedman, Nobel Laureate and a founding father of the influential Chicago School of Economics, argued that certain government activity in the realm of social welfare was justified on paternalistic grounds. Friedman understood that this principle was troublesome for conservatives, who might well agree that government should take responsibility for children and mentally incompetent adults. Once this portal to government assistance was opened, however, they would have some difficulty in deciding who to keep out.[24] At what age does childhood end? How do we determine incompetence? Friedman believed, for example, that social security programs were not a legitimate function of government. Yet one of the standard arguments for government's forcing workers to contribute toward their old age retirement is based on the paternalistic view that people are myopic and would not behave responsibly in this regard.[25] Plainly put, normal adults are not competent to plan and save for their old age.

A realist, Friedman understood that the welfare state was here to stay. Softening his stance on the legitimate functions of government, he came out in support of a negative income tax scheme that would provide a guaranteed annual income of $1,200 to a family of four.[26] At the time it was proposed in 1962, Friedman's guaranteed income was $200 below the average payment to public assistance recipients.[27] In 2006, Charles Murray crafted a more generous proposal for a guaranteed income of $10,000 per year for every US citizen 21 years and over, of which $3,000 would have to be used to purchase health insurance.[28]

Both Friedman and Murray's guaranteed income proposals came with the proviso that they would replace all the other public social welfare benefits. The welfare state as we know it would be scrapped along with the entire federal bureaucracy that distributes its benefits. In 1969 President Nixon announced support for the Family Assistance Plan, a guaranteed income program offering $1,600 in cash plus $800 in food stamps for a family of four, which was equivalent to several hundred dollars more than the average welfare grant at that time. This scheme was promoted by Senator Daniel Moynihan, arguably the liveliest intellectual politician of that era. Milton Friedman testified before Congress against the plan because it left many of the existing welfare programs intact. The Family Assistance Plan was defeated, in part, because while it went too far for conservatives like Friedman, it did not go far enough for many on the Left. The National Welfare Rights Organization demanded that the guaranteed income be raised to more than double the $2,400 for a family of four that was on the table.[29]Since the mid-1990s, a long line of proponents across the political spectrum have supported the general idea of a guaranteed income, but not always for the same reasons.[30]

The various schemes set forth in the United States and the fate of Nixon's plan reveal that although progressives and conservatives may move in the same direction, conservatives are driving with one foot on the brake, so to speak, trying to contain the size of government. Progressives are accelerating to reach the next level of social well-being. Like the forces of capitalism, they are incessantly on the move. Inspired by utopian tendencies and a passion for equality that fuels a perpetual search for disparities, the progressive spirit is temperamentally discontent with the current state of affairs. In the constant quest for a better future, progressives are inclined to discount past achievements that quickly form the status quo. In this sense, their glasses are always half empty, which may be why no matter how much social spending increases progressives find that the welfare state never seems to be doing quite enough to address poverty, inequality, and social mobility.

With the rise of corporate capitalism in the twentieth century, the progressive agenda concentrated on strengthening the role of the state vis-à-vis the market economy. Life under capitalism was seen as red in tooth and claw. In 1942 Schumpeter observed a widespread hostility to capitalism that every writer and speaker hastened to emphasize. "Any other attitude," he claimed "is voted not only foolish, but anti-social and looked upon as an indication of immoral servitude." By "every writer and speaker" he was no doubt referring mainly to progressive intellectuals—not those of the free market persuasion, which in that period included liberal economists such as Lionel Robbins, head of the London School of Economics and Friedrich Hayek (whose classic *Road to Serfdom* came out a few years later).

Indeed, capitalism has been viewed in many different lights. From an historical perspective Albert Hirschman argues that the creation of markets redirected human "passions" for honor and glory, typically displayed on battlefields and dueling grounds, into personal "interests" in material gain pursued through commercial channels governed by reason.[31] Thus, capitalism exerted a civilizing influence on humanity by sublimating the instinctual aggression of competitive energies into productive activities.[32] According to Max Weber, capitalism advanced a rational and systematic attitude that restrained impulsive behavior. Under the founding spirit of capitalism, human appetites were tempered by the Protestant ethic and Puritan prudence. In the early stages, work assumed the character of a religious calling, and the accumulation of wealth was evidence of virtue.[33] Daniel Bell suggests that over time those admirable qualities were undermined by the capitalist invention of instant credit. By doing away with the need to save before buying, credit cards permitted the immediate gratification of consumptive urges. As the Protestant ethic eroded, "only hedonism remained, and the capitalist system lost its transcendental ethic."[34]

Whatever the intellectual disdain for capitalism in the 1940s, the collapse of command economies in the Soviet Union in the early 1990s elevated the level of public appreciation for the tremendous productive capacity of the market economy. Hostility toward capitalism, which Schumpeter observed earlier, softened even among progressives on the far Left as the once fashionable thought of replacing the free market with a state-run command economy was consigned to the intellectual dustbin of really bad ideas. But a heightened regard for the material benefits of capitalism only served to enlarge the lingering animosity toward how these benefits get distributed through the free market. Of the many social causes embraced over the decades, none conveys the essence of the progressive spirit more than the continuous effort to regulate what is seen as the distributional problem of a free market.

Although progressives continue to press for more social welfare transfers, political leaders and the general public are concerned about meeting the current and projected costs of what has been already promised for the first half of the twenty-first century. Tony Judt's analysis acknowledged the fading support for social democratic welfare states in the advanced industrial countries. Looking to the future, he called for progressives to bear in mind the achievements of the past, to conserve the gains of modern welfare states, and to ask the questions, What is the good society? and What can the state do well?[35]

These are important questions, which elicit different answers today than in the days before the establishment of modern welfare states. Beyond supporting civil rights for minorities, throughout the twentieth century the progressive vision of what the state can do to advance the good society largely concentrated on assurances of material well-being. Progressives fought to create a broad base of welfare entitlements that would address long-standing concerns about poverty, inequality, and social mobility. The success of these initiatives has been typically measured on a scale of relative income and consumption—having enough to live comfortably, having as much as others in society, and having more than one's parents. At its core, then, the definition of progress rested on solving the economic problem of how to insure a decent standard of living. This is understandable given the wretched slums, minimum standards of living, and daily struggles for survival at the turn of the twentieth century. Adjusted for inflation, the poverty line of $460 per year for a family of five developed by Robert Hunter in 1904 equaled about 43 percent of the official US poverty line for a family of five in the 1960s.[36]

Prevailing Assumptions

To what extent do the economic problems of material need that sparked the mid-twentieth-century progressive welfare state reforms continue to afflict postindustrial countries? This question directs our attention to the ongoing tensions between capitalism and the progressive spirit, which are expressed in prevailing assumptions about what ails modern society. These assumptions guide progressive views on the scale and consequences of the distributional problems of a free market. Capitalism is seen as an economic system that generates widespread social and economic distress.

This progressive view draws on more than just a set of beliefs fashioned to support antipathy toward capitalism. It is based on analyses of social research that are continuously cited to create a shared perception that the distributional flaws of the market economy are responsible for intolerable levels of poverty and inequality, which hamper social mobility and call for additional public spending on universal social programs. A critical reading of the research suggests that while these problems have not been entirely resolved, they are far less serious than contemporary progressive claims would have the public believe. In the modern age of abundance, the twentieth-century struggles for material well-being no longer pose a compelling cause to animate the next generation of progressive thinkers—that is, at least in regard to the wealthy postindustrial democracies. (The next generation is likely to focus increasingly on the crushing poverty and inequality in the less developed countries.)

However, many, if not most, of the current generation of progressive intellectuals, academics, policy experts, and political leaders remain firmly wedded to the established agenda, embracing measures to reduce poverty and economic inequality and to accelerate social mobility through increased public spending on universal benefits. Seeking to eliminate material need through public transfers, this agenda conveys a vision of the good society that disregards the historically unprecedented and widespread abundance in the advanced postindustrial countries. At the same time it inadvertently caters to the corrosive effects of insatiable consumption and the commodification of everyday life, which are encouraged by modern capitalism and from which it profits.

When it comes to dispensing the fruits of capitalist production, conservatives place their faith in the market, imperfect as it may be, to achieve greater efficiency and economic justice than government. Progressives are equally convinced that, left to its own devices, distribution through the market creates unacceptable levels of poverty and inequality. In the name of social justice they argue that these problems need to be addressed through a wide range of institutional transfers by the welfare state. In fact, as it rapidly expanded throughout the twentieth century, the modern welfare state has done just that—delivering massive transfers to mitigate the distributional issues of a free market. A crowning achievement of progressive efforts, the modern welfare state is here to stay. Exactly how much it has accomplished and what else needs to be done about the issues of poverty and inequality are judgments for the reader to make after considering the evidence put forth in this volume.

Challenging the prevailing assumptions about poverty, inequality, social mobility, and welfare spending, this book takes a hard look at issues such as: What does the government's definition of poverty signify in an era of abundance? Are the rich getting richer and the poor getting poorer? To what extent are appraisals of social welfare need an expression of institutionalized discontent? Is the rate of social mobility in the United States on the decline? How does it compare to other wealthy nations? Does economic inequality affect the health and well-being of a wealthy society? To whom does inequality really matter? Is there a political advantage to universal benefits? What is the good society? These questions are addressed to gain a clear understanding of what the empirical evidence tells us about the current state of social and economic affairs in America and its implications for the role of government in cultivating the good society.

Poverty

2

Poverty Amid Abundance

Although the poor may have always been with us, it was not until the late nineteenth century that Charles Booth made the first scientific effort to determine their numbers. From his seminal 1880s survey of the working classes in London up to the mid-twentieth century, the condition of poverty was typically understood as a level of subsistence that barely afforded sufficient food, lodging, and clothing. Booth's estimate put the first poverty line at about 1,000 shillings a year.[1] Around the same time in the United States, Robert Hunter reckoned the figure to be $460 per year for the average family of five in the industrial northern states.[2]

One can quibble about exactly where these lines were drawn, but the living conditions of the poor at that time were such that you knew it when you saw it. Life in poverty was a palpable circumstance visually documented, for example, in Jacob Riss's images of the squalid tenements on Manhattan's Lower East Side and in the Great Depression newsreels of people standing in bread lines and living in Hoovervilles.[3]

Up through the 1930s, progressive reformers campaigned for government to eradicate poverty, an agenda that gained impetus as poverty rose during the Great Depression. With the coming of the New Deal, the principal responsibility for welfare passed from the hands of local communities to federal bureaucracies as the Social Security Act of 1935 laid the foundation of the American welfare state. By the 1940s political concerns for the poor took a back seat to more pressing matters of survival during the years of World War II. Poverty as a public issue continued on the wane throughout the prosperous 1950s.

There was a revival of interest in the early 1960s, when Michael Harrington's evocative account of life in *The Other America* drew public attention to the plight of the poor. The "other America" was a bleak place where at least half of the aged could not afford decent housing, proper nutrition, and adequate medical care, and low-income farm families suffered from "hunger in the midst of abundance."[4] According to Harrington's calculations, about

25 percent of the American people were poor at that time. His work signaled a resurgence of publications that raised national awareness about the conditions of poverty in the United States. Two of five major books on poverty were on the American Library Association's list of the best books in 1962.[5]

Against this tide, however, stood another highly regarded progressive thinker, Harvard professor John Kenneth Galbraith, who cofounded Americans for Democratic Action in 1947 with Eleanor Roosevelt and Arthur Schlesinger Jr., among others. His best-selling 1958 book, *The Affluent Society*, challenged the conventional view of poverty as a major social problem in the United States. Galbraith maintained that in a society where the median family income was $3,960, poverty "can longer be presented as a universal or massive affliction. It is more nearly an afterthought."[6] He was not alone in this judgment. Also writing in the mid-1950s another Harvard professor Alvin Hansen noted, "In the last-half century the American Economy has lifted the standard of living of the mass population to undreamed-of-levels of comfort and luxury. Mass poverty has largely been wiped out."[7] He did allow, however, that a "submerged tenth" of the population remained in need of assistance.

Recognizing that poverty in the United States had not been entirely eliminated, Galbraith described that which remained as falling into two broad categories: insular poverty that stemmed from living in economically depressed regions like Appalachia, and case poverty that was rooted in personal handicaps such as "mental deficiency, bad health, inability to adapt to the discipline of modern economic life, excessive procreation, alcohol, and insufficient education."[8] But in neither instance, he reasoned, could poverty be remedied by government transfers of income that would lighten the hardships and increase the consumption of the poor.[9]

At the turn of the twentieth century, H. G. Wells predicted that industrial society would give rise to the "people of the abyss," a group he described as criminal, immoral, and parasitic and those born with disadvantages that would allow no opportunity to enter the world of work.[10] While Wells flirted with eugenics, which at that time was vaguely fashionable in his circle of Fabian Socialists, Galbraith's solution for addressing the problem of highly disadvantaged groups emphasized social services and educating their children.

From a typically progressive viewpoint, Galbraith envisioned government as the vehicle to advance the good society. But his particular view of what made for a good society did not follow the usual prescription for material betterment through redistribution of income to the poor. Instead, he favored curbing what he saw as the mindless materialism spawned by the market. Galbraith argued that modern consumer demand was driven not by the spontaneous needs of individuals but by the calculated contrivances of advertising, a phenomenon he labeled the "dependence effect." Galbraith's book appeared shortly after Vance Packard's popular 1957 expose, *The Hidden*

Persuaders, which unveiled the advertising industry's psychological efforts to manipulate consumer appetites.[11] There is no reason to think that Packard formed Galbraith's view; it merely deepened a long-held conviction. If he were writing today, Galbraith would no doubt mention that modern technology has taken these efforts to another level of sophistication as consumer tastes are increasingly being fed by online advertising that targets messages closely tailored to previous purchasing patterns.[12]

Not everyone agreed. The conservative economist Friedrich Hayek dismissed the "dependence effect" as a non sequitur, since consumers have no innate or spontaneous desires for any of the amenities of modern civilization, from Apple iPods to the novels of C. P. Snow. As Steve Jobs observed, "A lot of times people don't know what they want until you show it to them."[13] Advertising is simply the method producers use to provide this information in the most favorable light. Hayek might have added that today online shopper services such as Yelp and Trip Advisor allow consumers to learn more about the quality of products and services from the experiences of others. Given a choice between public and private spending, Hayek would leave the money in the consumer's pocketbook.[14]

In contrast to Hayek's case for private spending, the thrust of Galbraith's analysis supported trimming private consumption that satisfies manufactured desires for all sorts of trivial stuff that add little to the quality of life. Thus, although he proposed increased taxation, it was not for direct cash transfers to the poor but rather for greater investment in public services that would enhance community life and build human capital through, for example, educational programs for disadvantaged children. Galbraith's appeal to boost public spending and his inclination to deal with poverty through increased investment in services rather than cash transfers foreshadowed a major shift in the nature of modern welfare states toward social investments to enable productivity and individual responsibility. But in the early 1960s, his view that poverty had become and should remain an "afterthought" in federal policy fell behind the curve when President Johnson declared the War on Poverty in 1964. Galbraith's assessment of the relation between increasing affluence and the state of poverty in America was premature, though not that far off the mark.

During the two decades immediately following publication of *The Affluent Society*, public spending on social welfare programs in the richest Western democracies nearly doubled as a proportion of their gross domestic product (GDP), climbing from an average of 13 percent in 1960 to 23.3 percent in 1980.[15] By 2009 the rate of public spending on social welfare had reached around 30 percent. Among these high-roller welfare states, the United States is often seen as a miser because it spends a lower percent of its GDP on social welfare than most other countries—a distorted perception of social accounting (to be addressed in Chapter 8). But more important by far is the significant rise in the general level of material well-being. A conservative estimate suggests that the median US household income in 2010 afforded 25 percent more purchasing power than the median household income in Galbraith's affluent society of the late 1950s.[16] The purchasing power per capita climbed even higher, since the average household size declined from 3.6 to 2.6 people between 1958 and 2010. Added to that is the sizeable increase in employee benefits, which are not reported as income. Between 1960 and 2003, employer spending on fringe benefits, mainly for health care and retirement, almost tripled from 8 to 23.6 percent of total employee compensation.[17] Although those in the upper income brackets gained the most, the nonwage compensations were widely spread among employees.[18] These significant economic gains tend to be ignored in stories about the stagnation of middle-class income, which exclude the value of employee benefits.

Between increasing affluence and the growth of federal spending on welfare since 1960, the tangible signs of material deprivation faded. By the 1990s, American political discourse on welfare policy was no longer animated by the progressive agenda that emphasized cash transfers to alleviate poverty, which held sway from the mid-nineteenth century. It was a worthy agenda buttressed by the moral force of biblical edicts to comfort the weak and assist the needy.

But as the twenty-first century dawned, the campaign against poverty in the United States had almost vanished from the public square. Bill Clinton's celebrated (by some, condemned by others) campaign promise to "end welfare as we have come to know it" was not a pledge to eradicate poverty but to alter the behavior of welfare recipients. In 2008, John Edwards's campaign staked on addressing the needs of the poor failed to gain political traction. The $500 haircut did not help; nor did his sordid affair comport with the populist message.

When the Census Bureau reported that the national poverty rate climbed from 13.2 percent in 2008 to 14.3 percent in 2009 (about what it was fifteen years earlier), media coverage was brief and perfunctory. Responding to the report, *The New York Times* editorial page addressed the loss of health insurance more than the increase in poverty.[19] In 2010, a poverty count of 15.1 percent made headlines that quickly faded—a twenty-four-hour story that gained little purchase in the public square amid the worst economic downturn since the Great Depression.[20] When the official explanation of the 2009 Recovery Act referred to "vulnerable" people rather than the poor, Peter Edelman expressed dismay that President Obama "seldom said the 'p' word."[21] Indeed, with no sign of an economic recovery in sight, Obama's 2011 State of the Union address marked the second time since 1948 that such an address by a Democratic president excluded any mention of poverty or the plight of the poor.[22] Again in the 2015 address the president made no reference to poverty in the United States, though he commented on the need to stamp out "extreme poverty" around the globe.[23] And Hilary Clinton announced her candidacy for the 2016 presidential race in a video that focused on the struggles of the middle class.

Between the 1960s and the early 1990s, we anguished over poverty even as the levels fell. But since the mid-1990s, there has been little discussion about it, even as poverty rates as officially measured were rising.[24] At first glance this appears very strange. A closer look, however, puts the issue to rest. Concerns about the twenty-first-century level of poverty in the United States have been tamped down for basically two reasons: practical considerations that resonate with Galbraith's notion about the complex nature of poverty in modern times and widespread reservations about what the official US government poverty rates actually measure.

Who Is Really Poor?

The Census Bureau's official poverty line rests on a formula devised by labor economist Mollie Orshansky in 1963, adjusted over time for inflation.[25] In 2015, this line was drawn at a pretax cash income of $24,250 for a family of four.

However, across the political spectrum the overwhelming majority of policy analysts doubt that this measure accurately reflects the number of people who are poor and the essential condition of poverty—as it is understood throughout much of the world. Not to put too fine a point on it, Rebecca Blank described the official poverty measure as "nonsensical numbers."[26] One reason is that it excludes the value of social benefits from programs that assist poor people. If these benefits were counted, Sheldon Danziger, president of the Russell Sage Foundation, calculates that the 2012 official poverty rate would have declined from 15 percent to 11 percent.[27] Christopher Jencks, the doyen of US social policy, offers a more startling analysis. Correcting the official measure for the value of food stamps, rent subsidies, refundable tax credits, and adjustments for inflation, he estimates the rate of poverty plunged to 4.8 percent in 2013.[28]

In light of these uncertainties, the Census Bureau has considered a range of alternative poverty measures since the 1980s. Efforts to revise the established index intensified after a 1995 report by the National Academy of Sciences, which addressed the many technical issues involved in developing a more rigorous measure.[29] Drawing heavily on that report, in autumn 2011 the Census Bureau unveiled the supplemental poverty measure (SPM). Calculating the poverty rate is not only technically challenging; it is a politically charged exercise that could redirect the current flow of federal funds among the states and counties. The new measure was tagged "supplemental" to stipulate that it would not replace the official count in determining eligibility for government programs. Offering a more sophisticated formulation than the established poverty index, the supplemental measure calculates income using a wider range of family resources, while making adjustments for taxes, certain costs of living, family composition, housing status, and geographic areas. It fixes the poverty line according to the amount spent on food, clothing, shelter, and utilities by families at the 33rd percentile of the income distribution plus a small allowance for other needs. Thus, the new poverty line represents a basic standard of living just below what two-thirds of American families routinely enjoy.

An aura of scientific authority surrounds the SPM generated by the imprimatur of the National Academy of Sciences and the exemplary academic credentials of the Panel that contributed to the report. They applied techincal computations to complicated problems. Yet those engaged in the process of measurement well know that the further the definition of poverty moves beyond subsistence, the more subjective and arbitrary the results. Suffice it to say that, as Rebecca Blank put it, "those who engage in poverty measurement can often be quite influenced by their sense of where they want to wind up."[30] Echoing these sentiments, Stanford University professor John Cogan, a member of the NAS Poverty Panel (and former associate director of the US Office of Management and Budget) registered his dissent to the recommendations of the National Academy of Sciences 1995 Report. He believed that these recommendations were not scientific judgments but "value judgments made by scientists—with a particular point of view."[31] Of course, Galbraith's claim that poverty was no longer an issue of pressing concern in the affluent society of the late 1950s was also a subjective judgment, but he presented it as such— unlike the SPM, which carries the weight of scientific endorsement.

What new insights emerge about who is poor in America when the results of the supplemental measure are compared with those of the official poverty index? As it happens, the differences between these measures are small in number but significant in distribution. When the alternative measure was initially reported in 2010, the overall rate of poverty in America registered 15.2 percent on the official index and 16 percent on the supplemental measure. Most striking, however, were the differences in the composition of those designated as poor. The percent of elderly poor people increased significantly under the SPM, whereas the percent of children deemed to be living in poverty declined. Moreover, the SPM showed an increase in the percent of poor White, Asian, and Hispanic people, but a decline in the percent of Black people in poverty.[32]

The AARP (formerly the American Association of Retired Persons) was quick to confirm the SPM rates as an authoritative account of poverty, whereas children's advocates challenged its veracity.[33] To complicate matters, a few days after publication of the supplemental poverty rates, a Pew Research Center analysis of government data showed that older adults have made spectacular gains in wealth relative to younger adults over the past quarter of a century. The age-based wealth gap of 10:1 in 1984 climbed to 47:1 by 2009.[34] And in contrast to the relative increase in poverty among White people, the median wealth of White households rose from 7.5 times that of Black households in 2005 to 20 times that of Black households in 2009.[35] To further complicate matters, as the cohabitation rate of unmarried couples climbed tenfold from 1.1 percent in 1960 to 11 percent in 2011, it has become increasing difficult to take an accurate measure of household income.[36]

Far from settling the debate about how to gauge the degree of poverty in America, the Supplemental Poverty Measure highlights a range of thorny issues in defining and computing the rates: Where does wealth enter the equation? What is the value of leisure time for those voluntarily out of work? How should in-kind benefits such as health care be counted?[37] Should interest payments on consumer debt be subtracted from income?[38] But above all, the new calculations underscore the inherently arbitrary (some might say political) nature of the measurement process. Paradoxically, both conservatives and progressives have an interest in accepting the government's relatively high estimates of poverty. The numbers allow progressives to claim that a massive problem continues to exists, the amelioration of which demands greater public spending. And conservatives can charge that the vast amounts already spent on social welfare have only made the problem worse, proving of course that prevailing assumptions may cut both ways in skewing one's interpretation of social issues.

Beyond normative concerns about how values and subjectivity may affect where the poverty line is drawn, there are several persuasive reasons for healthy skepticism about what the official measures represent. First, there is a huge gap in the data between the earnings of those who are identified as poor and what they spend annually. The 2010 Bureau of Labor Statistics Consumer Expenditure Survey reveals that low-income families, those in the bottom 20 percent of American households, made purchases that were more than twice (212 percent) as high as their reported incomes before taxes.[39] This excess of spending over reported income has grown dramatically since the early 1970s, when it amounted to 139 percent of reported income.[40] For the poorest families, those in the bottom 5 percent of the income distribution, expenditures were more than seven times their reported income.[41] Actual consumption of goods and services may be higher than the out-of-pocket spending suggests, since these figures exclude a vast array of public benefits dispensed to low-income households through eighty income-tested programs such as school breakfast and lunch programs, nutrition programs for the elderly, housing vouchers, legal services, home energy assistance, and day care.[42]

What accounts for this startling gap between income and expenditures? Some of it no doubt reflects increasing debt. Although having limited access to credit markets, low-income people would encounter difficulties sustaining such high levels of expenditure over income. More important, at any point in time, low-income households include a high proportion of families experiencing a temporary reduction in income. These families typically seek to maintain their standard of living by borrowing or spending down assets— smoothing out consumption to match their wealth and expected earnings over time.[43] In addition, there is a marked tendency for people to underreport income.[44] Only 36 percent of food stamp dollars received by families were reported in the 2010 Current Population Survey.[45] Moreover, it is well documented that a significant proportion of welfare recipients regularly worked for pay that was not reported.[46] Obviously, part of the reason for this is that when a welfare recipient's reported income rises above the eligibility threshold, benefits are withdrawn.

Indeed, recent social reforms designed to promote labor force participation in many welfare states are a response to the recognition that welfare benefits can affect economic behavior in undesirable ways. For all intents and purposes, Charles Murray's claim that public welfare benefits bred disincentives to work, which was viewed as heresy by progressive advocates in the mid-1980s, had become received wisdom by the late 1990s.[47] Among Europeans this idea was expressed as welfare provisions creating "poverty traps" or "enforced dependency"—phrases prudently crafted to avoid blaming the victims.[48] One report by the Organization for Economic Co-operation and Development (OECD) went so far as to say that "dependency traps are an unintended outcome of most social security systems."[49]

Another partial explanation for the gap between reported income and expenditures among those in bottom fifth of the income distribution involves the hidden system of intrafamily transfers through which a considerable amount of money flows to young households. In 2010, for example, more than 50 percent of households with members between the ages of 50 and 64 years made cash transfers to their children and grandchildren, which averaged about $8,000 a year over the previous two years. Neither earned income nor public benefits, these private transfers are excluded from the standard accounting for poverty. Although some of these private transfers went to young households in the low-income bracket, the amount they received is not clear.[50]

There is no firm explanation for the vast discrepancy between income and consumer expenditures. And neither of these metrics is the embodiment of precision. As with the measure of poverty, the accuracy and meaning of data on consumption are open to question. It is difficult to obtain an all-inclusive account of how much families actually spend over time. And what this spending represents is not self-evident. Do low levels of spending signify living in poverty, practicing a frugal lifestyle, or saving for future consumption? The data do not tell us. In the short run a household's expenditures on certain durable goods, such as an automobile, is not closely related to its normal level of consumption. And in the long run, some goods, such as owner-occupied housing, are consumed without registering as expenditures.[51] Yet evidence suggests that in regard to characteristics such as home ownership, automobile ownership, and level of education, a consumption-based poverty measure captures people who are on the whole more disadvantaged than those included in either the official poverty index or the SPM.[52]

In addition to higher than expected levels of expenditure, the abundance of material possessions enjoyed by people supposedly living below the poverty line also casts serous doubt about what the official measure represents. Thus, for example, in 2009 at the height of the recession, 40 percent of the families officially designated as poor owned their own homes, which were mainly single-family units and had a median value of $100,000.[53] Most of these are three-or-more-bedroom homes, with a porch or patio and a garage. The median size is 1,470 square feet. Although smaller than the homes of Americans with reported incomes above the poverty line, they are equal to the average size of new homes in Denmark and larger than the average newly built homes in France, Spain, and the United Kingdom.[54]

Moreover, 92 percent of poor households had microwaves; 76 percent, air conditioning; 50 percent, computers; 64 percent, washing machines; 99 percent, a refrigerator (23 percent an additional freezer); 98 percent, color televisions (70 percent more than one television); and 77 percent owned a car, truck, or van (22 percent owned two or more vehicles).[55] This describes a level of material well-being that corresponds with neither public perceptions of poverty nor biblical dictates to aid the needy.

Drawn from scientific surveys conducted by federal agencies, these facts raise credible doubts about the extent of material deprivation among those counted as living under the official poverty line in the United States. The conservative Heritage Foundation concludes that most of the people designated as poor by the official measure are not seriously deprived.[56] The progressive response does not challenge the facts but disputes their interpretation, arguing that despite the abundant possession of household amenities, life on an income under the poverty line remains a disagreeable struggle to make ends meet. Chiding the Heritage Foundation analysis, Katrina vanden Heuvel, editor of *The Nation*, suggests that if living below the poverty line is so cushy, the foundation should consider paying its researchers $22,000 a year to support their families.[57]

Whether or not it can be characterized as a cushy life, the fact remains that the majority of people currently deemed as poor in the United States have access to the basic necessities of life—food, clothing, shelter, entertainment, education, health care, and transportation. By basic necessities I am referring not only to what is needed for subsistence, but to those commodities that symbolize the proverbial linen shirt without which Adam Smith's day laborer would have been ashamed to appear in public. Or as Smith put it, "whatever the custom of the country renders it indecent for creditable people, even of the lowest order, to be without."[58] There are, of course, differences of opinion about the exact bundle of goods and services embodied by this standard in twenty-first-century America—and the contents change periodically. It is indeed the case that today's luxuries have a way of becoming tomorrow's necessities.[59] It is also true that production costs of conveniences that may seem lavish today tend to decline over time.

The Temporal Dimension

In considering what it means to be poor, it is important to recognize that material possessions associated with luxury and necessity are not the only reference points that may change over one's lifetime. The official measure of poverty ignores a temporal dimension that implicitly governs the public's understanding of this social condition. Are you living in poverty if your income falls below the line for a week, a month, or a year? When people think of poverty as a social problem, they generally assume a long-term or chronic condition. But how many middle-class professionals reading this today can look back to some period in their life when they would have qualified as being poor based on their income—if only through their graduate school days, in the first year after graduation, or during a spell of unemployment? Between 2009 and 2011there were 2.9 million college students residing off-campus who were counted as living below the poverty level.[60] Although they constitute a relatively small percent of those deemed as poor according to the federal standard, this group embodies the larger issue of how to interpret fluctuations of lifetime income.

An intriguing analysis of longitudinal data reveals that over the life cycle 58.5 percent of Americans adults between 20 and 75 years old will experience a spell of poverty as measured by the official standard—an experience that confronts 68 percent of the people if the level is raised to 125 percent of the poverty line.[61] On face value, these figures appear to confirm an argument that the US system of welfare capitalism is basically flawed and in need of a major overhaul.[62] Yet with Americans enjoying among the highest median household incomes in the world, the fact that a shocking proportion of the population spends some time living below the federal line is perplexing. What exactly does this signify? Is the high incidence of poverty indicative of a major social problem, a normal part of the life course on the path to prosperity for many if not most of the population, or perhaps, for some people even a character-building life event? Before balking at the suggestion that an experience of poverty might be construed as a character-building event, remember we are not discussing the World Bank's $1.50 a day criterion for developing countries, but poverty as defined by the contested US measure.

Another story emerges from the analysis of economic well-being over the life course. The same data showing that more than half of American adults endured a period of poverty also reveal that 76.8 percent of the adults between the ages of 25 and 60 enjoyed a year or more living in a household whose annual income exceeded $100,000—and 50.9 percent lived in a household with an annual income of $150,000.[63] By this account over the course of their lives at least one-half of the people living in poverty also lived for some time in relatively well-off households. With three-quarters of the population experiencing such prosperity, the US system of welfare capitalism looks a lot less defective than one might infer from the lifetime *poverty* rates.

Efforts to gauge the significance of economic hardship in the United States cannot ignore the temporal dimension of poverty. Many households endure brief spells during which their incomes fall beneath the poverty line, just as many people experience periods of unemployment. Chronic poverty, though, is relatively rare. Only 6.1 percent of Americans between the ages of 25 and 60 years spend five or more consecutive years in poverty and 1.7 percent spend ten years or more.[64] On a monthly basis between 1996 and 1999, the household income of 34 percent of the population dipped below the poverty threshold for two months or more, while only 2 percent of the population remained below the poverty line for the entire period.[65] Similarly, from 2004 thru 2007 the income of 31.6 percent of the population fell below the poverty line for two or more months, but just 2.2 percent of the population remained under the poverty threshold for the full four years. The median time in poverty was around 4.4 months for all the individuals officially designated as poor between 2001 and 2006.[66] In 2009, with unemployment hovering around 9 percent, only 7.3 percent of the population was under the poverty line for the entire year.[67]

Frictional, Cyclical, and Structural Poverty

The swings in economic fortune and misfortune are extraordinarily complex phenomena to encapsulate in a poverty index. At any given point in time, low-income households include a high proportion of families experiencing a temporary if sharp reduction in income due to a loss of employment, changing jobs, divorce, returning to school, and dropping out of the labor force to raise children, among other bumps and detours along the life course. These families typically seek to sustain their standard of living by borrowing or consuming assets, which smooths out consumption to match their expected earning when life returns to normal. But data collection and reporting on poverty are not sensitive to the duration of a family's status below the poverty line or to savings and other resources that may be available to see them through an interim downswing.

In contrast to the typically unidimensional portrayal of poverty, economists identify several types of unemployment. The most prominent distinctions are among frictional, cyclical, and structural unemployment, the causes
and duration of which vary. Frictional unemployment represents the temporary period between jobs when workers are entering and moving around in
the market. As such, it is considered inevitable due to the normal voluntary
turnover in the labor force. Cyclical unemployment involves job layoffs in
response to downturns in the business cycle. Though reoccurring, these too
are usually short term with employment rebounding as the economy picks
up steam. Structural unemployment is considered more problematic, involving long-term or permanent job loss, which results largely from a discrepancy between available skills and those required to fill existing jobs as well
as a geographic mismatch between the location of workers and available jobs.
The increase in unemployment between 2007 and 2010 is attributed more to
cyclical than structural forces.[68] These different kinds of unemployment are
related to the official poverty rates, which sheds a discerning light on their
interpretation.

Thus, from a temporal perspective, the official rate of poverty consists
of groups of people experiencing temporary, sporadic, and chronic events in
their lives. Frictional unemployment is associated with the group for whom
being counted as poor is a temporary and usually a once-or-twice-in-a-
lifetime event due to voluntary choices or unanticipated incidents. This group
includes, for example, people going on to higher education and changing jobs
or experiencing an unexpected detour in the road of life, such as divorce and
accidents that may require adjustments in their occupational status. Like the
60–70 percent of my students who raise their hands when I ask how many of
them have ever experienced poverty, most of this group's members consider
it a passing phase. In general, this group tends to possess the educational and
social skills required to succeed in the job market.

Cyclical unemployment can also impact those who experience temporary spells of poverty. However, these fluctuations in the business cycle are
more closely related to the group whose members are sporadically counted
among the poor. Their human capital is generally lower than that of the temporary poor, which makes them more vulnerable to economic downswings.
Their annual income intermittently crosses above and below the poverty line
over the life course. This group also includes many seasonal workers.

Unlike workers whose incomes temporarily or periodically fall below the
poverty line, the chronic poor consists of those who are marginally, if at all,
capable of functioning in the modern market economy. A substantial proportion of this group is subject to structural unemployment stemming from
social, physical, psychological, and educational deficits that are not easily rec-
tified. It is a group whose members possess very little human capital. Their
income is usually far below the poverty line for many consecutive years. As

such, they are among the most destitute who have been classified as in "deep poverty."[69]

The personal problems and financial hardships of the chronic poor are qualitatively different from the conditions of others whose incomes occasionally dip below the poverty line. Yet public agency and media reports about the high official rate of poverty in the United States rarely distinguish between these groups. The failure to make this distinction serves at once to exaggerate the problem of poverty and to thwart its solution.

3

No Longer a Massive Affliction

ARE YOU BLIND?

When I suggested to one of my colleagues that the real scale of poverty in the United States is considerably below the rate typically depicted, he stared in disbelief, blurting out, "What are talking about? Use you eyes, for God's sake! Are you blind?" Of course, one need only take a short walk from our campus, down Telegraph Avenue in Berkeley, or stroll around in downtown San Francisco to see what he means.

Throughout the country on a given night there are approximately 650,000 homeless people wandering the streets in ragged attire, many of whom do not know where their next meal will come from. Most studies show the vast majority of homeless people are not only impoverished but suffer from at least one disabling condition such as alcohol addiction, drug abuse, or mental illness.[1] In short, what we are seeing are examples of Galbraith's "case" poverty.

Homeless people represent the most visible and severe expression of those chronically living in abject poverty—grim testimony to the fact that a large number of citizens continue to suffer significant long-term privation. Just how much case poverty exists in the United States is an open question. Various estimates would put the current rate of chronic poverty somewhere between 2 and 7 percent.[2] At the middle range, if 5 percent of the population experienced this condition, we are talking about 15.5 million people. Just a fraction of the official poverty rate, this relatively small percent nevertheless signifies a huge number of people living in distress—a figure that would pack the seats of roughly 200 major league football stadiums. As with the homeless, a large proportion of this group suffers from poor health, mental illness, addictions, and other disabling conditions.[3]

Thus, when consumption patterns, material possessions, and the persistence of low income are drawn into the frame, what appears is a picture of poverty in America that is indeed large enough so that one would have to be blind not to see it, but still small enough so that it bears little resemblance to the massive affliction portrayed by the official measures of poverty. And when we look more closely, we see a chronic poverty problem restricted largely to people with physical and psychological conditions that make it difficult to engage in productive activities—people in need of intense services, rehabilitation, and care. From this perspective, not only does the size of the problem become more manageable, but the solutions take on a different hue from those mainly seeking to provide additional cash for low-income people. Within this wider frame we also find that an affluent society has a significant proportion of people with relatively low incomes who own homes, cars, televisions, computers, clothes dryers, dishwashers, and air conditioners. It is true that low-income people as well as many not-so-low-income people (including most of you reading these words) struggle daily to make ends meet. But this is a struggle to match resources with modern appetites for material consumption—not to put a roof over their heads, clothes on their back, and food on the table.

The picture drawn here confirms Galbraith's perception of poverty in the United States as an afterthought, restricted mainly to cases involving personal limits and hardships that preclude individuals from partaking in the general well-being and the disinclination of some people to move away from geographically depressed areas. It was not a structural failure of capitalism. Indeed, as he saw it, by the middle of the twentieth century the increased output of industrial society effectively eliminated poverty for all who worked.

It is therefore noteworthy that in the 1998 revised edition of the *The Affluent Society*, Galbraith deleted his "afterthought" comment, one of the several revisions in the text on the subject of poverty. Thus, the 1958 edition declared, "The most certain thing about modern poverty is that it is not efficiently remedied by a general and tolerably well-distributed advance in income."[4] In the 1998 edition a similar view is expressed ("The most certain thing about poverty is that it is not remedied by a general advance in income"),[5] only to be contradicted a few pages later: "The notion that income is a remedy for indigency has a certain forthright appeal." Advocating for a guaranteed minimum income, which he had earlier rejected as politically unviable and socially problematic, Galbraith now finds that "the provision of such a basic source of income must henceforth be the first and the strategic step in the attack on poverty."[6] In the 1958 edition, he argued that the first and key strategic step in an attack on poverty was to ensure that children in poor families attend first-rate schools, where they would be well educated and nourished.

Although continuing to describe the causes of poverty in terms of personal deficiencies as well as social barriers, by 1998 Galbraith concluded that "most modern poverty is insular involving forces that restrain or prevent participation in economic life." In general, the 1998 version of *The Affluent Society* appears to have moved toward the more conventional progressive view of poverty, emphasizing social causes and market flaws that can be mitigated by the transfer of income—a curious shift when one considers that government spending on social welfare programs had more than doubled as a percent of the GDP between 1958 and 1998, unemployment was at its lowest level in 30 years, and according to the official measure, the national rate of poverty was 73 percent higher in 1958 than 1998. These facts suggest that despite having coined the term, even Galbraith was not personally immune to the sway of "conventional wisdom."

It is tempting to assert that he had it right the first time. Although the current data support Galbraith's 1958 observations about the state of poverty in America, his explanation for how we eventually got here has turned out to be only partly correct. The Affluent Society came to press at the dawn of what some describe as the "Golden Era" of welfare state expansion. According to the official index, the poverty rate in 1960 was over 22 percent or almost 50 percent higher than the official rate in 2011.[7] The battle against want of basic necessities was powerfully reinforced by social expenditures on a broad package of benefits that has increased vastly since the 1950s. This package includes Social Security; unemployment; public assistance; Supplemental Security Income for the blind, aged, and disabled; daycare; subsidies for low-wage earners; child care credits; subsidized housing; food stamps; meals for the elderly; medical care for elderly and low-income people; early education; job training; and many other social benefits. The cost of these social benefits multiplied almost tenfold (in constant 2011 dollars) from $235 billion in 1963 to $2.3 trillion in 2011.[8] Taking the population change into account, these social welfare transfers rose from about $1,168 to $7,000 per capita.

Although some of these benefits such as Social Security, unemployment, and Medicare are distributed across the board to people with varying incomes, a large part of the package is designed expressly to assist low-income people. Allowing for inflation, federal and state spending on income-tested programs climbed by 557 percent between 1968 and 2004; over that period the US population grew by about 46 percent.[9] In 2009, thanks to the economic stimulus from the American Recovery and Reinvestment Act, the federal government alone spent $708 billion on eighty income-tested programs, a 23 percent increase over the amount spent on this population in 2008.[10] These need-based benefits were limited to people with low incomes, but not all below the poverty line. However, for a rough idea of the potential boost offered by this set of programs, if the benefits were divided only among those identified as living below the poverty line in 2009, the federal expenditure would have amounted to nearly $16,000 per person or $64,000 a year in benefits (not all cash) for a typical family of four. The impact of the 2008 recession on low-income people was clearly cushioned by this array of social programs. Although all low-income groups benefitted significantly from these cash transfers, those at the bottom of the income distribution did not gain as much as the people whose incomes hovered just above and below the poverty line.[11]

Fifty years ago Galbraith proposed a cyclically graduated unemployment scheme under which benefits would rise in periods of high unemployment and decrease as jobs became available. In recent years Congress has essentially complied. During the recession, Congress temporarily raised the unemployment payments and extended the time limit to 99 weeks. Once firmly in place, the social safety net expanded to cover necessities such as food and shelter. According to the US Department of Housing and Urban Development annual count, even the rate of homelessness continually declined between 2008 and 2011.[12] Although this decline started before the implementation of the Homelessness Prevention and Rapid Re-Housing Program in 2010, the $1.5 billion funding of this measure surely reinforced the downward trend.

Finally, funding for food stamps more than doubled from $27.6 billion in 2007 to $57.8 in 2011, at which point the average recipient's household benefit amounted to $3,400 a year.[13] Indeed, low-income Americans are far more likely to experience obesity than hunger.[14] Some assume that this is due to the poor quality of food available in low-income neighborhoods and the higher cost of a healthy diet compared to junk foods. Reliable empirical findings reveal this is not the case.[15] Very much like their fellow citizens in the middle classes, a high proportion of low-income Americans eat too many fatty and sugary foods and exercise too little. Although women in low-income families are more likely to be obese than those in high-income families, the reverse is true for men.[16] In the modern era of abundance, the problem is simply that people are consuming more calories and burning fewer. In 2010, Colorado with a 21 percent rate of obesity was the thinnest state in the union—the same rate would have made it the fattest state in the union only 15 years earlier.[17] All of this eating is accompanied by a great deal of waste. The United States Department of Agriculture estimates that 133 billion pounds of food, about 30 to 40 percent of the total supply, never make into people's stomachs.[18] While two-thirds of American adults are overweight, many European countries are close behind.[19] Heart-wrenching palpable images of the poor—malnourished children, gaunt with bone-protruding poverty—emanate almost exclusively from the developing countries in which it is estimated that 900 million people were living on less than $1.25 a day in 2010.[20]

By any historically literate measure, the rise of modern welfare states accompanied by the decline of material deprivation in the United States and many other advanced industrial democracies is an extraordinary achievement of the twentieth century.[21] We have witnessed the realization of the progressive agenda to alleviate the most tangible adversities of poverty. But having won the battle against want elicits little celebration. The progressive spirit is temperamentally disposed to relentless discontent stoked by utopian ideals. In response to the unprecedented level of material well-being among low-income people, those seeking to advance the human condition have moved the goalposts. They now find that conventional measures of poverty neglect to capture the real material adversities of modern life or the basic failure of capitalist society. If want of basic necessities is no longer the issue, how do progressives convey the nature of twenty-first-century poverty in economically developed countries? This starts with a new perception of the problem, which recalibrates its scale and magnifies its intensity to heighten public awareness and revitalize the case for still more government action.

Reframing the Problem: Institutionalized Discontent

To solve a jigsaw puzzle, people usually start by connecting the pieces with straight edges to form the frame. This creates a visual boundary for focusing their attention. In the nineteenth and twentieth centuries, the progressive outlook was framed by the economic problem delineated along the plumbed lines of poverty, hunger, dilapidated housing, and disease. By the twenty-first century the frame for this problem has lost its edge in the advanced industrialized world. In Western Europe, 50 percent and then 60 percent of the median income once defined the straight edge of poverty.

The work of the European Union Social Protection Indicators Committee and publications by the OECD now argue that the measure of twenty-first-century poverty in the advanced industrial countries is more complicated than the lack of income for the fundamental needs of modern life.[22]

It is not unusual for academics studying social issues such as poverty, hunger, and abuse to broaden the conceptual boundaries as the depth of the problem declines. This is evident in the way that advocacy researchers continue to address the issue of rape on college campuses. More than twenty years ago, for example, a widely-cited study claimed that 27 percent of college women were victims of rape or attempted rape; critical analyses revealed this figure to be an immense exaggeration.[23] Since then, the rate of forcible rape documented in the FBI Uniform Crime Reporting System declined by 30 percent;[24] similarly, the Bureau of Justice Statistics' annual National Crime Victimization Survey reveals that the rate of rape and sexual assault on college campuses fell by more than 50 percent from 9.2 per thousand in 1997 to 4.4 per thousand in 2013;[25] because these data are collected the same way every year, it is reasonable to assume that their biases are constant and the findings provide a reliable guide to *trends* in the rate of rape, even if they might underestimate the magnitude. As the rate of the problem diminished, the conceptual boundaries of sexual violence on campus were reframed under the heading of "sexual assault," the precinct of which extends far beyond the legal borders of rape. Applying this broader formulation, a highly-publicized 2015 study reports that 25 percent of college women have experienced a sexual assault—the definition of which includes forced oral, anal, and vaginal sex as well as unwanted kissing, grabbing, and rubbing up against a person in a sexual way, even if it is over one's clothes.[26] Mingling an unwanted kiss or dancing too closely with forcible rape inflates the numbers as it trivializes sexual violence. More gravely, it distorts social policy by shifting public resources to middle-class college students and away from those who are in greater need of assistance.[27]

Hunger in the United States is another problem where defeat has been snatched from the jaws of victory. In 1995, federal agencies launched an annual "Food Security Survey," which was just around the time that Rebecca Blank, then a member of President Clinton's Council of Economic advisers, observed that severe health problems related to malnutrition had virtually disappeared in the United States.[28] Yet by 2013, the federal survey found 14.3 percent of households suffering from "food insecurity." As Douglas Besharov explained, "many think that this is an artificial construct, as it is based on answers to eighteen different questions that express some uncertainty about having sufficient financial resources to obtain enough food to meet the needs of all household members *even once in the past year.*"[29]

This propensity to stretch the boundaries to encompass milder forms of social distress is inspired by layers of motivation—a curious blend of opportunism and idealism. Public funding to examine and alleviate social problems has created a large class of professional researchers and service providers with a vested interest in keeping the numbers high and on the rise. "It is a question," as Irving Kristol observed, "of jobs and status and power."[30] To say the problem is diminishing, but we need more funding for research and service is a hard sell. The media are inclined to report on problems that are growing and affect large numbers of people, while ignoring the exact definitions and measurements on which the numbers are based.[31] This encourages broad definitions that embody as many cases as possible, since proposals to study and remedy the problem of poverty, for example, compete for public attention and financial support with other social problems such as sexual assault, bullying, micro-aggression, discrimination, child abuse, mental health, and physical illness—the definitions of which are also being extended.[32] Under these circumstances professional ambitions and competition for public funding spawn a market of institutionalized discontent.

At the same time, many come to the study of social problems with an idealistic inclination to shape a kinder, gentler world. It is easy to agree that amid the abundance of American society no one should go hungry or even be uncertain about having enough money for food once in the past year. But this ideal should not obscure the harsh meaning of poverty in a world where 3.1 million children under 5 years of age die from undernutrition.[33]

Beyond a mixture of academic self-interest and idealistic dispositions, the Europeans had practical political reasons to broaden their definition of poverty, which was set at 60 percent of each country's median income. When the European Union's (EU) membership spread eastward, the conventional poverty index proved awkward, since countries such as Hungary, Slovakia, and Slovenia registered lower rates of poverty than Finland, Luxembourg, France, and Germany.[34] This did not bode well for sensible decision making about economic transfers to assist the EU member nations most in need. Not only that, but when researchers took a hard look at the resources available to households typically identified as poor according to the European index, in many OECD countries the numbers shrink to what Galbraith described as an afterthought in the United State. For example, in Australia the official rate of poverty in 2007 declines from 13.7 percent to 2.5 percent after calculations of household consumption and wealth are factored into the measure. In Germany when just wealth, but not household consumption, is included, the 2005 poverty rate falls from 17.2 percent to 7.9 percent.[35]

With the rates of income-related poverty falling to very low levels when gauged by comprehensive empirical indicators of financial resources, those promoting progressive policies to reduce suffering have sought to reframe the problem of human need in the twenty-first century. The concept of "poverty" is no longer considered adequate to express the breadth of the hardships that must be addressed by government intervention. Major international bodies such as the International Labor Organization, the OECD, and the European Union have contributed to reformulating the modern European view of poverty around the idea of "social exclusion."[36] In 1992 the European Commission asserted that the term "social exclusion" conveyed a more adequate depiction of deprivation than the term "poverty."[37] A few years later, in the same vein the International Labor Organization affirmed that social exclusion can be seen as a replacement for poverty, one that provides a multidimensional view of impoverishment.[38]

As interest in this perspective gained momentum, the Center for Analysis of Social Exclusion was established at the London School of Economics and Political Science in 1997, which guaranteed a proliferation of research and publication. At the March 2000 Lisbon Summit of the European Council, social "inclusion" (an affirmative reformulation) was identified as one of the main policy areas for cooperative exchange. Endeavoring to clarify what this expansive concept actually included, members of the European Union Social Protection Committee empirically defined a portfolio of indicators.[39] The portfolio consists of eleven primary and six secondary indicators, including unemployment, education, health care, housing, child well-being, the employment gap of immigrants, and material deprivation along with the conventional 60 percent of median income measure, which is now used to identify those being "at-risk-of-poverty."[40]

Some of these indicators are puzzling, particularly the nine-item material deprivation index, which asks respondents whether they can afford: (1) a washing machine; (2) a personal car; (3) a color television; (4) a telephone; (5) one-week annual holiday away from home; (6) to face unexpected expenses; (7) to pay for arrears (rent, utilities, etc.); (8) a meal with meat, chicken, or fish every second day; and (9) to keep a home adequately warm. The question of whether one can "afford an unexpected expense" might elicit respondents' thoughts about everything from the costs of replacing a dead car battery to a new roof. (Arguably their answers reflect levels of optimism about unanticipated losses more than anything else.) One week's annual holiday away from home can range from camping in the forest to a luxury cruise in the Mediterranean (where incidentally it costs much less to keep a home adequately warm than in Scandinavian countries). Even a color television may vary in price from less than $100 to more than $5,000. Because there are no stable values associated with these items, it is difficult to decipher exactly what individual responses mean.[41]

On top of this imprecision, the use of these indicators creates a perplexing question: How do we interpret discrepancies that arise between the nonmonetary index of material deprivation and the income-based measure of being at risk of poverty? According to these indicators, the risk of poverty in Hungary, Slovakia, the Czech Republic, and Slovenia, for example, is *lower* than in many other countries such as Finland, France, Germany, Ireland, Luxembourg, and the United Kingdom. At the same time, however, the four Eastern European countries have *higher* levels of material deprivation, as measured by the percent of their populations that could not afford at least three of the nine items in the deprivation index. Comparisons that show countries with relatively *lower levels* of being *at risk of poverty* having relatively *higher levels* of *material deprivation* bring to mind an Orwellian narrative on the meaning of poverty and material deprivation—as these terms are commonly understood.[42]

There is almost no end to the list of items one might incorporate in an index of material deprivation. One effort to elaborate and refine this index increased the original list to seventeen items. This expanded version includes questions about living in noisy areas and districts suffering from pollution and grime caused by traffic or industry—upscale parts of Manhattan Island would probably qualify.[43] Such measures reflect a vision of social inclusion that aspires to an environmentally pristine, peaceful middle-class life for all. This is a highly desirable objective in its own right, but one considerably removed from authentic material deprivation as it was evident in the nineteenth and twentieth centuries, as it is evident today in many parts of the developing world, and as it is understood by the public in advanced industrial nations.

Although the European idiom of social inclusion has drifted into academic discourse, it has yet to gain the same currency among progressives in the United States. Here as serious concerns about poverty recede, the topic of public conversation has shifted to insecurity and inequality. Insecurity can be awakened without much effort. It reflects a state of uncertainty tinged with anxiety about what the future holds in store, which lurks in the back of most people's minds, except for the pathologically optimistic. The modern welfare state in wealthy countries has done much to diminish the levels of physical and economic insecurity typically experienced in the nineteenth century. Driving over Donner Pass on highway 80 in California in a heated four-wheel-drive SUV, it is hard to imagine that in the middle of the nineteenth century after traveling more the 2,000 miles in covered wagons almost half of the Donner Party perished just uphill from what is today the town of Truckee. This is a reminder that the modern discourse of heightened insecurity may be expressed in response to the 2008 recession, global competition, uncertainties of rapid technological changes, and the like, but it is conducted in the context of a historically unprecedented expectation of material comfort and economic security.

The Challenge of Abundance: Having Too Much

With the US economy on the road to recovery, insecurity fades into the wings as the broader issue of how to divvy up the wealth takes center stage.[44] Should government be taking more to rejuvenate the public sphere? Is there a pressing need to reduce economic disparities among citizens? The practical meaning of income inequality depends in large measure on how it impacts people's lives. The perennial question of whether money buys happiness has generated a large body of research, which correlates the observable measurement of money with elusive definitions of happiness.[45] Although the results are inconclusive, they lean toward the answer of "yes, but only up to a point." Daniel Kahneman and Angus Deaton, both Nobel Prize winners, analyzed more than 450,000 survey responses distinguishing two ideas of happiness: how satisfied respondents were with their lives as a whole and their emotional well-being as reflected in the frequency and intensity of feelings such as enjoyment, happiness, anger, and sadness. These notions distinguished between thinking about life and living life.[46] The findings revealed that beyond a certain threshold, about $75,000, additional money does not buy greater happiness in the feelings people experienced in their daily lives, but it did continue to make a difference in their global judgments of life satisfaction.[47]

From another perspective, Tyler Cowen points out that despite the widening difference in income, the inequality of material consumption has narrowed remarkably over the past century.[48] Short of taking a voyage in outer space, there are few forms of travel on this planet—from bicycles, to automobiles, jet planes, and ocean liners—beyond the reach of the middle classes. From the profile of a Toyota that looks like a Mercedes to Asian knock-offs of designer apparel, modern production has blurred the distinction of up-market goods that once proclaimed an accredited position in society. People enjoy almost universal access to entertainment and the comforts and conveniences of modern amenities. Even as they struggle to make ends meet, average Americans are instinctively aware that their living standards are pretty good.

Widely broadcasted in the media, egalitarian indignation over the increasing disparity in income does not appear to coincide with views expressed by the populace at large. The Gallup poll taken at end of 2011 reports that while more than two-thirds of Americans thought it was very or extremely important to grow the economy and increase equality of opportunity, only 46 percent believed it was that important to reduce income inequality. Surprisingly it turns out that Americans were less likely to agree that the discrepancy between the rich and the poor represents a problem that needs to be fixed in 2011 than in 1998. On the heels of the worst recession since the Great Depression, a majority of respondents believe that income inequalities are an acceptable part of the economic system.[49] Even amid the Great Depression, only 42 percent of those surveyed thought that government should limit the size of private fortunes.[50] An analysis of surveys conducted between the 1970s and 2012 offers strong evidence that Americans registered no increase in support for redistribution despite rising inequality over the decades.[51]

To be sure, it is advisable to read these polls with a cautious eye. As anyone who has composed surveys can attest, the way issues are phrased can sway the answers. Respondents are sensitive to the placement and wording of questions. "Should government increase taxes to help the poor?" (How much might this cost me?) "Should government raise inheritance taxes on estates worth over $10 million?" (Not a bad idea.) Still, the general tendency reflected over recent decades of polling seems to confirm an historical impression that American individualism engenders a good deal of allowance for economic disparities. Alexis De Tocqueville took note of this ingrained belief in the United States almost two centuries ago, commenting that he knew of no other country where greater "contempt is expressed for the theory of the permanent equality of property."[52] Public tolerance of economic inequality resonates with the "difference principle" in John Rawls's theory of justice, under which inequality is acceptable as long as the standard of living at the bottom improved as those on the top rungs of the economic ladder climbed higher.[53] Acceptance of inequality does not mean that the middle class is disinclined toward raising marginal tax rates a few points on those in the highest bracket. It appears that in some states even a majority of Tea Party supporters would back a 5 percent income tax increase on millionaires.[54]

Although increasing inequality is generally undesirable, the preference for equality is ultimately contingent on other choices; in other words, one's sense of economic inequality is largely contextual. Where one stands depends upon the reference group against which comparisons are made. Thus, it has been observed that most members of the "Occupy Wall Street" movement claiming to be among the 99 percent look a lot more like the prosperous 1 percent when compared to the world as a whole. Some Americans may be astounded to hear that Hungary has greater equality and less poverty (as measured by the European index) than the United States. Whether Hungary is deemed a more just society than the United States depends upon what one makes of the fact that Hungary's median monthly income of roughly $800 is approximately 55 percent of the poverty line for a two-person family in the United States—and less than half the unemployment benefit in Wyoming.[55]

Writing in the late 1950s, Galbraith detected little interest in inequality as an economic issue for a variety of reasons. At the time, first of all, inequality did not seem to be getting worse. Moreover, the rich had become a less visible annoyance as the ostentatious display of wealth had lost the power to convey membership in a privileged caste—and gained the reputation of vulgarity. Increasing prosperity allowed so many people to indulge in the purchase of luxury goods, or copies of them, that they ceased to serve as a mark of distinction. (Today in some enclaves of wealth, status-driven consumption is more likely to result in "conspicuous conservatism"—acquisition of a Prius instead of a Cadillac.) But above all, Galbraith maintained that the material gains of increasing output eliminated the social tensions associated with inequality—rising income dulled envy. Still, he recognized that while the progressive attitude toward inequality was no longer as outspoken as in the past, antagonism toward the wealthy simmered. The good liberal, as Galbraith explained, was haunted by "the cynical Marxian whisper hinting that whatever he does may not be enough. Despite his efforts the wealthy become wealthier and more powerful."[56]

The general lack of concern about inequality was acknowledged by Galbraith in the late 1950s, during the post–World War II period of optimism and relative prosperity.[57] The sharp economic downturn in recent years has raised simmering resentment over inequality to a boil, fueled in part by the wildly disproportionate compensation awarded to the captains of finance and industry as their boats went down. Many Americans felt there was something unseemly about rewarding the failures of what had come to be seen as a corrupt corporate elite. In this context latent antipathies aroused by economic inequality have bubbled to the top of the progressive agenda.

The irony in all this, however, is that resentment over inequality seems to have displaced concern for the truly impoverished members of society. In the 2011 White House address on economic growth and deficit reduction when President Obama insisted that the wealthiest people pay more taxes, his demand was couched in the language of equity for the middle class. The "Buffet rule" as he called it, argued that "Middle-class families shouldn't pay higher taxes than millionaires and billionaires. That's pretty straightforward."[58] There was a passing reference to the poor in this address, a fleeting afterthought at most. While conservatives charged Obama with stirring up class warfare, it was a battle line drawn between the upper and the middle classes, not the traditional struggle of the rich against the poor. Following this address the 2011 Occupy Wall Street movement sought to pit the 99 percent of Americans who are not spectacularly rich against the top 1 percent. The President's 2012 State of the Union Message again warned of the growing inequality in the United States.

Alarm over the widening gap between the highest income earners and everyone else is rooted in a materialistic ethos that calculates well-being not as the absence of privations but as the relative position one holds in relation to others in the possession of worldly goods. What becomes most important is having as much stuff as the next guy, regardless of how much. The focus on redistribution to achieve economic equality does little to alleviate the disabilities of the chronically poor. It does not develop opportunity, strengthen family life, educate children, create satisfying work, or encourage the civic virtues that are independent of market capitalism. It does nothing to address the acute suffering of those afflicted by case poverty. Instead, it conveys an image of the good society as one dedicated to increasing private consumption. It reinforces the unbridled materialism that Galbraith saw as irrelevant, if not detrimental, to the essential quality of modern life.

Galbraith's condemnation of rampant materialism was in keeping with good company. Ever since the Industrial Revolution social critics have recoiled from the base life-draining sterility of the purported satisfactions of material accumulation. In recent times Amitai Etzioni argues for restraining materialistic consumption and investing more human energy in social and cultural pursuits.[59] Even Adam Smith, often hailed the father of economics, was deeply ambivalent about the material culture of his time, cheering on economic progress while deploring the mounting desires for "trinkets of frivolous utility" that accompanied the new prosperity. As Albert Hirschman points out, "Smith's ambivalence reflects that of generation after generation of Western intellectuals both celebrating and vilifying material progress."[60] Like Smith, Galbraith's views were not firmly aligned on either side.

To redress what he deemed a disproportionate emphasis on the production of material wares and individual consumption, Galbraith argued that the good society required greater social balance between public and private spending. To this end, he advocated the expanded use of state and local sales taxes as the best way to enlarge and enrich public goods and services: recreation facilities, public safety, community services, transportation, and most of all education. He was adamant about the advantages of this tax to create human and social capital despite its potential impact on the distribution of income and financial costs to low-income people.

Along with improving the social balance of public and private consumption, Galbraith was concerned about the balance of work and leisure and how to limit the drudgery of manual labor. Amid modern affluence he observed the rise of a "New Class," for whom agreeable work is a rich source of satisfaction that lends purpose and structure to life. Among this class the professoriate stands out as an example in which the leisurely activities of reading and contemplation have been elevated to the status of strenuous toil in the groves of academe. Galbraith's call for the expansion of the New Class as the major social goal of society reflected the utopian tendencies of the progressive spirit. There is, of course, much to recommend the work of reading and contemplation interrupted every so often by a sabbatical—during which these efforts continue uninterrupted by occasional meetings with students. Yet until technology relieves the need to drive nails into wood and handpick grapes off the vine, much hard labor will remain to be done.

Reflecting on the implications of unprecedented prosperity, Galbraith outlined an alternative progressive agenda that included making work easier, more pleasant, and personally satisfying through greater investment in human capital and increasing leisure. His agenda transcended the conventional materialistic concerns about poverty and inequality, the social urgency of which weigh lightly on the modern scale of affluence. It concentrated instead on the profound issues of what makes a good society and the purpose of human labor after survival in modest comfort is no longer at stake. This agenda mirrored the existential challenge foreseen by John Maynard Keynes.

Writing in the midst of the Great Depression, Keynes peered into the future, confidently predicting the level of economic life a hundred years hence and what that would mean for the well-being of the grandchildren waiting to be born. What he saw was an age of abundance where the average standard of living in the industrial democracies would be four to eight times higher in 2030 than it was in 1930. This was virtually on the mark. In the United States the per capita family income in 2013 was five-and-a-half times greater than 1930.[61] At this level, according to Keynes, for the first time since creation, people would be free from the spur of economic necessity. To some extent the process of creating freedom from want relies on the capitalist treadmill of accelerating consumption. Yet he imagined the possibility of a fifteen-hour work week as a rising standard of living satisfied human needs and lowered the pressure to earn more money. In fact, leisure time has increased in the twenty-first century. Although the fifteen-hour work week is nowhere on the horizon, the adoption of a thirty-five-hour work week in France is at least a symbolic step in that direction.[62]

In the course of eliminating economic hardship, Keynes believed the age of abundance would create an unprecedented challenge. With the economic problem solved, "man will be faced with his real, his permanent problem—how to use his freedom from pressing economic cares, how to occupy the leisure which science and compound interest will have won for him, to live wisely and agreeably and well."[63] The enriching use of leisure, the purpose and meaning of a noble life, and the values that define the good society, these are the salient issues that demand our attention as the US economy's revival lifts material well-being to the heights that Keynes envisioned. Yet, as the economic problem of material well-being fades, the progressive agenda has recast the distributional problem of capitalism from concerns over people not having enough to distress that some have more than others.

Inequality

4

The Root of All Evil

For most of the twentieth century, poverty represented the root of all evil—sprouting criminality, violence, hunger, disease, stunted achievement, and premature death. As such, progressive initiatives to eradicate poverty tapped into a gripping social issue. From Roosevelt's New Deal to Johnson's War on Poverty, these initiatives expanded the institutional edifice of the modern welfare state and in the process not only abolished the struggle for subsistence but assured most US citizens a minimal standard of living. Although poverty has not been entirely eliminated, the relative success of the modern welfare state has stripped the progressive movement of a compelling cause, one which derived moral force from religious edicts to assist the poor and needy.

Of course, there are other concerns, such as protecting the environment and securing the rights of sexual minorities, around which progressives continue to mobilize. Important as they may be, however, these issues are peripheral to the progressive ambition of altering the free-market distribution of resources through government transfers to the poor. To realize this ambition amidst declining political interest in poverty, progressive reformers increasingly have come to argue that the root cause of social distress is embedded in economic inequality, which represents the critical distributional defect of capitalism.

Although political efforts to reduce income inequality do not carry the moral weight of scriptural pronouncements (leaving aside those for whom *Das Kapital* assumes biblical status), they have an intuitive moral appeal. Long before any academic exposure to ideas of social justice, one typically hears young children yelling, "That's unfair!" when a pie is divided unequally among them; the quickest to complain are those handed the smallest slices. If Wordsworth's reflection that "the child is father to the man" carries any weight, then these early responses to inequality continue to filter our moral perceptions of what is a fair and just distribution of goods.[1]

Why not? All other things being equal, there seems to be little ethical justification for one child to get a bigger slice of the pie. However, as adults, **45** we come to recognize it is rarely, if ever, the case that all other things are equal. Karl Marx got around this problem by arguing that "the secret expression of value, namely that all kinds of human labour are equal and equivalent, because in so far as they are human, labour in general cannot be deciphered until the notion of human equality has acquired the fixity of a popular prejudice."[2] All human labor has the same value because we are all equal in what he deems people's most important characteristic—their humanity. This tautological formulation skirts the issue of how to or even whether to adjust for merit.

The question of how to deal with merit was addressed by another influential voice arguing for equality in the late nineteenth century. In Edward Bellamy's immensely popular utopian novel *Looking Backward*, the state guaranteed the "nurture, education, and comfortable maintenance of every citizen from cradle to grave." When this sweeping guarantee is explained to the novel's protagonist Julian West (who had awoken in Boston in 2000 after sleeping for 113 years), he asks how the workers' wages or benefits are regulated:

> "By what title does the individual claim his particular share? What is the basis of his allotment?"
>
> "His title," replied Dr Leete (Julian's guide) "is his humanity. The basis of his claim is the fact that he is a man."[3]

And as with Marx, it was on the basis of their humanity that everyone received an equal credit by which to acquire the resources for a comfortable standard of living. If every man's income was the same, Julian wondered what inducements were there to put forth one's best endeavors and how was merit rewarded? Dr. Leete explained that status and recognition were conferred through a system of distinguishing the best workers in every field and awarding them badges of iron, silver, and gold, proudly worn in daily life. The award of blue and red ribbons represented the highest honors, which were reserved for the most creative contributions and accompanied by "special privileges and immunities." There were also many minor distinctions of standing within ranks so that no form of merit went unrecognized.

Thus, even Bellamy's vivid egalitarian impulse could not escape the need to compensate merit and penalize sloth. Divorcing status from wealth, his utopia was organized on the principle that merit should be recognized mainly by rewards of honor and status rather than material compensation. As for the material life, everyone deserved an equal share—more or less. Bellamy was vague about the "special privileges and immunities" provided to members of the highest rank in the industrial army, noting only that they were intended to be modest enough so as not to create invidious comparisons with those in lower ranks. And there was one explicit exception to the guaranteed standard of living, as Dr Leete made clear, "a man able to do his duty and persistently refusing, is sentenced to solitary imprisonment on bread and water till he consents."[4]

Since classical antiquity, the balance between merit and equality has animated philosophical debate about what constitutes a just distribution of material goods. Aristotle, for example, believed that a fair and just distribution could not ignore merit, which once taken into consideration made a fair distribution essentially an unequal one. He squared the intuitive sense that "equal" is just by differentiating between numerical and proportional equality.[5] The former dictates that everyone gets the exact same basket of goods; while latter prescribes that the amount of goods received by different people is relative to the amount of effort each contributed to their production. With this deft distinction, Gregory Vlastos observes, "the meritarian view of justice paid reluctant homage to the equalitarian view by using the vocabulary of equality to assert the justice of inequality."[6]

How these things are expressed is important. Arguing to increases taxes on the wealthy, President Obama's "You didn't build that" statement during the 2012 election campaign was seized by conservative opponents as a virtual denial of just rewards for individual merit. His progressive supporters rebutted that the sentence was being quoted out of context, which was frequently the case. Since different interpretations are possible, readers may judge for themselves the extent to which this statement esteemed individual merit.

> If you were successful, somebody along the line gave you some help. There was a great teacher somewhere in your life. Somebody helped to create this unbelievable American system that we have that allowed you to thrive. Somebody invested in roads and bridges. If you've got a business—you didn't build that. Somebody else made that happen. The Internet didn't get invented on its own. Government research created the Internet so that all the companies could make money off the Internet. The point is, is that when we succeed, we succeed because of our individual initiative, but also because we do things together.[7]

It is certainly true that along the way successful people receive help from others, usually starting with their parents, and that entrepreneurs along with everyone else benefit from public order and the physical infrastructures of modern societies. A forceful expression of these truths, the President's statement gave little voice to the role of individual talent, hard work, and enterprise in creating successful businesses. The mild credit granted to individual initiative was wrapped in communal aid.

Although basically of one cloth, the progressive argument for raising taxes on the wealthy and increasing income equality is woven from several strands of political and academic thinking. On the street, populist demands for equality tend to be justified in the prickly idiom of "Wall Street vultures" and "capitalist exploitation," which peppered the placards of the short-lived but widely covered Occupy Wall Street gathering. A more refined and forceful case for reducing inequality is made in the established political arena, where the discourse appeals to the intuitive sense that equal equals fair. All that is being asked is that millionaires and billionaires pay their fair share. This leaves aside the meritarian question of how much they made it on their own and legitimately deserve to possess this wealth in the first place, which critics on the right read into the widely publicized "you didn't build that" statement. It is a question that animates Robert Nozick's entitlement theory of distributive justice.[8] As long as someone has come by financial gain through either the lawful application of his or her labor or by way of a voluntary gift, the person was entitled to keep it—plain and simple. The resulting distribution in society was just, he argued, regardless of how much diligence, skill, or just plain luck had been involved and the amount of inequality generated.

Proposals to advance equality by taxing tycoons evoke little public opposition, Nozick's ideas of entitlement notwithstanding. Perhaps it is because some would question how lawfully the super-rich came by their wealth in the first place. And whether or not targeting this group is just, few would argue that the millionaires are unable to easily afford it. The progressive case for income redistribution gains added support from the prevailing assumption that economic inequality is inherently bad. This assumption is tied into the intuitive perception that equality is just, based on the incontestable fair-mindedness of equal opportunity, which is easily conflated with economic equality. Champions of economic equality have an emotionally compelling argument that assures the moral high ground to those making the case. It is not an argument which any sensible politician (or aspiring academician) wants to enter on the other side. Thus, in political discourse, equality is so thoroughly vested as an abstract good that questions are rarely raised about exactly how much economic *inequality* is unacceptable, how much is fair, or even how much really exists. The nature, extent, and implications of inequality are not topics for critical appraisal in the political arena. This leads to some fuzzy ideas of fairness.

Thus, in the name of fairness, Presidents Obama's call for billionaires to pay no less than 30 percent in federal income taxes was justified as "asking a billionaire to pay at least as much as his secretary."[9] Some might argue that billionaires should pay a much higher rate than their secretaries. Certainly that is the case in France, where 30 percent is a paltry sum compared to French President Francois Hollande's campaign vow to impose a 75 percent tax on all incomes over 1 million euros. True to his vow, Hollande passed the 75 percent tax. After it was struck down by France's constitutional council, he compromised, shifting the burden from the millionaires to the companies that employed them.[10] One might imagine that inequality in France was much greater than in the United States, which is not the case according to the measures that academics typically employ when addressing this issue.

In contrast to the moral appeals and vague calibrations of fairness in political discourse, the academic arguments for progressive policies to advance equality are grounded in systematic measures of both inequality and its impact. Quantitative metrics of social science impart an aura of precision to estimates of inequality . However, as with measures of poverty, the empirical estimates of inequality and what they signify rest on loose soil that offers fertile diggings for economists and philosophers. To grasp the essential meaning of inequality requires examining income measurements along with demographic changes, geographic differences, and shifting fortunes over the life course.

Measuring Inequality: More or Less

Income inequality in the United States is generally perceived to have increased over the last thirty years. But the degree and implications of this trend remain much in dispute. The disagreement reflects, in part, differences in the way economists measure inequality, which are rarely aired outside of technical publications.[11] And even when the different measures are reported, what they signify is difficult to discern beyond whether the numbers are going up or down. If some degree of inequality is inevitable, the question remains as to how much is acceptable. The next time someone explains to the reader about the need to increase equality, you might try asking: How much should we have? (As little as Sweden, is one likely response. But inequality has been on the rise in Sweden as in most other industrialized countries—so is the acceptable level that of Swedish inequality in 1995 or 2010?).[12] The standard indicators of inequality offer no widely agreed-upon answer to this issue. Instead, they convey a general impression of the distribution of income in society, which summarizes the degrees to which some people have more money than others.

The merits of scientific debates and philosophical arguments about the benefits of income equality cannot be fully understood without a fundamental grasp of the core measures around which the battle lines are drawn. Alas, it is a topic that will probably test the reader's concentration.

The most commonly used computations include the Gini index and a comparison of income quintiles. They vary in convenience and transparency. The Gini index provides an expedient summary, which ranges from zero to one; zero denotes perfect equality of income—everyone has the same amount—and one represents a distribution in which all the society's income is possessed by one member. These extremes, of course, do not exist in the advanced industrialized world. In 2011 Gini coefficients ranged from .342 to .568 based on the market incomes in twenty-eight member countries of the OECD.[13] By summarizing the dispersion of income in one number, Gini coefficients are useful for comparative purposes. Offering numerical precision, they clearly show whether economic inequality is increasing or decreasing over time and higher or lower among countries.

However, the numerical precision veils the existential reality of inequality, particularly in a country as large and diverse as the United States. That is, the numbers reinforce the intuitive sense that those with an annual income of $100,000 are better off financially, have say a higher standard of living, than others with an income of $85,000. If this were not the case, why be concerned about income inequality? But in fact it is often not the case. The US Bureau of Economic Analysis documents strikingly large differences in the cost of living throughout the United States.[14] Thus, for example, when regional prices differences are factored in, a $100,000 income in New York State is worth less than an $85,000 income in Montana. Understandingly, some might argue that it is worth the difference to live in New York. Having come from New York City, like many of my friends, I once believed that civilization ended on the east bank of the Hudson. Yet people have different preferences for cultural amenities and natural beauty—and different levels of tolerance for traffic, noise, smog, and cramped apartments. Montanans typically refer to their state as "the last best place," which may explain the influx of wealthy people over the last few decades. Cost-of-living differences are even more extreme among metropolitan areas. The San Francisco bay area is almost 40 percent higher than Rome, Georgia—a charming locale nestled in the foothills of the Appalachian Mountains. Because the cost of living is usually higher in states and metropolitan areas where the average household income is above the US median, the Gini coefficient tends to exaggerate differences in the levels of material comfort and well-being implied by economic inequality. Consider, for example, what $1 million will buy in housing in Dallas, Texas, and San Jose, California (see Figures 4.1 and 4.2).

FIGURE 4.1   A 5-bedroom, 4.5-bathroom brick home in Dallas, Texas—with an extravagant iron staircase, soaring ceilings, and landscaped backyard complete with a pool and spa.

FIGURE 4.2 A 3-bedroom, 2.5-bathroom home in San Jose, California, has a private courtyard entrance that leads to a completely remodeled interior with an open floor plan, with updates such as a large gourmet kitchen with high-end appliances.

The interpretation of the Gini index is opaque in that it fails to capture the actual shape of the distribution of income. Thus, two countries may have the exact same Gini coefficient, but different configurations of inequality among lower, middle, and upper income groups. Despite the suitability of Gini coefficients for comparing levels of economic inequality over time and among countries, the findings expressed by these comparisons can distort or obscure their implications for economic well-being. The prevailing assumption pictures increasing economic equality as a social improvement. Yet during a recession economic equality as measured by the Gini index may well increase in a country where everyone is getting poorer. Earnings fall for people in both the upper and lower income brackets, but the decline is steeper for those at the higher end—who have more to lose in the first place. By the same token, a country could experience rising inequality according to its Gini index, yet everyone is becoming better off. The rich are getting richer as the poor are also getting richer, just not as much. In this case the experience both satisfies the distribution clause in Rawls's second principle of social justice and exceeds the criterion of what economists call a Pareto improvement, which involves any change in the distribution of income that leaves at least one person better off and no one worse off.[15] Yet even in these situations progressives lend less weight to the overall increase in material well-being than to the negative social effects presumably generated by heightening inequality (an issue more closely examined in Chapter 5).

As with the measure of poverty, the degree of inequality revealed by the Gini index depends upon how income is defined. The working definition of inequality varies according to economists' choices about the components of income that enter their calculations.[16] Two of the definitions most widely employed are categorized as "market income" and "disposable income," which conceptually distinguish between household income generated solely from employment and investments and that which also includes the redistributive effects of the welfare state via taxes and social spending. As such, Gini coefficients based on disposable income are lower than those of market income, which does not include welfare benefits. Both measures are usually adjusted for household size, when the data allow.[17] Neither of the measures includes the monetary value of unpaid domestic production that the Canberra Group of international experts identify as a theoretical component of household income but consider too difficult to measure for practical calculations.[18]

In contrast to the conceptual line separating market and disposable income, the practical definition of the income components within these categories is open to interpretation. The narrow interpretation of market income includes the sum of all earnings, which would appear as gross income on US tax returns, excluding capital gains.[19] A more expansive view is taken in a US Census Bureau study that, in addition to earnings from work and property, interprets market income to encompass realized capital gains, government cash transfers, and the imputed value of rental income for homeowners, which can be seen as an investment return on home equity.[20] By including cash transfers this interpretation straddles the conceptual divide with disposable income.

The standard OECD definition of disposable household income takes account of the posttax sum of wages and salaries, net property income, net cash transfers, and social benefits other than social transfers in kind.[21] However, the most comprehensive estimate draws upon the Haig-Simons definition under which annual income amounts to the total value of what a person could consume in that period, without reducing his or her net worth.[22] In practice this total corresponds to the sum of the standard OECD measure plus the value of in-kind social transfers and the accrued value of capital gains.

The Value of Leisure

Even the most rigorous efforts to operationally define inequality using comprehensive measures of income are apt to disregard the monetized value of an essential commodity: leisure time. Ben Franklin's dictum that "time is money" captures the general point, but the specific amounts elude precise calculation. Leisure is a hazy concept, variously defined as time not spent in paid work, time devoted to engaging in enjoyable activities, and time consumed free of obligation and necessities. More precisely, leisure is seen as the period during which one is not engaged in compulsory activities that involve market work, household chores, home production, and errands to obtain goods and services. But these definitions beg the question of exactly where to draw the line between work and leisure. Those familiar with Thornstein Veblen's *Theory of The Leisure Class* have sometimes characterized the labor of academics attending learned gatherings in Paris or Rome as the leisure of the theory class.[23] Indeed, a good deal of professorial life involves activities associated with leisure such as sitting around engaged in lively conversation and leafing through interesting books.[24] This may be what California's Governor Jerry Brown had in mind when he opposed raising academic salaries because of the added compensation professors reaped from their "psychic income."[25]

Although the definition of leisure time embodies a degree of conceptual ambiguity, alternative measures reveal consistent empirical trends. As Keynes predicted, analyses of surveys over five decades show leisure time for working-aged people has increased; these findings hold whether measured by the highly simplistic definition of time not spent in paid work or by a more intricate appraisal based on the period during which one is not engaged in compulsory activities that involve market work, household chores, home production, and errands to obtain goods and services.[26]

Findings based on detailed time-use diaries of daily activities in the United States cast a long shadow of doubt on popular depictions of being overworked in modern life.[27] Yet, despite persuasive empirical evidence of increasing leisure, the sense of being overworked no doubt resonates today with the existential experience of many people, for whom the exigencies of working life fifty years ago is ancient history. Feeling short of spare time in the twenty-first century may have less to do with a decline in the supply of leisure and more with increasing internal demands aroused by the endless opportunities to invest one's free time checking Facebook, i-Phones, Twitter, Netflix, YouTube, and GoogleCircle, not to mention surfing 100 channels of television. The harried life of leisure is a paradox of the digital age. It has eliminated many time-consuming chores while opening vast possibilities of choice that have accelerated our internal clocks. Research suggests that the time during which online shoppers were likely to abandon a site if the page did not load declined from four seconds to two seconds in less than a decade.[28]

Along with the unforeseen results of technological advances, the dramatic increase in labor force participation of women since the 1960s has created the widespread feeling of continually being pressed for time. This is particularly experienced by well-educated professionals in two-income households with children—a profile that no doubt fits many readers of this book.[29] Between 1965 and 2010, the percent of mothers in the labor force more than doubled from 35 percent to 71.3 percent. It is important to recognize, however, that this movement into the labor force was not so much from a life of leisure to work as from household work to paid employment. This shift was accompanied by a loss of temporal autonomy, which heightens the constraint of work time.

Unlike the company employee tied to a desk from 9:00 to 5:00, the household worker can choose when to clean, go shopping, prepare food, or visit a friend for coffee—her time is "free" in the sense that she owns it.[30]

Although temporal autonomy creates flexibility around the use of leisure time, it does not increase the total hours available for these pursuits. Moreover, in 1960 household work involved preparing food, cleaning, and other activities for much larger families than in 2010, and without the widespread benefit of fast food delivery, microwaves, dishwashers, clothes dryers, self-cleaning ovens, and other time-saving devices.[31] For women the increase in hours consumed weekly by paid employment was more than offset by the decrease in time spent on household work, which fell by 50 percent between 1965 and 2003.[32]

The substantial data from time-use surveys show that since the 1960s leisure increased more for men than for women across all measures. The largest gain in leisure, however, was experienced by the less educated adults, an increase that favored people in the lower income brackets. This raises the question: Would income inequality decline if the Gini coefficient included the monetized value of this gain in leisure time? The answer depends on how the economic value of leisure time is defined. If hours of leisure were simply valued at the average market wage, income inequality would decline, since low-income people gained more leisure time than those in the upper brackets.[33]

However, most of the increase in leisure for women came from a decrease in household production and other nonmarket work. It is not clear how much of this work would command the average market wage. More to the point, conventional estimates of the economic value of leisure are usually based on opportunity costs, appraised by what one could have earned during an hour devoted to leisure or the price one would be willing to pay for leisure time.[34] By this definition the monetary value of leisure time is closely linked to earned income. As income inequality increases, the monetary value per unit of leisure also rises for those at the top of the ladder. Although the number of leisure hours has been declining for these high-income earners, it is still conceivable that the total economic value of their leisure time is increasing. Thus, even if the definition of income used to calculate the Gini index of inequality were expanded to include the monetized value of leisure time, the impact of increasing leisure inequality on income inequality remains an open question.

This landscape survey of income definitions stakes out the dense conceptual terrain that underlies the basic arithmetic of Gini coefficients. The devil is in the proverbial details of these conceptual accounts, which may excite professionals engaged in measuring income but makes dry reading for others.[35] The point of this excursion is to highlight the variability of what Gini coefficients represent based on technical choices about which professionals often disagree and to which the general public is rarely privy.[36] Thus, for example, according to OECD, measures of the Gini index of inequality for the United States vary by 36 percent, depending on whether income is defined as market earnings before taxes and transfers or disposable household income after taxes and cash transfers.[37] And these definitions exclude the value of in-kind transfers and capital gains, which would have yielded still different results. No matter which of the conventional income definitions is used, however, the results show that income inequality in the United States has increased over the last several decades and ranks among the highest in the developed countries of the world.[38]

In making international comparisons it is important to recognize that the Gini index conveys an incomplete view of social justice and little substantive insight into matters of economic well-being. For example, the .378 Gini coefficient for the United States represents a much higher degree of income inequality than the .257 computed for the Slovak Republic. As for economic well-being, a look at how much money is actually available reveals that the Slovak Republic's median disposable household income amounts to 29 percent that of the United States.[39] Their middle class would be on welfare in the United States. Beyond efforts to balance merit and equality, the quest for social justice also pays regard to an adequate standard of living. As Frankena argues, it includes "a vaguely defined but still limited concern for the goodness of people's lives as well as for their equality."[40]

Are the Rich Getting Richer and the Poor Getting Poorer?

A 2012 survey by the Pew Research Center found 76 percent of the public expressed the prevailing assumption that the rich are getting richer and the poor are getting poorer, which was about the same as the 74 percent that held this view in 1987.[41]

The abstract degree of inequality summarized by the Gini index, however, does not convey any information about whether the rich are getting richer while the poor are getting poorer. In contrast to the Gini coefficient, the analysis of income quintiles entails a direct examination of how money is distributed among the different groups, revealing the extent to which incomes are rising or falling. Calculating the financial resources of five groups that range from the top to the bottom 20 percent of the income distribution, this approach illuminates the economic well-being of families and how they fare over time. Here, too, the results will vary according to the alternative definitions of income. Thomas Piketty and Emmanuel Saez's well-known study of income inequality in the United States, for example, was based on the market income of tax filers.[42] According to this definition of income, from 1979 to 2007 there was a 33 percent decline in the mean income of those in the bottom quintile in contrast to a 33 percent increase among those in the top 20 percent of tax units.[43] Thus, left entirely to its own devices, the market allocation of income generated a pattern of increasing inequality wherein the rich got noticeably richer and the poor got poorer—a bleak testimony to the distributional problem of capitalism. This account reveals a trend that clearly violates the principle of social justice, which accepts economic inequalities as long as they are to everyone's advantage.

However, as Richard Burkhauser pointed out in his presidential address to the Association for Public Policy Analysis and Management, the market income of a tax unit is a poor indicator of how much money families actually have to live on.[44] A more inclusive measure of the income that remains in households after subtracting what they must pay in taxes and adding the money they receive through government transfers transmits a different image of the American experience. Applying these criteria, instead of a decline, we see a 32 percent increase in the mean income of the poorest fifth between 1979 and 2007 (Table 4.1). Overall this broader measure still reveals a rise in inequality during that period as the mean income of those in the top bracket climbed by 54 percent.[45] But it too is incomplete.

Along with taxes and transfers, the most authoritative and extensive measure of income also incorporates capital gains. The nonpartisan Congressional Budget Office as well as Burkhauser and his colleagues agree that a comprehensive definition involves the sum of market income adjusted for taxes, household size, cash and in-kind transfers, and capital gains.[46] However, the consensus unravels over the issue of how to value capital gains. The basic choice is whether to focus on the total taxable gains realized in the year capital assets are sold or the annual change in value of capital assets whether or not they are sold. This is not just a matter of bookkeeping. The choice to include either realized or accrued capital gains in the calculation of annual income has a considerable impact on the rates of inequality.

The Congressional Budget Office (CBO) favors the use of realized capital gains that are reported on tax returns. After factoring in the impact of taxes, capital gains, and government transfers, the CBO data reveal a sharp decline in inequality compared to when it is measured solely by market income. According to their figures, between 1979 and 2010 the household income in the bottom quintile increased by 49 percent, the income in the middle three quintiles increased on average by 40 percent, and those in the highest bracket increased by 71 percent.[47] While incomes increased across the board, these figures indicate that the largest gains were experienced by those on the two ends of the income distribution.[48] These findings temper progressive arguments that focus on the increasing inequality of market incomes to demonstrate the need for greater social welfare spending.

All of the income measures cited earlier (Table 4.1) indicate a rising level of inequality, which varies only in the rate at which it seems to have increased over the last three decades. In contrast, a different picture emerges

TABLE 4.1

Alternative Measures of Income Growth and Inequality

Population Quintiles	Change in Income 1979–2007– Based on Tax Unit, Unadjusted, Market Income*	Change in Income 1979–2007– Based on Household Size Adjusted Posttax, Postcash, and In-Kind Transfer*	Change in income 1979–2010– CBO Measure Column (2) plus Realized Capital Gains**
Poorest 20 percent	−33.0	31.8	49
Next 20 percent	0.7	31.3	40
Middle 20 percent	2.2	34.4	40
Next 20 percent	12.3	38.8	40
Richest 20 percent	32.7	54.0	71

Sources:
*Philip Armour, Richard V. Burkhauser, and Jeff Larrimore, "Deconstructing Income and Income Inequality Measures: A Crosswalk from Market Income to Comprehensive Income," *American Economic Review* 103 (May 2013), Table 1.
**Congressional Budget Office, *The Distribution of Household Income and Federal Taxes, 2010* (Washington D.C.: Government Printing Office: December 2013).

if accrued capital gains, which include housing, are substituted for realized taxable gains. This approach yields a reversal of income trends between 1989 and 2007, which shows a decline in inequality as the household income in the bottom quintile climbed at a rate considerably higher than the increase experienced in the top quintile, which was hit much harder by the housing market crash in 2007.[49] Introducing a plausible variant of the CBO's treatment of capital gains, this analysis challenges the dominant narrative about the rising tide of inequality. Needless to say, the choice between these methods of valuing capital gains is highly contested.

The Congressional Budget Office prefers to use realized capital gains partly because those data are readily available.[50] This practical consideration must be weighed against the concern that counting taxable capital gains in the year they were taken ignores the fact that often these assets have appreciated over many years. Although realized gains can be discounted for inflation over the previous year, the actual inflation has accumulated since the purchase date, which could have been decades earlier. Moreover, realized capital gains are usually taken sporadically, forming a volatile portion of income that varies from year to year, which can spike depending on the performance of the stock market and changing tax laws. Thus, the unusual jump in income inequality in the period immediately following the 1986 Tax Reform Act, which dropped individual tax rates beneath corporate tax rates, is more likely attributed to a shift from corporate to individual income than a material change in inequality.[51] Most important, perhaps, is that accounting for taxable realized capital gains ignores the increased value of stocks and bonds that are not taxed until they are sold and overlooks up to $500,000 of profit on the sale of housing, the average citizen's primary capital asset. These are significant shortcomings.

Yet to its advantage, the calculation of realized capital gains from tax returns is exact and relatively straightforward compared to the intricate estimates of accrued capital gains on which economists disagree. These estimates first require making assumptions about the rate of return on assets in order to compute a periodic change in values to stocks, bonds, housing, and other capital assets. Then the imputed gains or losses are allocated based on the arguable assumption that everyone receives the same rate of return for similar assets. Some would question including the appreciation of housing among accrued gains because the increased value does not affect the owner's standard of living and selling one's home is quite a different matter than cashing in stocks and bonds.[52] Others might compare gains on housing to an accumulation of income in a savings account that could be drawn down if needed over the life course. With real estate values booming in the 1980s, for example, many elderly Californians sold their homes and retired to Oregon and Washington, with a comfortable nest egg.

Every pertinent measure of income quintiles, especially the widely acknowledged comprehensive assessment by the Congressional Budget Office (CBO), dispels the notion that within the United States over the last three decades the rich have been getting richer as the poor have gotten poorer. The CBO measure reveals that from the highest to the lowest quintile, the mean household income of every group was lifted amid a rising tide of inequality—among the bottom fifth the mean income increased by 49 percent.

Another Dimension: Looking Within the Groups

Although the analyses of change since 1979 illustrate the extent to which household incomes climbed while the gap between the bottom and top fifths widened, it is a one-dimensional picture that discounts what was happening within these economic bands. This image conveys a static impression that the same households within each quintile were experiencing these changes over time. In fact, a lot more was going on among the households within these five divisions, the particulars of which lend depth to the one-dimensional story of increasing economic inequality.

To grasp the full implication of the rising inequality in household income, it is important to recognize that during the period in question young workers were continually entering the labor force as the older generation retired and died. A twenty-five year old who began working in 1979 while living on his own with an income in the bottom 20 percent would be very likely to reach a higher bracket by the time he was fifty-three years old in 2007. So not only did entry-level income rise between 1979 and 2000, but over the course of time many of those who started out at the bottom climbed toward the top. In just the period from 1996 to 2005, for example, the US Treasury Department estimates that about half of the taxpayers starting in the bottom 20 percent moved into a higher income bracket.[53] Of course, we do not know how many members of this upwardly mobile group were young scions spending their first year out of Princeton as shipping clerks in their fathers' factory, serving Teach for America in a poor rural area, or lolling on the Left Bank—a reminder that numbers can impose a surface on patterns that shields us from the underlying reality.

Yet there is more to this story. As the time passed, the twenty-five year old was married and had two children. Thus, what started in 1979 as a single-person household in the bottom fifth of the income distribution had morphed into a middle-income household with four people by 2007. This change illustrates an important characteristic of the income quintiles. Although they represent five groups with an equal number of households, the average number of persons per household within these groups varies as do other characteristics such as family structure and employment. The top fifth of households contain 82 percent more people than the bottom fifth.[54] The proportion of married couples in each group ranges from 17 percent in the lowest income quintile to 78 percent in the highest. At the same time, single men and women living alone account for 56 percent of the households in the bottom fifth, but only 7 percent among the top group. And no one was employed in more than 60 percent of the households in the bottom quintile; while 75 percent of the households in the top quintile had two or more earners.[55]

Taking account of the household characteristics within each quintile reveals that to some extent the increasing level of income inequality since 1979 coincides with the changing demographics of family life, particularly the smaller number of persons per household, the decreasing rate at which couples form and maintain stable marriages, and the increasing number of two-earner households.[56] On that score, Bradford Wilcox and Robert Lerman estimate that 32 percent of the growth in family income inequality since 1979 is linked to the retreat from marriage and the decline of stable family life.[57]

Concentrating on advances within just the top quintile offers a different perspective, which sharpens our understanding of what is behind the rising level of economic inequality in recent years. Two prominent findings based on the Congressional Budget Office's (CBO) all-inclusive measure of income tell the story: From 1979 to 2010 the after-tax income of the top 1 percent increased by 201 percent (compared to the 49 percent increase for households in the bottom quintile and the 65 percent increase for those in the 81st to 99th percentile).[58] Research focused on the pretax market income of the top 1 percent generates an even higher level of inequality than the CBO findings.[59]

Thus, a disproportionate degree of the increasing level of inequality was due to significant financial gains made by those at the apex of the income pyramid. As for the rest, a careful analysis matching data from the US Census Bureau and Internal Revenue Service demonstrates that after 1993 there was no palpable increase of inequality among the bottom 99 percent of the population.[60] Because the pretax incomes of the top 1 percent started at $388,905 in 2011, many of these families would not be considered the super-rich. It is around the top one-tenth of 1 percent, where pretax incomes start at $1,717,675, that we begin to cross the line between relatively well-off and truly affluent.[61]

As soon as the conversation on inequality begins to concentrate on the wealthiest households, the question increasingly comes to mind: What do these people do to deserve such immense rewards? A 2013 study commissioned by *The New York Times* discloses a median executive pay of $13.9 million among the CEOs of 100 major firms—described by one journalist as a "new class of aristocrat."[62] Although not terribly harsh, this description connotes a privileged class more renowned for its leisure pursuits than productive labor. But it does suggest how easily personalizing the numbers can transform a dispassionate report on the top 1 percent into bitter accounts of debauchery and corporate corruption. The likes of Bernie Madoff, Tyco's Dennis Kozlowski, and Ken Lay of Enron supply no shortage of infamy on which to justify a denial of merit. But then there are the brilliant hard-working multimillionaires who created Apple, Google, and Microsoft, not to mention our favorite movie stars and athletes. Though even here some might question why in the world grown men should receive immense sums of money to stand around a few afternoons a week waiting for a chance to hit a ball with a big stick? Major League players were paid on average $3.39 million in 2013. In contrast, for the same activity most minor league players earned between $2,500 and $7,000 for a five-month season—talk about inequality.[63]

Closer to my home and at a much lower rate of compensation than Major League players, all the faculty at the University of California, Berkeley, are on the same pay scale, except our colleagues in a few departments such as Business, Law, and Engineering. Their pay scale is higher, reflecting in part what an authority in these fields might reasonably expect to be paid on the open market compared to what an expert in Elizabethan poetry or child welfare policy could command. In a capitalist system, the criterion for reward is ultimately associated with what the market will bear. Of course, many people doubt just how well this standard works in practice. They wonder, for example, how difficult it might be to replace a CEO earning $20 million a year with an equally qualified executive who would accept half that salary. Also, market demand is no guarantee of social value or cultural enlightenment. A writer's worth varies by the number of readers that are willing to plunk down the price of a book, regardless of how crass or meaningless the content. Alas, *Fifty Shades of Gray* has earned millions, while my publishers will be fortunate to clear the modest advance awarded for this work. What the market will bear is certainly an imperfect calibration, but it is preferable to having the standard set by bureaucratic quotas or political bargains, though both are often in play.

How Has the Middle Class Fared?

Countless reports contend that the middle class is being crushed by inequality and diminishing income. Addressing these claims, the President's 2015 State of the Union message frequently mentioned the need to shore up the American middle class. In contrast, his sole reference to the poor was the call for a global effort to eradicate extreme poverty around the world.[64]

With household incomes increasing amid rising inequality, what do the facts tell us about the state of the middle class? There are several ways to answer this question, depending on how the middle class is defined and the benchmarks against which its progress and well-being are measured. The historical absence of an aristocracy has bred a fluid sense of social class and a democratic ethos that imparts a degree of reluctance for Americans to identify as "upper class." Thus, the middle class is a well-regarded, if ill-defined, status, to which most Americans subscribe. It is typically associated with one's income, education, and occupation. Numerous polls capture the propensity of Americans to identify themselves as somewhere along the spectrum of lower middle to upper middle class. Between 1972 and 1994, for example, no more than 10 percent of those responding to the annual General Social Survey saw themselves as either lower class or upper class.[65] Gallup polls taken from 2001 to 2012 show a solid majority of respondents self-identified as middle or upper middle class, though over this period the figures declined from 63 to 55 percent.[66]

When policymakers and the media talk about the middle class, however, it is usually defined by economic divisions. Estimates vary regarding the range of income that delineates the middle class, as well as the interpretation of how the economic fortunes of this group have changed over time. Thus, reviewing the same Census Bureau data, *The New York Times* decries, "Middle Class Shrinks Further as More Fall Out Instead of Climbing Up," while ten days later the Pew Research Center announces, "America's 'Middle' Holds Its Ground After the Great Recession."[67] Both of these captions are correct and neither highlights the larger story in the data, which only underscores how those who write the headlines may parse the numbers to express the points they wish to publicize. The economic definitions of the middle class in these reports differ—$35,000–$100,000 in *The New York Times* and $40,667–$122,000 in the Pew study. But the findings are very similar. Both show a substantial contraction of about 10 percent in the size of the middle class, which started shrinking around 1970. Though it sounds ominous, this decline of the middle class is not necessarily a distressing trend. It depends on where those who were squeezed out of the middle class ended up. If they all moved into the upper income brackets, everyone is better off.

So where did they go? The answer hinges on the years in question. *The New York Times* headline focused on the period from 2000 to 2013, the decade of the Great Recession during which the middle class declined by around 2 percent, the upper income group also declined by about 3 percent, while the lower income group increased. The Pew caption referred to the period from 2010 to 2013, just after the Great Recession. Over this interval the size of the middle class remained stable, and there was even a small uptick in the upper income group and a slight decline in the lower income group.

Despite the fluctuation of a few percentage points during the Great Recession, the larger story in *The New York Times* report is that between 1967 and 2013 both the lower income and the middle-income groups contracted while the size of the upper income group expanded by 15 percent. From this perspective the shrinking of the middle class (and of those in the lower income bracket) is directly connected to a significant advance in economic well-being as the combined size of the middle and upper income groups grew by 5 percent.

Thus, while *The New York Times* headline evoked a disheartening picture of middle-class decline, the data easily yield a more promising interpretation of the middle-class experience since 1970. The Pew findings offer a somewhat different conclusion, in part because the middle-class definition was pegged at a higher level of income. Although the middle-income group fell by 10 percent, about 6 percent of those who left had climbed into the upper income category. But since the other 4 percent had dropped into the lower income category, the combined size of the middle and upper income groups fell by 4 percent.

Of course, there are other benchmarks against which to evaluate the economic progress and status of the American middle class. Certainly, those concerned about inequality would judge that the middle class has not fared very well in comparison to the income gains realized by the country's top 1 percent. But consider everyone else on this planet. The American middle class boasts the fourth-highest disposable household income in the world. The United States finishes behind only the Grand Duchy of Luxemburg (a country of half a million people)l Norway with 5 million people awash in North Sea oil; and Switzerland, which stayed out of both world wars and imposes the strictest immigration laws in Europe. The average US family has 38 percent more disposable household income than a family in Italy, 25 percent more than a family in France, and 20 percent more than a household in Germany, when adjusted for differences in purchasing power.[68]

Although some academics invest considerable intellectual energy in debating how to quantify inequality and the significance of change in measures

such as the Gini coefficient, most members of the middle class have no idea
whether this index is going up or down, unless they read about it in news. And
even then the average middle-class citizen is more interested in how much
money remains for her family to live on after the give and take of government taxes and transfers than whether or not the Gini index rose or fell by
three-tenths of a point. If there is any doubt, ask yourself if given the choice to
dwell in one country as a member of the middle class knowing only the Gini
coefficient of inequality and the median household income, where in Table 4.2
would most politically middle-of-the-road Americans want to settle?

A number of issues have been raised about the divergent approaches to
the measurement of inequality, the disparate characteristics of those in different income brackets, the absence of cost-of living adjustments, the plight
of the middle class, the soaring 1 percent, and the sobering impact of international comparisons. Some are more arcane than others. On the whole these
issues serve not so much to dismiss concerns about rising economic inequality as to calm public apprehensions about the rate, degree, and implications
of this trend. The disparities related to the changing distribution of income
in the United States look a lot more acute before taxes and benefits are taken
into account. As such, it can be said that the capitalist market generates and
the welfare state mitigates inequality. Recounted in its most auspicious light,
the story of this interaction over the last three decades reveals that while inequality increased so did household incomes at every level. Measured by disposable household income, the US standard of living is among the highest of
all the advanced industrial democracies, not to mention the rest of the world.
Indeed, reflecting on the rest of the world, Tyler Cowen urges us to preface all
discussions of inequality with a reminder that although economic inequality

TABLE 4.2
Inequality and Household Income, 2010

Country**	Gini Coefficient	Median Disposable Household Income*
A	.38	29,100
B	.29	24,200
C	.27	24,300
D	.26	23,700
E	.30	23.300
F	.34	20,100
G	.32	21,000
H	.34	23,200

*US dollars controlled for purchasing power parity.

**A-U.S.; B-Germany; C-Sweden; D-Finland; E-France;
F-Japan; G-Italy; H- U.K.*Source*: OECD (2014), *Society at a
Glance 2014: OECD Social Indicators* (Paris: OECD). http://
dx.doi.org/10.1787/soc_glance-2014-en

has been increasing among advanced industrialized nations, over the last two decades global inequality has been falling.[69]

Could We Ask for More?

Of course, in an ideal world everyone would have been even better off if the top 1 percent had taken home less than 13 percent of all the income and the bottom 20 percent had gained more—while the economy grew at the same rate. Not to promote the best as an enemy of the good, there is nevertheless a convincing case to be made for social reforms that would to some degree shift the distribution of income away from the top. Progressives and conservatives agree on the need to rein in government transfers received by wealthy citizens, particularly the special benefits derived from favorable tax treatment afforded homeowners. These benefits, known as "tax expenditures," allow homeowners to deduct the interest paid on mortgages and to net up to $500,000 of capital gains tax free on the sale of their homes.[70]

The amounts are not trivial. In 2013, the Congressional Budget Office estimates that the tax expenditures for mortgage-interest deductions amounted to $70 billion, almost 73 percent of which went to households within the top 20 percent of the income distribution, while those in bottom 20 percent received no benefit.[71] Peter Peterson, Secretary of Commerce in the Nixon administration, declared these benefits a "perverse subsidy" and proposed limiting the amount of mortgages that would qualify for a deduction to $250,000.[72] Similarly, policy councils established under both President George W. Bush and President Obama have also recommended capping the size of mortgages that qualify for deductions. In theory one might argue for the continued support of these tax preferences if they functioned as incentives to promote the socially desirable end of home ownership. This argument would not apply to the mortgage deduction on second homes. But research finds that by and large most of the assistance is going to upper income families who would have purchased homes in the absence of these tax breaks. The main difference being that they probably would have bought slightly smaller homes.[73] Although there would be some downside for the home-building industry, limiting tax subsidies to wealthy homeowners could lower the level of inequality without seriously adverse consequences for the rate of home ownership.

Yet even if these adjustments were made, much income inequality would still remain, which takes us back to the question: Could we ask for still more? Obviously there are many ways for government to appropriate additional money from those in the upper income brackets and deliver more to those on the bottom. Raising income taxes, lifting the ceiling on taxable income for Social Security, increasing the Earned Income Tax Credit and eliminating its marriage penalties, boosting the minimum wage, means-testing

Social Security benefits, and taxing the fringe benefits of employment are among the evident alternatives. Progressives and conservatives argue about whether such measures would kill jobs or grow the economy, discourage work or stimulate activity, generate class conflict or enhance social solidarity, and advance social justice or deny the just deserts of individual merit. A vast literature on these issues has generated mixed findings about the implications of various measures.[74] Thus, for example, Congressional Budget Office estimates indicate that while increasing the minimum wage would raise the pay of low-income workers, it would also eliminate some low-wage jobs, causing a substantial decline in the income of those who became unemployed. Moreover, a considerable portion of the increased earnings would go to families already earning well above the median income.[75] In a similar vein, studies published in reputable journals evince more than a dozen different estimates of the behavioral consequences of tax increases.[76]

Considering the uncertainty surrounding these issues, the degree of support for additional measures to spread the nation's wealth is heavily influenced by one's answer to the question: How serious is the problem of rising economic inequality amid increasing household incomes over the last three decades? The answer rests on competing ideas about the current state of material well-being in America, the integrity of free-market capitalism, and above all the putative consequences of inequality. As long as household incomes are increasing at every level (as measured by the CBO), conservatives are less concerned about rising economic inequality than progressives. They accept inequality as the tribute equality grants to merit, productivity, and luck in the free market, recognizing that this transaction is sometimes distorted by discrimination, exploitation, and larceny, which need to be checked by government.[77] With the average family's disposable household income in the United States among the highest in the world, inequality is perceived less as a source of social friction between the "haves and the have-nots" than as an imbalance between those who have a lot and others who have more. From this perspective it could be said that the age-old problem of scarcity has morphed into the contemporary challenge of abundance: The critical issue is no longer how to assist those whose resources are too meager to live on, but how to deal with those who have a disproportionate slice of the economic pie. This is an issue that fails to agitate conservatives.

Progressives abhor inequality. Compared to conservatives, they lend greater credence to the idea that inequality stems as much (if not more) from exploitation, discrimination, and larceny as from merit and productivity. Pointing to ample cases of corporate disregard for consumer protection and environmental degradation, many would accept the view of competitive markets as places where "dishonest and inhumane practices will drive out the honest and humane ones."[78] Joseph Stiglitz observes that many of the brilliant contributions that have advanced social well-being in modern society were made by scientists whose rewards were relatively modest compared to corporate executives at the top of the income ladder. As for those at the top of the distribution, he contends, "more than a small part of their genius resides in devising better ways of exploiting market power and other market imperfections—and, in many cases, finding better ways of ensuring that politics works for them rather for society more generally."[79]

Progressive leaders have declared income equality in the United States to be the defining challenge of modern times, one which threatens "the very essence of who we are as a people."[80] These pronouncements may herald the launch of a progressive initiative to increase social transfers or merely reflect routine rhetoric to fire up populist sentiment for the next election. In either case, they convey less concern about the average standard of material well-being, whether compared to what it was thirty years ago or what it is today in other wealthy countries, than about a disagreeable disparity between the amounts of income earned by the wealthiest people in the country and everyone else. How much is too much? What determines when the level of economic inequality becomes objectionable from the progressive perspective?

Imagine if we could erase the slate and the first study of the distribution of income in the United States has just been published revealing that the top 1 percent of tax units took home 10 percent of all the market income (or one-half of the amount they actually take home today). How would progressives respond to this imbalance? They would probably still be inclined to call for less because progressives see economic inequality as inherently toxic, which voids the questions of what caused it and how much might be acceptable.[81]

Temperamentally indisposed to any inequality, the progressive outlook is intellectually supported by more than the mere assertion that economic inequality is wrong. The progressive disposition is justified by five prevailing assumptions about why inequality is socially harmful: it spawns social ills, hinders economic growth, warps democracy, defies individual preferences, and impedes social mobility. As we shall see, despite repeated claims in a large body of social science literature, there is less here than meets the eye.

5

Inequality Amid Abundance

WHAT'S THE HARM?

In a free society some degree of income inequality is inevitable. But how much is socially acceptable? This is a contested issue that reflects one's views about the consequences of economic disparities. Progressives contend that inequality is the essential incubator of social ills, even within wealthy countries where the floor of material well-being is high. This outlook frames much of the writing on economic inequality by academics and members of the media.[1] As they see it, a vast body of research testifies that inequality breeds human miseries and economic stagnation while undermining democracy and retarding social mobility. These studies reinforce each other, lending the appearance of a rigorous scientific consensus. A probing analysis of the empirical evidence, however, tells another story.

A Seedbed of Social Ills

What is arguably the foremost prevailing assumption about the impact of economic disparities encompasses a broad band of social, psychological, and physical suffering. These detrimental outcomes are widely broadcasted as scientific truths to the general public. In addition to those who have actually read Joseph Stiglitz's popular 500-page volume *The Price of Inequality*, many others just having scanned the dust jacket will get the message that "the social impacts of inequality are now increasingly understood—higher crime, health problems, and mental illness, lower educational achievement and life expectancy."[2] The same can be said for Richard Wilkinson and Kate Pickett's provocative study, *The Spirit Level: Why Great Equality Makes Societies Stronger*, which claims that "almost every modern social problem is more likely to occur in a less-equal society. This is why America the richest nation on earth has per capita shorter life spans, more mental illness, more obesity and more of its people in prison than any other developed nation."[3]

One of the most talked about and frequently cited works on this topic, Wilkinson and Pickett's study linked levels of economic inequality among twenty-three countries (and among states within the United States) to a litany of social ills, including higher rates of homicide, infant mortality, obesity in children and adults, childhood conflicts, imprisonment, teenage births, mental illness, and illegal drug use, along with lower levels of educational attainment, trust, life expectancy, foreign aid, women's status, recycling, and social mobility. The links were empirically forged with a massive amount of data and reinforced by references to numerous studies, creating a body of evidence, which ostensibly confirms that economic inequality spawns considerable social distress.

Having confirmed what egalitarians believed in their bones as the abiding truth, these findings were endorsed by the progressive press without reservation. Writing in the *New Statesman*, Roy Hattersley, a leading figure in the British Labor Party, attests, "The correlation is near to absolute. Inequality goes hand in hand with the social diseases that blight whole communities." He concludes that "unless progressive politicians are stupid as well as craven they will seize the moment to argue for the egalitarian alternative."[4] Likewise, *The Guardian*'s editorial goes on record insisting, "The Spirit Level's inconvenient Truths must be faced."[5] On the opinion page of *The New York Times*, citing John Steinbeck's dictum that "a sad soul can kill you quicker, far quicker, than a germ," Nicholas Kristof verifies that the book offers "growing evidence that the toll of our stunning inequality is not just economic but also is a melancholy of the soul."[6] Admitting in *The London Sunday Times* that "The Spirit Level merely formulates what everyone has always felt," John Carey, a distinguished professor of English literature, finds what is new about this book is that "it turns personal intuitions into publicly demonstrable facts."[7] That one finds not a grain of salt sprinkled among these journalistic encomiums suggests the potency of either the research findings or the capacity of the prevailing assumption to extinguish critical scrutiny. I leave it to the reader to judge the evidence.

Before examining the empirical evidence, however, ordinary curiosity implores us to consider the common-sense logic of the prevailing assumption: What precisely is it about income inequality (not abject poverty, mind you) in wealthy countries that cultivates the bristly garden of social ills described by Wilkinson and Pickett?[8] Their answer to this question rests in part on a firm body of scientific data documenting the deleterious effects of psychological stress on physical and mental health.[9] On the back of this hard evidence they graft the flimsy speculation that psychological stress is directly related to the level of income inequality in society. "Greater inequality," they assert, "seems to heighten people's social evaluation anxiety by increasing the importance of social status. Instead of accepting each other as equals on the basis of our common humanity as we might in more equal settings, getting the measure of each other becomes more important as status differences widen."[10] (Note how agreeably the acceptance of equality on the basis of "our common humanity" resonates with the earlier discussion of Marx and Bellamy's utopian musings.)

In countries with higher rates of income inequality, Wilkinson and Pickett see "social position as a more important feature of a person's identity."[11] According to this view, a professor or an industrial magnate's social position would be a more important feature of his or her identity in the United Kingdom (where the Gini measure of income inequality is .34) than in Germany (where the Gini index is .29), and so on down the line among other countries with lower levels of inequality.

These speculations deny the obvious truth that income inequality is at once a palpable and amorphous condition. The average US citizen recognizes, of course, that there are differences in income throughout the world, within her own country, in her immediate neighborhood, and among friends and family members. That some people have more money than others is a tangible reality. But most people have no idea about the actual distribution of income and their position in the population. An analysis of several surveys of ordinary citizens in up to forty countries reveals widespread misperceptions about the degree of inequality, how it is changing, and where they fit in their country's income distribution. For example, in the countries surveyed, an average of 7 percent of respondents owned a car and a second home, yet on average 57 percent of this group thought they belonged in the *bottom half* of the income distribution. Among low-income respondents receiving public assistance, a majority placed themselves *above* the bottom 20 percent of their income distribution. In light of these and other findings, the researchers conclude, "it seems doubtful that the median voter generally knows whether she would lose or gain from redistribution."[12]

And most people who do have ideas about inequality rely on reports from the progressive media, which gets its information from a relatively small group of researchers in universities, the Congressional Budget Office, and think tanks. And even then, what does this information tell the average citizen? The standard index of inequality signifies at best a fuzzy abstraction, which conveys nothing about one's economic position in society or how it might be changing.

If income inequality generates stress through creating insecurity, dissatisfaction, and low self-esteem based on how well one's income measures up to that of others, then much depends on the boundary that frames this comparison. Exactly what is the reference group for these "others"? Do middle-class elementary school teachers in El Paso, Texas, for example, compare their incomes primarily to those of their coworkers, neighbors, the oil barons within the state, Wall Street bankers across the country, Silicon Valley CEOs in California, insurance salesmen in Manhattan, the Mexican workers just across the Rio Grande, or the income of their fathers and siblings? Some may well relish the thought that they are doing better than their fathers and their neighbors just across the border. Others might feel satisfied or dissatisfied by comparisons to their coworkers and fellow citizens in the local community. It is unlikely that on their way to work many are disheartened by the thought that Mark Zuckerberg is now on a yacht somewhere in the Mediterranean. People generally compare themselves to others in similar economic circumstances rather than to dot-com moguls and movie stars. "What matters," Richard Layard submits, "is what happens to our 'reference group,' because what they get might have been feasible for you, while what Tom Cruise gets is not."[13]

The point is that it is hard to imagine why all the teachers in El Paso would compare themselves to the same reference group and why any of their comparisons would encompass the income distribution of the entire country. In 2013 the median salary of elementary school teachers in El Paso was $51,170. How would they judge their level of material well-being against that of teachers in San Jose, California, whose median salary was $70,720? Would it change their assessment to know that after being adjusted for the cost living, the San Jose teachers' median falls to $23,352 and the El Paso median climbs to $55,862?[14]

Indeed, beyond the difficulty of knowing how people grade their economic circumstances, the idea that personal security, satisfaction, and self-esteem all ride on where one's household income is positioned relative to a nebulous group of others exemplifies a narrow materialistic assessment of human nature which denies the diverse motives, ambitions, desires, and beliefs that animate people's lives. It is a mental attitude that reminds me of a woman I once saw in a shiny red convertible sports car with a license-plate frame that proclaimed, "She who dies with all the toys wins." She was stopped at a light next to another woman in an eight-passenger SUV with a prominent bumper sticker that announced, "Proud Parent of Two Miramonte High School Honor Students." The equation of individual stress with the overall level of income inequality in a society oversimplifies the way people score life. Although it may be the easiest to measure, material acquisition is by no means the only gauge of human achievement, self-esteem, and personal satisfaction.

Empirical observations further undermine the dubious notion that individual stress is somehow intensified by national levels of income inequality. Among the twenty-three countries analyzed in *The Spirit Level*, Japan ranks as having the lowest level of income inequality, yet it is widely considered to have one of the most stressful work environments in the advanced industrialized world.[15] And before entering the labor force, Japanese students encounter intense pressure to perform in school.[16] One might argue, however, that Japan's experience reflects an unusual sociocultural environment. Not only is the country's population declining, but more than half of the single people between the ages of 18 and 34 years are not involved in a relationship with the opposite sex.[17]

A more persuasive scientific repudiation of the inequality-spawns-stress hypothesis emanates from the by-product of research on poor people in rural Kenya, a region of the world where poverty signifies subsisting on less than $1.57 a day.[18] Based on a rigorous experimental design that included 1,372 rural households, this study examined the impact of a relatively large increase in income on a broad range of outcomes, including psychological well-being and the participants' levels of cortisol, a biological marker of stress. In sixty-three villages, participants were randomly assigned to treatment and control groups, the former received either small or large unconditional cash grants of up to $1,525 (almost three times the subsistence poverty line); about half of these grants were allocated in a lump sum and the rest in nine monthly installments. One of the central objectives of this study was to assess whether the alleviation of extreme poverty would reduce stress as measured by changes in the participants' levels of cortisol and their subjective responses to a research questionnaire. The findings revealed no significant difference in the cortisol levels between the treatment and control group. However, the treatment group registered significant improvements on subjective questionnaire measures of stress and psychological well-being, which offers partial support to the notion that cash transfers to those in abject poverty can reduce stress.[19]

Although focused on the alleviation of poverty, there is another way to look at this study and interpret its results. In the course of improving the economic circumstances of recipient households, the unconditional cash transfers created an immediate and palpable increase in the level of economic inequality between the treatment and control groups within each village. In these circumstances it was not necessary to understand the meaning of a Gini coefficient; in every village the members of the two groups could see that although they all lived in homes with thatched roofs at the beginning of the year, by the end of the year a large proportion of the transfer beneficiaries had metal roofs (and more livestock). With the obvious rise in inequality, would those who did not receive the grants experience an increase in stress and a reduction of psychological well-being? Indeed, the researchers recognized the possibility that increasing the income of some households in the village but not others might generate negative spillover effects. Contrary to the inequality-spawns-stress hypothesis, however, the study found no evidence of these negative effects.[20] Hence, neither logic nor systematic observation supports the alleged connection between income inequality and stress, which is typically put forth to explain many of the other problems attributed to inequality.

Although the underlying logic does not bear scrutiny, Wilkinson and Pickett's study offers hard numbers to buttress the prevailing assumption that economic inequality breeds a massive assortment of social problems. More than thirty-five graphs are displayed showing the degree to which the levels of economic inequality in twenty-three countries are statistically correlated to many adverse social conditions; all the graphs convey the same conclusion—the higher the degree of inequality the worse the problem. This striking visual representation may pose a convincing appearance of causality to the untrained eye. But every research student knows that correlations do not confirm causality, even if there are many leaning in the same direction. Countless illustrations show these statistical measures are readily susceptible to misinterpretation. Having found a fairly strong correlation between eighth-grade math scores in US schools and the distance of their state capitals from the Canadian border, for example, Daniel Moynihan submits the droll proposal that states seeking to improve their students' scores should consider moving closer to Canada.[21] *The Spirit Level*'s claims based on a string of simple two-variable relationships triggered a spirited debate, which exposed essential flaws in its design and implications.

Analyzing the connection between inequality and homicide rates in twenty-three countries, for example, the two-variable scatterplot illustrated in Figure 5.1 shows homicide rates rise as we move from countries with lower to higher levels of inequality (measured here by the ratio of the income between the top and the bottom 20 percent). This relationship is visually highlighted by a straight line drawn on the graph, which most closely fits the data points of all the countries.[22] However, in this distribution the United States' homicide rate lies outside the range around which all the other countries are

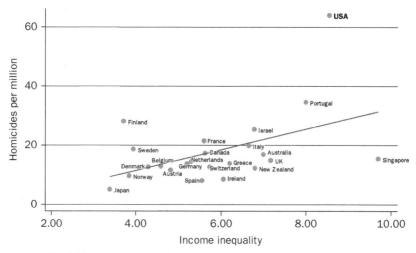

FIGURE 5.1 Homicide rates and inequality.

Data Source: EqualityTrust International Data Sethttps://www.equalitytrust.org.uk/civicrm/contribute/transact?reset=1&id=5

clustered. The US homicide rate is so high as to constitute what statisticians consider an extreme outlier that cannot simply be ignored.

When such outliers appear, it is customary to ask: What might account for such an extreme value? Would the relationship between levels of inequality and homicide still hold for all the other countries if this extreme case were taken out of the sample? One possible response to the first question is that as a result of permissive gun control laws, history, and cultural inclinations, the United States has the highest rate of firearm ownership in the world—almost twice that of the other twenty-two countries in the study; it also has the highest rate of homicide by guns, which is the way most murders are committed. In answer to the second question, when the United States is taken out the sample, the line fitted to the twenty-two remaining countries flattens out and the relationship between inequality and homicide is no longer statistically significant.[23]

The homicide example illustrates a serious problem in the research design of *The Spirit Level*; it completely ignores the potential impact of demographic, cultural, legal, and historical differences among a relatively small sample of countries in which a few cases can skew the findings. With a combined population of about 20 million almost entirely Caucasian people, for example, Sweden, Norway, and Finland have three of lowest levels of inequality among the sample countries; the United States has the highest level of inequality. But within the United States the state of California alone has almost twice the total population of the three Scandinavian countries and an incomparable degree of racial, ethnic, religious, and cultural diversity. With a sample of only twenty-three countries, many of the study's findings are disproportionately influenced by one or two extreme cases or by a small cluster of the Scandinavian countries.

In a dismissive critique of Wilkinson and Pickett's argument, Peter Saunders demonstrates how to generate an entirely different story about the consequences of economic inequality. By expanding the sample size to thirty-eight countries and correlating the countries' rates of inequality with their scores on a "Social Misery Index" composed of suicide rates, divorce rates, HIV infection rates, alcohol consumption, and racial bigotry, he discovers that "as countries become more equal, life gets more miserable." Reluctant to draw any meaning from this correlation, Saunders acknowledges the implausibility of marginal differences in inequality among relatively wealthy countries having a discernable impact on people's well-being.[24]

Ultimately if disparities in income spawned social pathologies, the consequences would show up not only among a range of countries with different degrees of inequality at a point in time but also within individual countries as levels of inequality vary over a period of years. That is, according to Wilkinson and Pickett's line of reasoning, a longitudinal analysis of individual countries should confirm that the intensity of social problems rises or falls directly in response to changing rates of inequality. Take, for example, teenage births, which represent a precise measure for comparative purposes. The cross-sectional analysis of the twenty-three countries reveals the higher the level of income inequality, the higher the rate of teenage births. However, from a longitudinal perspective the purported influence of income inequality evaporates. Between 2000 and 2011, despite the increase in income inequality in France, Sweden, and the United States, the teenage birth rates declined in each country. During the same period, the level of income inequality declined as did the teenage birth rate in Italy, Norway, and the Netherlands, whereas in Greece inequality declined but the teenage birthrate rose.[25] That is, in four of the seven cases the teenage birth rates change in the opposite direction of that expected.[26] A more startling contradiction appears in the long-term pattern in the United States illustrated in Figure 5.2, which shows the rate of teenage births rising as inequality declines from the late 1940s to the late 1950s and then falling as inequality rises through 2013.

According to Wilkinson and Pickett, a "vast literature" confirms what they describe as the "big idea" that income inequality is detrimental to health, particularly rates of life expectancy and infant mortality.[27] This reading of the evidence creates the impression of a scientific consensus that simply does not exist. It is based on a review of the literature in which Wilkinson and Pickett assess a large number of studies as supportive, partially supportive, or unsupportive of the hypothesis that inequality has a negative impact on a population's health.[28] Their classification ignores the comparative weakness of cross-sectional designs and takes advantage of the restrained discourse of

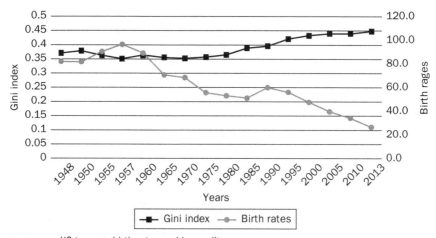

FIGURE 5.2 US teenage birth rates and inequality.

Data Source: S. J. Ventura, B. E. Hamilton, and T. J. Mathews. "National and State Patterns of Teen Births in the United States, 1940–2013." National Vital Statistics Reports 63, no. 4. Hyattsville, MD: National Center for Health Statistics, 2014; U.S. Census Historical Income Tables. http://www.census.gov/hhes/www/income/data/historical/inequality/

academic reporting. Thus, for example, Wilkinson and Pickett deem as "partially supportive" a study whose authors cautiously summarize their results as follows: "In contrast to most earlier studies, we find very little support for the view that income inequality is associated with variations in average levels of national health in rich industrial countries."[29] Likewise a systematic review of ninety-eight studies concludes: "Overall, there seems to be little support for the idea that income inequality is a major, generalizable determinant of population health differences within or between rich countries."[30] As Figure 5.3 indicates, over two decades the average rate of infant mortality for twenty-two OECD countries fell by almost two-thirds as the average level of inequality rose by 7 percent.

Indeed, an exacting body of longitudinal research offers persuasive evidence refuting the alleged effects of income inequality. A study of income inequality's impact on life expectancy and infant mortality in OECD countries, for example, found that over a period of twenty years life expectancy rose more in countries that had higher increases in inequality and infant mortality fell more in countries where the rise in inequality was highest—contrary to the big idea.[31] Similarly, an analysis of national trends in the United States between 1978 and 2000 reports that regions experiencing the largest increases in income inequality had the largest declines in mortality.[32] In 2002, an editorial in the *British Medical Journal* depicts Wilkinson's earlier findings on the impact of inequality as "an artifact of the selection of countries." It reports

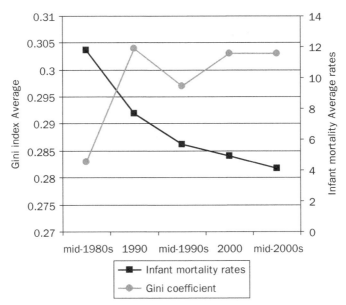

FIGURE 5.3 Average inequality and infant mortality rates for twenty-two OECD countries.
Data Source: OECD Factbook 2010.

that with better data, a larger sample, and controlling for other factors, more rigorous research shows "the association between income inequality and life expectancy has disappeared."[33] Thus, despite Wilkinson's assertions, numerous studies have failed to find any evidence linking changes in inequality to negative outcomes for life expectancy and infant mortality.[34] Summing up one of the most thorough assessments of the literature, Andrew Leigh, Christopher Jencks, and Timothy Smeeding's "reading of the evidence is that most studies of health and inequality find no significant relationship either across countries or over time." However, they add the judicious caveat that it may be premature to draw firm negative conclusions.[35]

The progressive indictment of inequality as the seedbed of social ills is sustained less by the accumulation of impartial scientific findings than by the sheer force of repetition riding on moral undercurrents that equate equality with fairness. This is magnified by conceptual confusions that conflate national measures of inequality with extreme poverty. By conventional standards of social science research, most of the empirical evidence for the adverse impact of inequality on a wide range of social problems is found wanting. But the arguments against inequality do not end here.

Promoting Plutocracy

Allegations that economic inequality threatens to undermine the political foundations of democratic society are as common as assertions that it fosters illness and mortality, though less amenable to measurement. The claim that inequality has an adverse effect on government's responsiveness to citizens is often expressed in the blunt equation: as wealth procures political power, plutocracy displaces democracy. The problem here is seen as a matter of immense wealth concentrated in the hands of the relatively few, allowing them to exercise undue influence on public decision making.

Certainly, invitations to influence peddling are ever present in the political arena, generating illicit temptations to which more than a few public officials succumb.[36] Just in the state of Illinois, between 1961 and 2009, more than half the governors ended up in prison. James Madison foresaw the problem, recognizing that human nature being what it is, "you must first enable the government to control the governed; and in the next place oblige it to control itself."[37] It might be argued that acts of outright political corruption, which are identified and punished, confirm the strength of democracy by penalizing those who govern for the inability to control themselves.

Charges of economic inequality's adverse impact on democracy tend to be framed less as unlawful acts of bribery than as the devious manipulation of voluntary contributions to sway elections and shape legislation and regulatory practices to suit the interests of those writing the checks. Regarding the electoral process, running for political office in the United States is an expensive proposition. Unlike the legal ceiling of $30 million on campaign spending by presidential candidates in France, the sky is the limit in the United States, where more than $6 billion was spent on the federal elections in 2012.[38] These costs have been increasing. Between 2000 and 2012, for example, total spending on federal elections more than doubled.[39]

Although hefty amounts are required to run for national and state offices, there is no evidence that the super-rich can buy elections. That does not stop them from trying. Many people on both sides of the political aisle are disturbed by billionaires donating vast sums to influence the electoral process, particularly when these contributions go to those in the opposing party. The Koch brothers pumped an estimated $407 million into defeating Obama in 2012, much of it their own money.[40] Progressives were no doubt displeased by the effort and overjoyed by the outcome. Now some are unnerved by the brothers' follow-up pledge to pour $889 million into the 2016 elections. But Willie Brown, who controlled the Democratic Party purse strings of the California State Assembly for decades, reminds us that if money were a deciding factor in politics, California would have had "Governors Al Checchi, Bill Simon, and the mother of them all Meg Whitman, who stuffed $170 million into the pockets of various consultants and lost by a landslide." Brown's response to the Koch brothers' pledge was "bring it on."[41]

Conservatives hold no monopoly on billionaires seeking to influence elections. George Soros and Tom Steyer spend generously on progressive candidate and causes. In 2014, Steyer reportedly donated $74 million in support of Democratic contenders vowing to combat climate change, with little electoral return on the investment.[42] Beside the partisans, many wealthy political patrons hedge their bets, investing in both parties to assure their tickets to the inaugural ball and a voice that will be heard when public policies have a bearing on their interests.

Although their sizeable donations often make the headlines, wealthy individuals are not the only players seeking to gain an advantage in the political arena. Special interest groups from all walks of life employ financial resources, moral persuasion, and constituent loyalties at their command to influence political decision making. Representing people from diverse segments of society—doctors, lawyers, teachers, auto workers, farmers, bankers, social workers, the elderly, children, ethnic groups, religious groups, and sexual minorities—these groups donate huge sums and often exercise considerable clout in the political arena. Between 1989 and 2012, public employee unions were among 6 of the 15 largest donors to national campaigns; it is no surprise that most of their money went to the Democratic Party, which typically supports government spending.[43] In 2014, about twelve thousand registered lobbyists spent about $3.2 billion plying their trade.[44] Some of the interest groups have a huge membership base. AARP (formerly called the

American Association of Retired Persons), for example, is among the most powerful interest groups in the country.[45] With a membership of 37 million adults over 50 years old and gross receipts of $2.2 billion, AARP is a major force to be reckoned with when it comes to social policies for the elderly.[46]

For decades, political scientists have been analyzing the levers of influence that bear on public policy decision making at the national and local levels. Initially much of this research was guided by a theoretical perspective that drew attention to the power wielded by the upper class while unintentionally and systematically neglecting other sources of influence.[47] In the late 1950s Nelson Polsby set out "to account for the extraordinary unanimity that scholars displayed in upholding certain propositions about community power— propositions, which according to a careful reading of the literature and independent research experience, seemed quite wrong."[48] His well-known study challenged the firmly held beliefs: "The upper class rules in local community life"; "political and civic leaders are subordinate to the upper class"; and "the upper class power elite rules in its own interests."[49] Based on a painstaking assessment of eight major studies of community power along with an independent analysis of public decision making related to urban development, education, and political nominations in New Haven, Polsby formulated a persuasive case for rejecting established views about the political dominance of an upper class power elite in local communities.

Employing a different research design on the national level more than half a century after Polsby's study, Martin Gilens's analysis offers another perspective on the relationship between economic and political inequality. In contrast to Polsby's case study approach that involved talking to local parties about their participation in decision-making activities, Gilens studied the policy preferences expressed by low-, middle-, and high-income respondents to national surveys. These preferences focused on four domains—foreign policy, economic policy, social welfare, and religious issues—spanning a period of years from 1963 to 2006. Overall he found a clear relationship between affluence and political influence. That is, the adoption of policies across all of the domains was most strongly aligned with the preferences of the high-income group. As Gilens notes, however, his sample of affluent respondents involved citizens at the 90th percentile of the income distribution who earned around $135,000 a year—a substantial sum in 2010, but hardly enough to qualify as the truly rich.[50]

Moreover, his evidence also showed that on the national level the preferences of these affluent citizens were far from decisive. The study identified other significant forces at play in the decision-making process. For example, inequality in political responsiveness to the low-income group declined when a presidential election was pending and if Congress was closely divided with a high level of policy gridlock. Policies favored by interest groups prevailed over citizen preferences on a number of specific issues, particularly in the domain of social welfare where interest group support helped to account for policy outcomes more favorable to the less well-off. To the extent that the findings suggest an unequal pattern of influence that favored the highest income group, the central question under consideration is whether this pattern was intensified by the increasing level of economic inequality between 1963 and 2006. On this matter, Gilens's data do not support the assumption that a rising degree of economic inequality fosters increasing political inequality. From 2001 to 2006, during the George W. Bush presidency, the difference between the influence attributed to the upper and lower income groups was relatively small, while the degree of economic inequality was at its highest level since 1963.[51]

Finally, there is a serious issue of whether a valid interpretation regarding political inequality can be drawn from survey data comparing policymakers' responsiveness to the preferences of upper and lower income respondents. The reason for this has to do with the numerical representation of groups that are defined by their level of income. Consider, for example, comparing political responsiveness to the preferences expressed by a random sample of citizens from the bottom 20 percent of the income distribution to preferences expressed by a sample of those in the top 20 percent. For argument's sake, let us say that the policy outcomes favor the preferences of the upper income group. The intuitive presumption is that the policymakers appear more responsive to wealthy people than to poor people, which may well be the case.

However, appearances can be deceiving. As noted earlier, when the population is divided into percentiles by income, although each percentile represents an equal number of households, there is considerable variation in the number of voting-age adults per household; the difference between the top and bottom 20 percent is particularly large, since the households in the top 20 percent of the income distribution contain 82 percent more people than those in the bottom fifth.[52] Thus, in favoring the preferences of the top 20 percent of the income distribution, it is not entirely clear how much policymakers are responding to the influence of the affluent or abiding by the tenets of representative democracy. Indeed, based on a broad review of the research in 2004, the American Political Science Association Task Force on Inequality and American Democracy concluded that "there is little evidence of a direct effect of rising economic inequality on widening political disparities."[53]

Of course, it is naïve to imagine that money is of little importance in politics, if for no other reason than so much of it is spent lubricating the electoral and policymaking processes. Democracy is an abrasive business, which is amplified by the American style of interest group politics. James Buchanan won the Noble Prize for his elaboration of public choice theory in which economic motives illuminate political behavior. "Much of modern politics," he says, "can be understood as rent-seeking activity. Pork-barrel politics is only the most obvious example. Much of the growth of the bureaucratic or regulatory sector of government can best be explained in terms of the competition between political agents for constituency support through the use of promises of discriminatory transfers of wealth."[54]

There is no utopian answer to the hunger of political and materialistic ambitions fed by wealth purchasing influence to further the buyer's social and economic interests. Shorn of utopian attitudes, James Madison sought the "defect of better motives," through a balance of powers held in check by opposite and rival interests built into the political system.[55] But as long as there is wealth, which presupposes some degree of income inequality, the affluent will test the restraints of our democratic system with varying degrees of success. Their impact depends on complex interactions among individuals, special interests, policy issues, timing, and shifting political divisions that are not fully understood. Indeed, with the explosive growth of social networks—Facebook founded ten years ago has 1.23 billion regular users monthly—we have yet to fathom the democratizing potential of the Internet age.[56] Although money counts, there is no persuasive evidence that an *increasing* level of income *inequality* has a direct bearing on the degree of political responsiveness to different economic groups in society.

Stunting Growth

Another frequent assertion about the detrimental effects of inequality is that it hampers economic growth. Several theoretical explanations are typically offered for this effect.[57] Pondering the psychological and political consequences, it has been said that economic inequality undermines trust, social solidarity, and a sense of fairness, which creates friction in the labor market and saps the motivation to work; politically, a high degree of inequality can create pressures for redistribution that lead to social unrest, which is detrimental to economic growth.[58] Trust, social solidarity, and a sense of fairness are states of mind that are difficult to separate from the context in which they are experienced. According to Emile Durkheim's classic analysis, solidarity germinates in the soil of moral and cultural homogeneity.[59] That is, small comparatively homogenous societies where a commonality of values, norms, and traditions is braced by ties of kinship, geographic proximity, and religion offer more fertile ground for a high degree of solidarity than large heterogeneous countries.[60] If this analysis is accurate, the question of distinguishing cause and effect arises. Does an egalitarian ethos promote social cohesion and trust, or does a preexisting level of social cohesion based on deep-seated cultural, kinship, and religious bonds generate more willingness to share the national wealth among citizens than in countries where these elements of social cohesion are less binding?[61]

In any event, the issue at hand is the extent to which the sense of trust and obligation to kith and kin associated with solidarity has an impact on productivity. Research suggests that the consequences for productivity are mixed, particularly for entrepreneurs in developing countries. Indigenous entrepreneurs in villages in Ecuador, for example, often converted to Protestantism to escape the numerous claims on their profits that came with the social and financial obligations of their membership in the Catholic Church. Along with the benefits of trust and normative obligations, solidaristic communities have been observed as giving rise to "a gigantic free-riding problem."[62] And although social solidarity imbues members with a positive sense of belonging and common purpose, it can also form a wellspring of conflict with outsiders, which is of growing concern as the rising tide of immigrant labor carries strangers across the borders of the global economy.[63]

In addition to the alleged impact on solidarity, inequality is seen to diminish economic development by impeding investment in human capital. If income were distributed more equally, those in the lower income groups would be better able to afford the costs of advanced education, particularly in the United States, where tuition prices have been skyrocketing. Yet the proportion of 18- to 24-year-old Americans enrolled in postsecondary education increased from 26 to 41 percent between 1967 and 2012; over the same period, economic inequality as measured by the Gini index climbed from .397 to .477. This experience fails to support the argument that increasing inequality exacerbates underinvestment in human capital.

However, the possibility remains that the spread of postsecondary education could have been even larger if the level of inequality had not increased. Besides, rising inequality was not the only change experienced over this period. Since the 1960s the feminist movement has propelled an increasing number of women on to higher education. And even if inequality had declined, one might still make an argument for a greater investment in education for low-income children.[64] It is often tempting to imagine how much better outcomes "would have been" if only a greater effort, more money, and a higher dose of some elixir were delivered—a musing that is immune to contradiction because the impact of heightened physical and economic stimuli cannot be firmly established in their absence.

Finally, what is perhaps the most persistent and contested account of how inequality stunts national growth involves the long-standing debate between supply-and-demand-side economics. Basically, one side of the argument holds that economic growth is driven by consumer demand for goods and services; low-income households tend to spend a higher proportion of their income on these goods and services than wealthy households, which have a greater propensity to save; all other things being equal, transferring income from those in the upper to those in the lower income groups increases aggregate consumption, heightening demand and reducing inequality. This transfer, of course, would impose higher taxes on the rich, which might create incentives to work less, to move out of the country, and to avoid taking entrepreneurial risks—though after the Great Recession one might argue that some restraint on risk taking among entrepreneurs is not such a bad idea.

Although economists have made many calculations to estimate the impact of financial disincentives, the precise effects of increasing marginal tax rates are elusive, in part, because of the various tax shelters available to wealthy people—exemplified in Warren Buffett's celebrated claim about paying lower tax rates than his secretary. But also because, as Eugene Steuerle puts it, "the failure to take into account other psychological and sociological motives for behavior, as well as the effect of complexity on the behavior that results, is a fundamental source of error in much of the economics literature."[65]

The case for supply-side economics maintains that expansion in the output of goods and services is fueled by investments in production that depend on the financial resources of the rich; if that pool of resources is drained through increased taxation, investment in productivity falls, constricting the creation of jobs and lowering the output of goods and services. In the modern global economy, however, both consumer demand for goods and services and capitalists' investments in their production increasingly transcend national borders. China's rapid economic growth, for example, has relied heavily on consumer demand from overseas. And with the accelerated mobility of capital, the worldwide level of foreign investment amounted to $19 trillion in 2011, of which the United States and China were both major recipients and providers.[66]

Globalization has been characterized by some as a logical progression to the next stage in the development of world capitalism;[67] others see it as giving rise to a fundamentally new system of capitalism that transforms the traditional division between workers and owners. The proportion of American households owning stocks, for example, climbed by over 200 percent between 1985 and 2013, giving rise to history's first mass class of worker capitalists.[68] In either case, whether globalization represents an advanced stage or a new form of capitalism, the growth of transnational corporations, the integration of capital markets, and the heightened mobility of labor have implications for theoretical assertions about how income inequality impacts a country's economic growth.

The various accounts for why inequality might impede growth—adverse psychological and political consequences, underinvestment in human capital, and curtailing consumer demand—form a backdrop to a body of research seeking to detect some empirical support for these ideas. An OECD report summarizes the results of 17 cross-country studies on this issue. Conducted between 1994 and 2014, most of these studies focused on between 40 and 80 countries over periods ranging from 25 to 40 years. The mixed results are inconclusive, if not bewildering. Inequality had a negative effect on growth in seven studies; at the same time, six studies revealed that inequality had a positive effect on growth in middle- and high-income countries; the remaining four studies were either insignificant or negative when inequality either increased or decreased. The report also included an analysis based on the author's research, which found that inequality had a negative impact on growth.[69] Some of the findings suggest that in low-income countries, where large segments of the population struggle to feed and clothe their children on $1.50 a day, the consequences of inequality may be politically more volatile, more detrimental to the development of human capital, and more likely to inhibit economic growth than in rich countries.

One hypothesis for the contradictory findings is that they reflect the different lengths of time over which the impact of income inequality was being measured; specifically that the short-term effects on growth were positive, whereas over the long term they turned negative.[70] However, additional studies by senior scholars focusing on the long-term experiences of wealthy countries fail to find a negative trade-off between inequality and economic growth. Controlling for a range of relevant variables, Lane Kenworthy calculates the effect of income inequality on growth from three perspectives: a comparative analysis of fifteen countries from 1980 to 2000, a comparative analysis of forty-eight US states over the same period, and a longitudinal analysis of the impact of inequality in the United States from 1947 to 2000. Carefully weighing the evidence, he concludes in each case that "income inequality appears to have had little or no effect on economic growth."[71] Another study using different measures reaches a somewhat more positive conclusion about the effects of inequality on growth in twelve rich countries over an average stretch of sixty-two years per country. This study found increases in inequality slightly boosted economic growth, though it was difficult to determine how much of the additional growth was eventually distributed among all the income groups.[72] In sum, assertions that income inequality stunts economic growth rest on evidence that is at best inconclusive, if not groundless.

Greed and Envy: It's Human Nature

The progressive conviction that income inequality is harmful to the social and economic fabric of society is reinforced by another prevailing assumption: most people care less about the absolute level of their income than about how much income they possess relative to others. That is, however much money they have, people are normally discontent when others have a great deal more than they do; it creates a sense of relative deprivation. This "normal" resentment of others who have more can be taken to imply that human nature prefers equality. The relative deprivation felt by those at the bottom can be allayed by having them move up the economic ladder past the others, but this imbues those being surpassed with a sense of relative deprivation. If everyone receives an equal income, everyone may avoid experiencing the psychological discomfort of having less than others. However, if people are really so concerned about how much income they possess relative to others, perhaps this state of economic equilibrium creates its own form of psychological discomfort, that which some people feel from not having more than others—the deprivation of relative advantage.

As the saying goes, if greed is the vice of capitalist society, envy is the sin of socialism.[73] The moral indictment of envy acquires semantic cleansing in the social science literature, where it is referred to as "positional concerns." Sara Solnick and David Hemenway's study has been widely cited as empirical confirmation of the idea that given the alternative, most people would prefer to receive less income as long as their position relative to others was more favorable than if they received a higher income. Their study asked 257 students, faculty, and staff at the Harvard School of Public Health to choose between living in two imaginary societies where a dollar had the same purchasing power:[74]

> Society A—here their yearly income would be $50,000, while others
> earned on average $25,000.
> Society B—here their yearly income would be $100,000, while others
> earned on average $200,000.

Loose interpretations of this study have advanced a misleading generalization about the clarity and meaning of its findings. Richard Layard reports, for example, that a majority of the Harvard students preferred to live in Society A. They chose to be poorer provided their relative position improved. Layard concludes from these findings that "people care greatly about their relative income and would be willing to accept a significant fall in living standards if they could move up compared to other people."[75] The way it was phrased conveys an impression that the findings clearly show most people prefer to live in Society A, where their income is much lower than in Society B, just to have more than the average. Although it is not what the authors conclude, this interpretation of the findings has been transmitted across disciplines.[76] The actual findings, however, tell a more ambiguous story. Preferences expressed in this type of survey are often sensitive to the order in which the choices are presented, with a strong bias toward selecting the first option listed; thus, the authors alternated the choices; and indeed, when offered as the first choice, 56 percent of respondents selected Society A, but when listed as the second choice, only 38 percent chose it. Although Layard was accurate to say that the majority of students, precisely 52 percent, preferred Society A, his description of the findings ignored the fact that a much larger majority, precisely 65 percent, of the faculty and staff chose to live in Society B. Moreover, when the preferences of the entire sample are tallied slightly, less than half (46 percent) of the respondents favored Society A.

Surveys of this sort are sensitive not only to the order in which choices are listed but also to their exact wording. Another study reports that when participants were given the choice of which job they "would choose to take," one where they are paid $35,000 and their coworkers earn $38,000 or one where their salary is $33,000 compared to coworkers earning $30,000, the overwhelming majority (84 percent) chose to take the higher paying job. But when asked to judge "at which job they would be happier," 62 percent selected the one that paid less.[77]

In contrast to these pencil-and-paper responses to hypothetical alternatives, a series of experimental games transmit a different impression of the importance people attach to their income relative to the income of others. When a player was given the choice between being paid 400 units of lab money and having another player also receive 400 units or being paid only 375 lab units and having another player receive 750 units, about 50 percent of the subjects in Berkeley and Barcelona labs took the lower sum, sacrificing their payoff to significantly increase the amount received by the other player. Over a range of experiments this study showed that subjects preferred to increase the overall welfare by taking a smaller payoff rather than preferring a payoff that denied any financial advantage to the other player.[78]

Of course, these experimental games were one-time exchanges, the sums involved were relatively small, and the other student volunteers could be seen as a limited and somewhat artificial reference group. Still the findings fail to confirm an instinctive preference for positional concerns. Although the research is hardly definitive, there is no compelling evidence to suggest that when it comes to income, most people would take less in order to prevent their neighbors from having more than they do—some would and others would not. To satisfy themselves on this matter, readers need only consider whether they would forego, say, a 10 percent raise to block their colleagues from receiving a 15 percent raise.

No doubt, most people, with possible exceptions for the likes of the Dali Lama, experience some degree of envy over what other people have, including income. The level of envy and how it might be expressed depend in part on who those others are and how much of a difference is at stake. Joseph Epstein observes that the Chicago Bears running back, the late Walter Payton possessed all the rewards to which his athletic ability entitled him: fame, money, and the love of beautiful women. But as Epstein, the one-time high school basketball sub and avid sports fan, sees it, if he envied Patton "feeling that what he had ought really to have been mine, I should have to be judged, rightly I think, insane." However, Epstein the revered writer asks, "am I insane to envy a not very good writer who wins a MacArthur Fellowship, which pays him roughly half-a-million dollars for doing absolutely nothing more than remaining his mediocre self?"[79]

Yes, the reference group counts—and so does the amount they receive. Epstein's point would have been blunted if the fellowship paid only $500. When it comes to income, the reference groups for most people involve neighbors, friends, family, and coworkers. Finding that a coworker doing a job similar to yours earns $8,000 a year more may arouse a vague sense of envy. However, income differences in this narrow range are not what propagate the popular discourse on the injustice of income inequality in America. If that coworker earned $800,000 a year more than you, the mild feeling of envy would be displaced by a strong sense of injustice. Envy and a sense of injustice, as Epstein says, "are not always that easily distinguished, let alone extricated, one from the other."[80] But within the US workforce this huge difference in reference group incomes is unusual, if for no other reason than an $800,000 income is exceptional. A difference that large is most likely to be experienced among the super-rich, the top one-tenth of a percent in the income distribution. But this is not a group that typically condemns the distributional flaws of capitalism and the injustice of income inequality in the United States. Such criticism emanates largely from what the economic theorist Joseph Schumpeter described as the intellectual class, "people who wield the power of the spoken and written word, and one of the touches that distinguishes them from other people who do the same is the absence of direct responsibility for practical affairs."[81] It does not take much imagination to recognize the main players in this cast: professors and journalists, whose occupations bear only the faintest resemblance to most work in the real world and among whom the progressive spirit is prominently represented.

According to Schumpeter, the material success of capitalism sows the seeds of its destruction by increasing the standard of living, leisure time, and educational opportunities for the masses and lowering the costs of books and newspapers, all of which cultivates the rise of an independent intellectual class. He was particularly unenthusiastic about the value of mass higher education, noting that the university graduate "easily becomes physically unemployable in manual occupations without necessarily acquiring employability in say professional work. His failure to do so may be due either to lack of natural ability—perfectly compatible with passing academic tests—or to inadequate teaching."[82] In any event, the increasing number of university graduates eventually swells the ranks of the intellectual class. Living by the written and spoken word, Schumpeter's intellectual is an "onlooker with a critical attitude that arises from the fact that his main chance of asserting himself lies in his actual or potential nuisance value."[83] Animated by a righteous sense of hostility that amounts to moral disapproval of the capitalist order, the intellectual class strives to influence public policies that would control the market.

Schumpeter was not far off the mark. But he failed to foresee that the evolution of the intellectual class was not immune to the culture of capitalism from which it sprung. Thriving on disagreement, intellectuals generated a competitive marketplace of ideas. By the late 1960s, wealthy private foundations, think tanks, and periodicals propagating the progressive critic of capitalism were confronted by the rise of alternative institutions of a conservative persuasion. *The Public Interest*, for example, an influential policy journal cofounded by Irving Kristol, was enlivened by neoconservative ideas emanating from think tanks and foundations on the Right.[84]

In line with Schumpeter's observation, Kristol viewed the class struggle for status and power, conducted under the banner of equality, as mainly a battle between intellectuals and the business community. Though a prominent New York intellectual himself, he was commenting on the predominant influence of the progressive faction—the unusually high proportion of the intelligentsia who are hostile to capitalism. Speaking of a group with whom he was intimately acquainted, Kristol writes, "Professors are generally indignant at the expense accounts which business executives have and which they do not. They are, in contrast, utterly convinced that *their* privileges are 'rights' that are indispensable to the proper working of a good society."[85] In speaking of academic privileges, he alludes to the well-kept secret that university teaching is entirely divorced from the normal discipline of everyday work. At elite universities the professoriate spends no more than four or five hours a week in the classroom for twenty-eight weeks, with another three hours per week advising students over a latte at the local coffeehouse and on a bad week, two or three hours of committee meetings. The rest of the time is divided between holding forth at learned gatherings in fashionable locations around the globe and conducting research for publication in jargon-laden journals, which may be cited by a handful of academics in their field. All told, pleasant work if you can get it. In many cases the privileges are well earned by brilliant advances, primarily in science, technology, engineering, and mathematics, the so-called STEM disciplines, which contribute to human progress and understanding of the modern world. In his treatise on why intellectuals oppose capitalism, Harvard philosopher Robert Nozick distinguishes between academics in these more exacting fields—the "numbersmiths" who do not disproportionately oppose capitalism—and the "wordsmiths" in the softer liberal arts disciplines and the applied social sciences, who tend to resent the capitalist system.[86]

As to the underlying source of the resentment among intellectuals living by the written and spoken word, a number of thinkers have arrived at the same conclusion: Average members of the middle-class workforce tend to judge their financial well-being against salient reference groups that have a relatively narrow range of income differences; in contrast, many members of the intellectual class cannot help but to compare themselves to wealthy capitalists, with whom they often rub shoulders. According to Thorstein Veblen, "people of scholarly pursuits are unavoidably thrown into contact with classes that are pecuniarily their superiors."[87] Ludwig von Mises also notes the tendency of intellectuals to mingle with successful capitalists, considering them as a reference group whose vast wealth creates resentment.[88]

Most members of the intellectual class do not enjoy the economic status of corporate lawyers, CEOs, hedge fund managers, and other captains of capitalism. However, in many cases the intellectual's connections to prestigious universities and the media, and the public's respect for purveyors of knowledge result in an elevated level of social status that rivals the economic status of the upper class and enables them to travel in the same circles.[89] The disequilibrium between economic and social status may incite resentment of the capitalist market for its failure to produce a more agreeable distribution of material resources that awards the intellectual's contributions to society. The professoriate, for example, are a privileged elite rewarded more highly in the currency of social status, relaxing sabbaticals, temporal autonomy, pleasant surroundings, and the veneration of aspiring graduates rather than hard cash. Still, their salaries are well above the average income, often in the top 10 percent. Yet it can be disconcerting when they find contemporaries who did not score as well in school or ex-students who only a few years earlier sat attentively at their feet now earning enough to afford summer homes in Italy.[90] They wonder, why can some coarse lawyer afford to buy a villa in Tuscany when a refined scholar who knows so much more about the art of the Italian Renaissance cannot? "What kind of society permits this state of things to exist?" asks Joseph Epstein. "A seriously unjust one, that's what kind."[91] The indignation expressed here stems from a mixture of individual envy and a larger sense of social injustice. In either case, the ingrained hostility to capitalism may help to explain why the progressive passion for equality is not deterred by the absence of scientific proof that income inequality has negative consequences for social, economic, and political life.

Social Mobility

6

Social Mobility

GOING UP AND COMING DOWN

Economic equality is concerned with reducing the distance between those in the highest and lowest income groups. Social mobility is about the rate of movement among these groups, from one generation to the next. Like diminishing inequality, advancing social mobility is a virtuous endeavor that elicits universal approval. Do you know anyone who is against increasing social mobility? It is a progressive cause that most people instinctively support without giving much thought to all that it signifies. Critical faculties are inhibited, in part, by the semantics—mobility is preferable to inertia. Also, the idea of social mobility conveys a righteous alternative to the rigidity and oppression of countries that historically were controlled by hereditary aristocratic rulers. And even in the absence of an aristocratic class, it has a particular appeal in the United States, an immigrant society, where people arriving at Ellis Island empty handed could anticipate seeing their children climb the ladder to middle-class prosperity. Although some people got stuck on the bottom and some ethnic groups moved up more quickly than others, the Horatio Alger myth remains a reality for many immigrants.

Intergenerational social mobility is deemed a marker of the extent to which a society affords all citizens an equal opportunity to rise above the economic station into which they were born. Thus, there appeared to be good reason for consternation when speaking to an audience at the Center for American Progress, President Obama decried the diminishing levels of upward mobility in recent years, pointing out that an American child born into the bottom 20 percent income group "has less than a 1-in-20 shot of making it into the top." Urging that we not pit the interests of the middle class against those of the poor, but try "to improve upward mobility for all people," he observes "that is it harder today for a child born here in America to improve her station in life than it is for children in most of our wealthy allies—countries like Canada or Germany or France. They have greater mobility than we do."[1] Hailed as "one of his strongest economic speeches" by *The New York Times* editorial board, not the faintest curiosity was expressed about the verity of the purported decline, the implications of the proposal to accelerate mobility, or the accuracy of the international comparisons.[2] Such is the self-evident good attributed to social mobility that any call for improvement is cause for applause.

The desire "to improve upward mobility for all" brings to mind Garrison Keillor's weekly musings about life in the town of Lake Wobegon, where "all the women are strong, all the men good looking, and all the children above average."[3] Only in a fictional world, however, can all the children be above average. In the real world the arithmetic does not pan out. The same must be said for the estimable intent of improving upward mobility for all, when it is defined by the rate at which people move from lower to higher income quintiles; judged by this standard, social mobility is a zero-sum game—for every winner there is a loser. The top 20 percent cannot accommodate all of society's households. Thus, any rise in the flow of children from the bottom 20 percent of the income distribution into the top income bracket is matched by an equivalent increase in the proportion of those who must drop out of the higher bracket into a lower one. As fair and beneficial as it may sound, an appeal to increase this measure of upward social mobility is perforce an inadvertent demand for escalating downward mobility.

This does not discredit the potential value of increasing social mobility. But it raises a critical issue entirely ignored in calls to lift the rate of upward mobility. How do we know what amount of movement up and down is fair and beneficial? Consider the results if, hypothetically, all the households in the bottom 20 percent of the income distribution today rose into the top quintile over the next six months, during which time all those in the top income bracket fell to the bottom. While the US rate of upward mobility would soar, the lift would be accompanied by a marked change in the size and composition of the top and bottom groups. Specifically, based on the actual size and composition of these groups as they are currently constituted, the total number of people in the bottom quintile would increase by 82 percent, the proportion employed full-time would climb by 400 percent, and the proportion of the college graduates would triple.[4] The size and composition of those in the top quintile would show a parallel change in the other direction, with fewer people, who were less educated and worked considerably less than households in the bottom quintile. It could also be said that those who fell into the bottom quintile suffered more misery than the happiness gained by who rose to the top. Citing the Daniel Kahneman and Amos Tversky's findings on psychological aversion to loss, Jacob Hacker observes, "both research and commonsense suggest that downward mobility is far more painful than upward mobility is pleasurable."[5]

In this imaginary case the improved rate of mobility elevates a group that is smaller, works less, and is less educated than the people on top whom they are displacing. It is difficult to see why the low-income group would merit moving into the upper income bracket. Thus, despite the higher level of mobility, on first glance many would deny that this "improvement" is fair or beneficial to society. Though on reflection, some might argue that since those in the upper income bracket were probably born into wealthy families, they had reaped unearned benefits from costly private educations and social contacts with the elite, which paved the way to lucrative accomplishments. In contrast, those in the lowest quintile probably came from poor families, which were unable to offer these advantages. From this perspective is seems only fair that the group on the bottom receive an extra boost up the ladder. Indeed, there is some truth on both sides of this argument. The side that one tends to favor reflects perceptions and beliefs about how much influence merit, privilege, and opportunity exert on the rate of social mobility. The relative influences are hard to measure and tough to untangle.

The progressive critique of how income is distributed via the free market contends that a substantial proportion of people in the top income bracket have arrived there through privileges of birth or devious dealings rather than diligence and hard work; as Robert Reich puts it, "a large and growing portion of the superrich have never broken a sweat. Their wealth has been handed to them."[6] At the same time those at the bottom are seen as handicapped by the lack of equal opportunities to move ahead. Consequentially, when contemplating the rate of social mobility, progressives are temperamentally inclined to want more, inevitably further displacing those at the top: Why should individuals born to wealth and privilege remain in the highest 20 percent of the income distribution? Of course, some proportion of the people in the top bracket rose from modest beginnings. And even coming from a privileged background, those who study long hours, work hard, exercise thrift, and postpone gratifications to build a successful business or professional practice should not be disqualified from the return on individual merit that is their due. The prevailing assumption that the current rate of intergenerational mobility is declining and needs to be increased fails to grapple with three complicated issues: What, if any, is the actual level of decline? How much upward mobility is generated by individual merit, and how much is arrested by inherited family privilege and lack of opportunity? What is the socially desirable rate of upward (and correspondingly downward) mobility?

As to the actual level of decline, highly publicized political claims have magnified public perceptions that intergenerational mobility is decreasing at an unprecedented rate. Yet there is persuasive evidence that the rate of social mobility in the United States has not changed since at least 1971, despite the rise in inequality over the last fifty years.[7] A team of leading economists from Harvard University, the University of California at Berkeley, and the US Department of the Treasury examined almost 50 million tax returns from 1971 to 1993 in what is arguably the most extensive and rigorous study to date.[8] They employed three different measures of social mobility to analyze the relationship between parents' incomes and the incomes of their children ages 26 years and older.[9] Among families whose children had not reached the age of 26 years, the analysis of these younger cohorts focused on the correlation between parents' income and their children's college attendance rates, another dimension of social mobility—and a realistic proxy for later earnings.[10]

On every measure, the findings revealed no significant change in the rate of social mobility for children born from 1971 to 1993.[11] When measured in terms of movement up the income ladder, for example, children born in 1971 to parents in the bottom fifth of the income distribution had an 8.4 percent chance of making it to the top quintile compared to a 9 percent chance for those born into the low-income families in 1986. How acceptable is this Horatio Alger index? The gut response depends on whom we ask. Many conservatives would be inclined to answer "that's not bad"; many progressives would tend to enquire, "What about the other 91 percent?"

In regard to educational mobility, the gap in college attendance rates between children from the lowest and highest income families narrowed a bit from 74.5 percent for children born in 1984 to 69.2 percent for the 1993 cohort. On this dimension, mobility remained stable and may even have increased slightly over several decades.[12] This study's findings confirm that children entering the labor market today have the same chances of moving up in the income distribution as those born in 1970s. Moreover, when these results are merged with evidence from other studies of children born in the 1950s, the team of researchers from Berkeley, Harvard, and the US Treasury Department conclude "that rank-based measures of social mobility have remained remarkably stable over the second half of the twentieth century in the United States."[13] These findings are supported by another large-scale study, which was based on a different longitudinal data set. Analyzing the relationship between parent and child incomes for twenty cohorts of children born from 1954 to 1974, Deirdre Bloome discovered there was no significant change in intergenerational mobility over this period.[14]

The experience of social mobility in the United States, however, turns out to be more complicated when examined in terms of both time and place. That is, although the rates of social mobility evidently have remained stable over recent times, they vary considerably among geographic areas. A companion study to the one noted earlier, for example, employs similar measures to compare the rates of intergenerational mobility among the country's fifty largest districts, which are geographic regions that resemble major metropolitan areas.[15] The results show that among children born into the bottom 20 percent of the income distribution in 1980 to 1982, the probability of rising to the top quintile ranges from a low of 4.4 percent in Charlotte, North Carolina, to a high of 12.9 percent in San Jose, California. Likewise there was considerable variation among the geographic districts in the relationships between children's and parents' income rank.[16]

These findings lend cause to wonder: Why were the rates of social mobility so much higher in some geographic areas than in others? In response to this question, the research team further analyzed data comparing the experiences of all 709 geographic districts in the United States. Seeking to identify the determinants of social mobility, they examined the extent to which several measures of mobility were associated with a range of characteristics that might have affected the differential outcomes. The four characteristics most significantly related to measures of social mobility were racial segregation, high school dropout rates, the percent of single mothers, and amounts of social capital. And among these characteristics, the fraction of children in single-parent families was the strongest and most robust predictor of differences in mobility across all the measures.[17]

In addition, income inequality was initially identified as an important predictor of the variation in rates of mobility.[18] However, the relationship between income inequality and mobility washed out when the statistical analysis included the other four characteristics. The data show a strong correlation between income inequality and rates of single parenthood. Although the researchers suggest that these results are "consistent with the view that inequality affects children's outcomes partly by degrading family structure," it is as likely, perhaps more so, that causality runs in the other direction. That is, inequality may not "degrade family structure" so much as the low incomes associated with the financial struggles of single parenthood drive up inequality.[19]

The intuitive hypothesis that rising economic inequality diminishes intergenerational mobility received an influential boost when Alan Krueger, chairman of the Council of Economic Advisers, pinned a dramatic label— "The Great Gatsby curve"—on a small graph (Figure 6.1). If, as it is said, language links perception to reality, the Gatsby curve fails the test on several accounts. The curve was, in fact, a straight line on a graph depicting a simplistic two-variable relationship between income inequality and intergenerational mobility based on a small sample of ten countries.[20] And it is unclear what the alleged relationship conveyed by this line has to do with the course of Jay Gatsby's life, which (leaving aside his romantic obsession) was more about a parvenu whose wealth was acquired through shady dealings trying to gain social acceptance than his social mobility being retarded by income inequality. As to the purported evidence for the impact of inequality on mobility, the largest and most authoritative studies of the US experience based on painstaking analysis across both time and geographic localities show no effects of increasing inequality on intergenerational mobility.[21] These commanding studies of mobility in the United States were not included in the Gatsby curve. Indeed, the researchers themselves admit that the measures used to illustrate

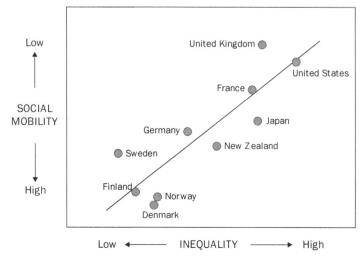

FIGURE 6.1 Great Gatsby curve.

the mobility rates in Figure 6.1 are so riddled with discrepancies as to cast considerable doubt on the veracity of theses international comparisons (as we will see in the next chapter).

Given the adverse impact of single parenthood on social mobility, it is curious that the rate of mobility in the United States has remained stable over the recent decades despite the huge increase in single-parent households. Between 1960 and 2011 the level of single parenthood soared from 9 to 33 percent of all households with children.[22] Single parents have lower levels of education than married mothers; this offers further reason to expect a declining rate of mobility.[23] However, it is possible that since the 1960s these downward pressures on the rate of social mobility were allayed by countervailing forces generated by civil rights legislation, affirmative action policies, expanded social welfare spending, and the overall rise in educational attainment.[24] Since 1960 social welfare spending more than doubled as a percent of the GDP and the high school completion rate went from 61 to 90 percent.[25] Hence, it would not be going too far out on a limb to predict that the future gains in these areas are unlikely to match previous rates of advancement.

Although there is still room for improvement in educational opportunities and other areas, it appears that the advantages and detriments of family life will come to exercise increasing influence on the rate of social mobility. Just talking to children counts, as revealed in Betty Hart and Todd Risley's study, which found that by age three children from professional families had heard 30 million words more than children from families on welfare.[26] There is a widening gap between children from upper/middle-class and working-class families in the socialization and life experiences that groom youth for success. Examining the landscape of family life from 1975 to 2009,

Robert Putnam and his colleagues find that "whether we measure parents reading Good Night Moon, or kids attending church, taking part in scouting or little league, playing high school football or soccer, participating in the school orchestra or other extracurricular activities, socializing with peers, or trusting other people, the differences between kids from upper/middle backgrounds and those from lower or working class backgrounds are steadily increasing."[27] And these differences mirror a growing disparity in academic achievement and completion of higher education.

The meaning of these trends is open to alternative interpretations. One view is that they forego the American ideal of meritocracy, fostering instead a system in which the accident of birth determines one's social standing and financial success in life.[28] Another way of looking at it, however, is that they reflect a system that delivers greater rewards to those who are better educated, work longer hours, attend more diligently to childrearing, and engage in civic activities. Both views are partly correct. No doubt, there are children of the rich who live a self-indulgent life of leisure. And wherever it is possible, some degree of nepotism is inevitable—what parent would condemn the mother who hires her daughter to help run the family business, particularly if the kid just received her MBA from the Stanford Graduate School of Business. Today's children of privilege are more likely to be burning the midnight candle studying for a graduate exam at Berkeley or Stanford than turning on, tuning in, and dropping out on a commune somewhere in Mendocino.[29] Their college degrees and acceptance into graduate programs are usually the result of talent, discipline, and hard work—bolstered by lifelong assistance from their families and the edge given to legacy status.[30]

The Kinship Factor in Social Mobility

Family has long been the principal channel through which privilege is transmitted from one generation to the next. It is also a tightknit interpersonal bond joined by blood that nurtures children, meets human needs for intimacy, and stands as a bulwark of social support between the individual and the state. Joseph Schumpeter believed that family bonds were a mainspring of the entrepreneurial drive to work, invest, and sacrifice for a future in which children would benefit from the gratifications their parents postponed. At the same time, however, he argued that the capitalist ethos encouraged calculating life's choices through a cost–benefit lens that magnified the costs and undervalued the benefits of parenthood, which would eventually undermine family life. He predicted that, along with the rise of the intellectual class, the erosion of traditional family life and parenthood would result in the eventual decline of capitalism. Although seventy years later capitalism continues to thrive, he was right about the disintegration of family life.[31]

Kinship loyalties and parental investments in children do not comple-
ment collectivist desires to have the state promote egalitarian objectives.
Marx and Engels portrayed bourgeois family as an exploitive institution in
which the wife is treated as a prostitute and "a mere instrument of production."[32] When the Bolsheviks came to power in 1917, they sought to transform
the bourgeois family by introducing legal measures under which divorce rates
soared. These measures, however, were later amended.[33] Today, the most progressive welfare states spend heavily on so-called family policies, the consequences of which are to reduce the individual's dependence on kinship and
increase reliance on the state.[34] This outcome is awkwardly referred to among
social scientists as "defamilialization."[35] It is no coincidence that the Swedish
welfare state is known as "the people's home." But even in Sweden, evidence
suggests that social mobility is not immune to the gravity of family rank.
Gregory Clark's research reveals "rates of long run social mobility are so low
that the 18th century elite in Sweden have persisted to the present as a relatively privileged group."[36] He documents similar results in eight other countries, including the United States, England, India, China, Chile, and Japan.

Clark's multigenerational study relies on the identification of surnames
prominent among the upper crust in each country. In Sweden the elite included those enrolled in the House of Nobility (Riddarhuset), untitled nobles,
and people with latinized surnames that were characteristic of the educated
class;[37] in contrast to this group, ordinary citizens were defined as those with
the most common Swedish surnames, such as Svenson, which were patro-
nyms formed by adding "son" to the father's first name. Drawn from sources
such as church registers, university enrollments, and tax records, the data
on elites and ordinary citizens were used to track and compare family earnings, occupational status, and education over many generations. Among the
typical findings, for example, the extensive records of enrolment at the prestigious Swedish universities of Lund (established in 1666) and Uppsala (established in 1477), and the membership rolls of the nine Royal Academies of
Sweden (founded in 1700s), reveal that for over three hundred years people
with elite surnames have been significantly overrepresented in these institutions. Analyses of these records also show a regression to the mean, marked
by a slow but steady convergence toward proportional representation between
members with elite and ordinary surnames. A similar pattern was found for
representation of the elites among physicians and attorneys.[38] The numerical documentation of how families with elite surnames have sustained high-
status positions over many generations is brought to life with sketches of
the lineage of famous figures such as Geoffrey Chaucer, Samuel Pepys, and
Charles Darwin. The reader learns, for instance, that the twenty-seven great-
great grandchildren of Charles Darwin "include six university professors,
four authors, a painter, three medical doctors, a well-known conservation-
ist, and a film director (now also an organic farmer)."[39] Moreover, two of

Darwin's descendants intermarried with families of John Maynard Keynes and Aldous Huxley.

Demonstrating that the elite have remained a highly privileged group for centuries, Clark offers some provocative thoughts about the causes, the consequences, and future prospects for social mobility. Similar to the Berkeley-Harvard team's examination of geographic differences in rates of social mobility, Clark's historical study confirms that, above all, family matters. His conclusion, however, emphasizes the beneficial impact of high-status families on intergenerational mobility rather than the adverse effects of single parenthood reflected in the geographic analysis—between these studies we have the heads and tails on the coin of family life.

According to Clark, the mechanism that conveys social status across generations is not inherited privilege per se but the innate talent inherited from parents, which is nurtured by the transmission of family norms, values, and investments in education and other beneficial activities. It is not the proverbial silver spoon in their children's mouths but the exceptional abilities in their genes that maintain the family status. Intuitively, this makes sense, although the inheritance of social privilege and innate talent are not mutually exclusive. And the extent to which economic success is attributable to one or the other is often indeterminate, on top of which physical effort and psychological resolve enter the equation. Chance also plays a role in the marketplace. Some success (usually other people's) is achieved by virtue of blind luck. But unlike genetic inheritance and patterns of family socialization, luck cannot be handed down over the generations. Over the long term, economic success is related to biology and family culture, which are passed on from one generation to the next. But in a sense, these too can be seen as luck that is just more enduring. Gary Becker describes inherited aptitude as the luck of endowment.[40]

Considering the interplay of nature and nurture, Clark poses the question: Which has a greater bearing on economic success: the genetic endowment of aptitude or the advantages of beneficial family socialization, which includes investment in education and other enhancements of human capital? Stopping short of genetic determinism, he ascribes the dominant role to genetics, which has several important implications for intergenerational mobility. It may seem counterintuitive, but genetic dominance assures the fluidity of social mobility. That is, no matter how consistently across generations the rich purchase tutors, music teachers, athletic coaches, elocution lessons, and placements in elite kindergarten and prep schools for their children, they cannot forestall the eventual regression to the mean of genetic endowments such as superior aptitude and intellectual capacity. But this is a slow process. Clark forecasts that it might take three hundred years for the regression to the mean to equalize the economic position of today's rich and poor families—a timeline of cold comfort to those currently at the bottom.[41] This convergence is predicated on Francis Galton's famous observation that the inheritance of human traits that have a continuous quality such as height and intelligence tend to cluster around the average, which he called the law of regression. "The law is even-handed," he explained, "it levies the same heavy succession-tax on the transmission of badness as well as of goodness. If it discourages the extravagant expectations of gifted parents that their children will inherit all their powers, it no less discountenances extravagant fears that they will in-herit all their weaknesses and diseases."[42] Although Darwin's descendants were a distinguished lot, none of their accomplishments achieved the heights of his scientific contributions.

But the dominance of genetic endowment has other less sanguine im-plications for the dynamics of social mobility. Just as the wealthy are unable to forestall the genetic gravity of downward mobility through large invest-ments in their progeny, Clark argues that government promotion of measures such as income transfers and early education are unlikely to have a significant impact on the upward mobility of the poor.

Early Intervention and Mobility

Yet there is some evidence that intense early intervention can produce ben-eficial outcomes, particularly with disadvantaged children. With a six-to-one student–teacher ratio, the highly acclaimed Perry Preschool Project was a two-year program starting at age 3, which provided 2 ½ hours of classroom ac-tivity on weekday mornings plus home visits with mothers for 1 ½ hours each week over the school year. The total cost per child was approximately $15,166 (in 2000 dollars). The children were from low-income African American families. The curriculum was intended to make a difference in their intellec-tual development as measured by IQ scores, which would enhance academic performance and later success in life. To evaluate the results, an experimental design was employed under which children were randomly assigned to the Perry Preschool program and a control group that did not receive this early intervention. With a remarkable sense of purpose, evidence was systemati-cally gathered comparing the two groups' earnings, education, employment, criminal activity, and other life outcomes up through age forty. The findings revealed that the Perry Preschool participants had significantly fewer arrests, higher earnings, and were more likely to have completed high school than members of the control group. Lending considerable academic stature to the project, James Heckman, the Noble Prize–winning economist, and others translated these gains into monetary figures based on cost–benefit analyses estimating the extent to which an early investment in preschool generated long-term returns to program participants and society.[43] Their elaborate cal-culations suggested that the program paid significant dividends to society.

However this widely-broadcasted valuation of Perry Preschool's economic re-turns veils serious concerns about the experimental fidelity of the preschool study and what the findings really measure. Critical analyses of the study reveal a long list of limitations in the research design and the appraisal of the evidence. For example, the sample of fifty-eight Perry Preschool students was a small group on which to peg the promised returns; the initial random assignment was compromised by a need to transfer two children from the program group to the control group because they had working single moth-ers who were unable to participate in the program's home visits and parent classes; about 20 percent of the sample was not randomly assigned because siblings were placed in the same group; some of the differences reported were not statistically significant and others, such as the difference in high school completion rates applied only to girls, not boys; the earnings were sig-nificantly higher than the control group for the previous month before but not for the previous year; the control group of boys (thirty-nine) was almost 20 percent larger than the number of boys (thirty-three) in the program group; and the cost–benefit analysis was heavily influenced by estimates of the potential costs of crime, which are difficult to assess and complicated by the fact that, although arrest rates differed between the groups, there were no differences in the number of convictions or the months sentenced to prison. Some also noted that, contrary to usual practice, the researchers responsible for evaluating the program worked for the foundation that developed the Perry Preschool curriculum.[44]

Beyond these issues of research design, implementation, and measure-ment, which might be dismissed as academic quibbling, a larger question of causality looms over the results of this project: To what extent did classroom exposure to the Perry Preschool curriculum make a difference? This question arises because, as initially conceived, the Perry project emphasized classroom activities that conveyed a "cognitively oriented curriculum" intended to en-hance children's intellectual performance. The anticipated boost in intellec-tual ability was to be the motor generating additional benefits throughout the participant's life cycle.

Indeed, tests showed that during the first few years the program group outscored the nonprogram control group on four measures of intellectual ability, including the Stanford-Binet IQ test. But between ages six and eight these differences faded to insignificance on almost every measure. And at age fourteen the two groups' mean scores on the Wechsler Full-Scale IQ test were virtually identical. These results created a proverbial black box between the intervention and its presumed consequences. If the classroom activity failed to enhance the program group's intellectual development, what was it about the preschool input at age four that could have produced the beneficial out-comes related to earnings, years of schooling, and number of lifetime arrests at age twenty-seven? The researchers evaluating this project offered a causal model, which suggested that the program group's initial very short-lived gain in IQ over the control group at age four generated heightened motivation, measured by teacher ratings from kindergarten through the third grade, which subsequently led to beneficial outcomes over several decades.[45]

However, the causal path from a brief gain in IQ to heightened motivation, which then generated positive outcomes for the program group, remains highly speculative, particularly since the teacher ratings of school motivation showed no significant difference between the program group and nonprogram control group. Having entered the realm of speculation, the data readily lend themselves to another interpretation that suggests the beneficial outcomes may have been influenced less by children's exposure to the preschool curriculum than by parental exposure to the home visits and the environment of family life.

During the two-year program, children in the Perry Project spent more than 90 percent of their time with their families compared to the relatively brief intervention of 2 ½ hours a day for eight months a year in the preschool classroom. One reason to consider the family environment is that the proportion of families with working mothers in the nonprogram group (31 percent) was more than three times as high as in the program group (9 percent).[46] Thus, not only was there a significantly greater presence of mothers in the daily lives of the three- and four-year-old program participants, but each week these mothers were receiving professional training and advice about how to create a stimulating learning environment at home. When surveyed years later, the mothers to whom home-visiting services were delivered had significantly higher aspirations for their children going to college than nonprogram mothers.

Considering how the long-term beneficial outcomes of the Perry Project may be related to the extensive work with parents rather than a result of the preschool curriculum, Yale University professor Edward Zigler and Victoria Seitz note: "If parents learned the benefits of becoming familiar with their child's teacher and trying to provide home activities that complemented what the child was learning in school, this could have led to the better early school motivation and performance these children later showed and to a consistently more supportive parental attitude toward schooling." They recommend that efforts be made to determine the relative impact of the classroom versus family interventions because "if the home visitation is a critical factor underlying the long-term benefits obtained, the particular educational curriculum employed may be relatively unimportant."[47]

A social intervention regularly referred to in the same breath as the Perry Preschool Project, the Abecedarian Project started at birth, delivered a more extensive package of services, and was arguably a more successful effort to improve the cognitive abilities of disadvantaged children. This was an all-day, year-round program that served poor, predominantly African American children at risk of developmental retardation from infancy until the age of five. The program included center-based activities focused on social, emotional, and cognitive areas of development, medical care, parent training, and extended supports through the second grade for a subgroup of participants.[48] In contrast to the Perry Preschool evaluation, the Abecedarian program participants consistently achieved statistically significant gains over the control group on measures of cognitive development and reading and mathematics achievement tests up through the age of twenty-one.[49]

Bidding to advance equal opportunity from the start of life, the Perry Preschool and Abecedarian programs set the standard for early interventions designed to increase the cognitive and social abilities of acutely disadvantaged children. These two highly celebrated programs delivered social and educational services of notably high quality and cost, which were linked to a number of positive outcomes in later life; however, for some of the Perry Preschool benefits it is uncertain how securely the chain of causality was fastened to specific interventions. The Abecedarian Project improved the cognitive abilities of participants by providing what amounted to a substitute family of highly motivated professional caregivers who worked to educate and socialize the children from 7:30 a.m. to 5:15 p.m. five days a week from infancy through age five.

Accepting at face value all of the benefits these programs claimed to achieve, it could be argued that they increased the opportunity for disadvantaged children to live a more wholesome and productive life than would have been the case in the absence of the preschool experiences. Even casting a critical eye on some of the benefits claimed, at the very least these programs furnished more competent care than the children would have received at home, in a safe, stimulating, and healthy environment that enriched their existential experience of childhood. As for moving the needle on the scale of social mobility, however, the financial differences between program and nonprogram groups were too small and tentative to have a potential impact on the intergenerational relationship between parent and child incomes.[50] It should come as no surprise that publicly organized preschool investments to compensate for cognitive and social deficits of children from underprivileged families are unable to match the spontaneous intergenerational transmission of attitudes, values, private investments, and genetic endowments that contribute to the social success of children born into privileged families.

At the same time that government interventions have failed to show a significant boost in the rate of upward mobility for children at the bottom of the economic ladder, the process of assortative mating continues to amplify the influence of inheritance, solidifying the position of those on the top rungs.[51] Noting the contemporary acceleration of this process, Charles Murray makes a plausible case that the rates of intergenerational mobility in the United States are likely to experience increasing downward pressure in the coming decades.[52] Many would assume that this foretells the narrowing of equal opportunity. Others might argue that it depends upon where one draws the starting line in defining equal opportunity. Does it start with removing obstacles to economic success such as parental neglect, inadequate education, and discriminatory labor practices, or must the line be pushed back into hearth and home, abolishing the effects of parental socialization, care, and the transmission of family values—or even earlier? There is credible evidence that the first nine months in the womb have significant implications for a child's future health.[53] Also, there still remains the matter of what to do about the inheritance of innate abilities.

7

The Arc and Ladder of Social Mobility

In *The Son Also Rises*, Gregory Clark depicts the inheritance of innate abilities functioning both to sustain the privileged positions of the elite and to slow the rate of intergenerational mobility for the poor. The "son" in this title refers to his conviction that over generations the inheritance of human traits, such as height and intelligence, gravitates toward the population average, insuring that the offspring of today's poor *eventually* will rise to an elevated social position.[1]

The work of an economist, Clark's study bears an interesting comparison to *The Rise of Meritocracy 1870–2033: An Essay on Education and Equality*, written over a half a century earlier by the British sociologist Michael Young—who coined the term "meritocracy." Both titles signify that something is ascending. Moreover, the title of Clark's scholarly research is a pun on a popular novel; the title of Young's well-known dystopian novel is cast as a scholarly essay. But the comparison reaches well beyond the titles. Young's story describes how the hereditary class system in England is upended by the creation of top-quality, state-supported grammar schools, which enroll only the most able students. The educational reform is accompanied by the development of highly effective methods of scientific selection based on aptitude tests given continuously throughout the school years. Thus, from an early age children of every class received the same opportunity to demonstrate their ability. Graduation from the excellent state schools determined the level of entry into industry, after which promotions were based on objective measures of innate ability and productivity. In this new system, merit, expressed through intelligence plus effort, had replaced kinship and seniority as the source of social and economic advancement.

Justified solely on merit, the rate of intergenerational mobility initially accelerated as clever, hard-working children of poor parents were lifted into the "thinking" class and dim, lazy offspring of the upper classes sunk into the manual occupations; soon these jobs were being squeezed out by technology, pushing manual labor into a menial class of domestic servants. With social stratification on the basis of merit welcoming the most capable children from the lower strata, the gap between the classes widened. Over several generations, the rate of mobility slowed to a crawl and then declined as those who rose to the top bequeathed their innate abilities and cultural competencies to their descendants—creating de facto a hereditary meritocracy. Conservative members of the elite proposed embalming the hereditary principle in law, although they understood that it could not go on forever because "intelligent people tend on the whole to have less intelligent children than themselves."[2] They recognized the regression to the mean as a brute fact that made some degree of social mobility essential. Over a stretch of time the sons of the lower class would rise. Though Young's tale of meritocracy is a long story that ends on an ominous note, the fictional dynamics of intergenerational mobility that he depicts closely parallels Clark's empirical observations, both of which question the prevailing assumption about the link between equal opportunity and mobility.[3]

Progressives take for granted that there is a linear relationship between equal opportunity and intergenerational mobility. That is, as equality of opportunity increases, the rate of mobility rises. Since equality of opportunity is less explicit and more difficult to measure than the correlation between the relative positions of parents' and children's incomes, the rate of economic mobility is often taken as a gauge of equal opportunity. The prevailing assumption is clearly expressed in Joseph Stiglitz's comment on the likelihood that the children of those in the middle and lower social classes will be better off than their parents: "If America were really a land of opportunity, the life chances of success—of say, winding up in the top 10 percent—of someone born to a poor or less educated family would be the same as those of someone born to a rich, well-educated, and well-connected family."[4] From this standpoint, equal opportunity is achieved when the government can insure that every child has the same chance of, not just doing well, but becoming wealthy regardless of his or her family background. Accepting that the genetic inheritance of some traits might influence the probability of a child's success, other academics explain: "If every adult wound up in the same relative socioeconomic position as his or her parents, there would be no mobility and no equality of opportunity. Perfect equality of opportunity however would not necessarily imply complete social mobility because mobility depends not only on parental socioeconomic status but on abilities some of which are inherited."[5] The sensitive question left hanging is: How much of social mobility might be attributed to inherited physical, psychological, and cognitive traits?

If inherited traits have a major influence on social mobility, there is a need to rethink the linear assumption that as equal opportunity moves toward complete parity, the rate of social mobility will continue to climb until there is no relationship between the economic positions of parents and children. People have different ideas about what exactly constitutes complete equality of opportunity. For argument's sake, let us imagine that it involves a state of affairs in which all children receive the equivalent food, clothing, and shelter; obtain a suitable education; and have access to adequate health care in a social environment where all offsetting discriminatory barriers to advancement are removed. Amid this egalitarian setting the children still vary in their inherited physical, psychological, and cognitive abilities, which give some an advantage that will be transmitted to their offspring.[6] The arc of social mobility will initially rise as opportunities increase for the most able children who were previously held back by limited access to education and health care as well as by discriminatory barriers. To the extent that high-achieving men and women marry each other, the process of assortative mating consolidates the transmission of aptitudes and talents among those who have made it to the top. As this group reproduces, the arc of mobility is approaching its apex, after which it slopes downward for the coming generations.

Evidence suggests that since the 1960s assortative mating has come to exert more intense influence on social mobility than ever before.[7] In part, this is because of a huge increase in the number of women going to college and entering the labor force. Women currently account for close to half the civilian workforce and more than half of the college graduates.[8] And admission standards have changed at prestigious colleges. Prior to the 1960s when Harvard men married Wellesley women, both were more likely to be wealthy than academically gifted. Today they both tend to be exceptionally talented and accomplished. As Charles Murray writes, "it means that very smart is likely to marry very smart."[9] At the same time the median age of marriage has gone from the early twenties in 1960 to the late twenties.[10] These six to eight initial years of adulthood are a formative period in the life course. In their early twenties, many, if not most, men and women are still in school, just graduating, beginning to work in entry-level positions, or hanging about looking to discover themselves. It is too early in the game to predict where they will end up. By the late twenties, those that were in college have completed their degrees and those at work have begun to advance; most are on course to their future stations in life. How far they will go remains uncertain. But one can estimate the initial velocity and direction in which they are headed. Thus, in today's marriage market, both partners have a lot more information on which to judge a prospective mate's prospects than was available in the past. Among two-earner couples, 40 percent are currently in the same or neighboring earnings bracket compared to 33 percent twenty years ago.[11]

This stylized account of the arc of social mobility needs to be modified by the recognition that although assortative mating may inhibit the rate of movement, some degree of mobility will continue to be driven by market luck, the regression of inherited abilities to the mean, and possibly by the outcomes of compensatory social interventions. Still, any effort to equate the degree of equal opportunity with the rate of intergenerational mobility cannot ignore the implications of parental endowments. Chances are that as the increasing knowledge of a potential partner's prospects in life continues to ratchet up assortative mating, the rate of social mobility will decline over the coming decades.

The extent to which genetic endowments influence individual behavior and intergenerational mobility is a contested issue fraught with social Darwinist implications for eugenics, racism, and other unsavory results. A century ago support for eugenics was bandied about not only among members of the British Fabian Society but in progressive circles in the United States. According to Richard Hofstadter, "Like the reform movements eugenics accepted the principle of state action toward a common end and spoke in terms of the collective destiny of the group rather than of individual success. This is significant of the general trend of thought in the Progressive era."[12] Although today the eugenics movement is universally condemned as evil, questions about the inheritability of various traits remain for many an uncomfortable topic susceptible to abuse on all sides. Genetic endowment in some ways remains the "third rail" of social mobility research around which one treads cautiously.

However, the success of scientific efforts to decipher the genetic code and the invention of new technologies for analyzing the genome have opened immense opportunities for the advancement of knowledge about the human condition. These developments have transformed medical research and expanded the purview of health practices. The profession of genetic counseling was launched in the 1960s, about ten years after James Watson and Francis Crick detected the structure of DNA. Genetic information is regularly used to help anticipate and resolve health problems in medical practice as well as to identify lawbreakers in the criminal justice system.

Advances in the study of genetics have also spurred scientific research on the interaction of nature and nurture. Intent on discovering how inherited advantages and disadvantages affect one's chances for economic success, social scientists are staking out an emerging field of research at the intersection of genetics and economics—genoeconomics. Beyond their strength in numbers, an assessment by twenty-two researchers from fifteen major universities and medical institutes lends a measure of scientific authority to the current state of knowledge in this field.[13] Summarizing the broad pattern of empirical findings over several decades based on studies comparing identical and fraternal twins, they note that "in modern Western societies, for most outcomes in life, over half the resemblance of two biological siblings reared in the same family stems from their genetic similarity." The research suggests that economic outcomes and preferences are almost as heritable as physical traits such as height and psychological traits such as cognitive ability and personality. In a study of more than 1,400 pairs of male Swedish twins raised at home, for example, the correlation of incomes averaged over twenty years for identical twins was .626

compared to .270 for fraternal twins. The authors note that these and other findings suggest many behaviors are influenced more by genetic endowment than common family environment; from this perspective nature trumps nurture. This challenges the "blank slate theory" of human development, which Steven Pinker describes as "the secular religion of modern intellectual life."[14] But to dismiss the blank slate theory is not to confirm that biology determines one's fate. A substantial amount of variance in economic outcomes remains unexplained by genetic endowment.[15] Moreover, the variable effects of genetic endowment do not exclude the possibility that inherited traits are susceptible to influence by compensatory social interventions, as seen in the results of the Abecedarian Project. The genoeconomic researchers warn against misguided attempts to draw social policy conclusions from heritability estimates.

A Poor Proxy for Equal Opportunity

To the extent that intergenerational mobility is influenced by genetic endowment and the transmission of family culture, it is difficult to formulate any firm conclusion about the degree of equal opportunity reflected in mobility rates. Nevertheless, in the wake of the Great Recession, the media widely publicized the idea that the United States is no longer the incomparable land of equal opportunity it once was; indeed, if anything, the United States was repeatedly exposed as the land of exceptionally unequal opportunity compared to European countries.[16] In this case, the media's proclivity to publicize misfortune was encouraged by a few studies revealing disturbing evidence that the US rate of social mobility fell far below that of other countries. Some see the comparison of mobility rates with other countries as a reliable benchmark against which to judge equal opportunity. The argument goes that because the parent–child transmission of genetic advantages is likely to be similar among human beings throughout the world, the extent to which rates of social mobility vary among rich countries could be taken as an empirical indicator of the different degrees of equal opportunity granted by these countries.[17] To make this judgment stick, however, requires taking comparable measures of social mobility in various countries.

There are several ways to compute social mobility. One approach frequently used by economists involves quantifying the relationship between the incomes of fathers and their sons. These correlations yield a number that predicts the average proportional difference in a son's income (usually in the late twenties) relative to sons about the same age from other families that is based on his father's earnings (at an earlier age) relative to that of other fathers. Thus, a correlation of 0.4 predicts that a 10 percent difference between two fathers' incomes will on average result in a 4 percent difference between their children's incomes. Another way to think about it is that

40 percent of the differences in parental incomes is passed on to their children. The higher a correlation, the more powerful the parental influence on their children's income and the lower the rate of intergenerational mobility. Technically, the correlation is referred to as a measure of "intergenerational income elasticity" and represents the slope of a simple linear regression calculated on father's and son's incomes.

Although the statistical methods convey an impression of numerical precision and reliability, the calculations of mobility rates are only as good as the measurements, and the measurements must contend with several issues. First, of course, is the challenge of linking parent and child incomes earned between twenty-five and thirty-five years apart. These data are typically drawn from administrative sources such as income tax records and longitudinal surveys. Surveys yield smaller sample sizes and less accurate reporting of income than administrative data. Once the data sets are identified, decisions have to be made about the specific periods in the parent and child life cycles during which their incomes should be compared, whether to include daughters and mothers, and whether to compare their incomes for a single year or take an average over several years and, if so, how many. Then there are arcane statistical concerns about how best to analyze the data.[18] Comparative analyses of mobility rates among various countries magnify some of these issues, since at the outset they rely on different sources of data.

Thus, despite the application of uniform statistical methods, there are wide variations among the findings of intergenerational mobility studies, even within the same country. Miles Corak's highly publicized comparative analysis of economic mobility rates in nine countries, which were used in the Great Gatsby curve (shown in Figure 6.1), identifies studies reporting twenty-eight different rates of mobility for the United States, with correlations ranging from .09 to .61.[19] These studies included Nathan Grawe's analyses of US mobility rates derived from two widely used data sets: the National Longitudinal Survey (NLS) and the Panel Study of Income Dynamic (PSID). The findings varied to such an extent that if one believed the result based on the NLS sample was accurate, the United States would have been tied with Denmark for the highest rate (.154) of intergenerational mobility among countries—upending the Gatsby curve. However, if one believed that the finding based on the PSID sample was correct, the United States would have come in with the next to the lowest (.473) rate of mobility. Much of the disparity here is attributed to the difference between the ages of the fathers in the two samples.[20]

As to which of these findings comes closest to the true level of intergenerational mobility in the United States, Grawe makes it clear "that it is impossible to confidently answer this question without data covering the entire life cycles of fathers and sons."[21] As if to drive home this point, a study by Markus

Jantti and his colleagues using the same data failed to replicate one of Grawe's findings.[22]

To compare the mobility rates for nine countries, Corak had to choose among a number of studies. For the United States, he selected Grawe's finding based on the PSID sample, which represented a minimal rate of mobility in comparison to the other countries. It was also well below the average rate for the twenty-eight studies of mobility in the United States. Several reasons were given for choosing to use this study. Corak explained, for example, that the other twenty-seven studies of the United States appeared to be more biased either upward or downward because of considerations involving the fathers' age, attachments to the labor market, and ethnicity. Further justification for the choice was offered based on a meta-analysis of the studies, the reliability of which suffers from the limited number of observations.[23] In response to the remarkable discrepancies in the research findings, he candidly admits the "range is so wide as to make international comparisons entirely questionable."[24] This is no secret among scholars who carefully study the topic. Summarizing the state of knowledge in 2013, Jantti and Jenkins testify that the evidence has "revealed few clear cut conclusions about whether mobility has been increasing over time or decreasing in particular and whether mobility is greater in one country rather than another."[25]

The uncertainty and imprecision signified by an array of discrepant findings stand in stark contrast to the confidence expressed by the progressive media and some academics in claiming that the United States has an exceptionally low degree of economic mobility.[26] Contrary to these claims, the findings from the Harvard-Berkeley study in 2014 tell another story. Based on a sample vastly larger than any of the previous US studies and led by two award winning economists, the Harvard-Berkeley research found a much higher rate of economic mobility than Corak reported as representative of the United States.[27] According to the Harvard-Berkeley findings, the United States should have been placed smack in the middle of the mobility rates on the Gatsby curve, just after the Scandinavian countries; compared to a larger sample of fourteen countries, the United States would rank fourth, again just behind Finland, Denmark, and Norway.[28] There is good reason to believe that this rigorous study of about 50 million children over more than two decades offers the most precise estimate to date of intergenerational mobility in the United States. Regardless of how accurate the numbers may be, from a comparative perspective there is a question of what exactly these measures signify.

The focus on empirical measures of intergenerational mobility generates numbers that have dominated the discourse of comparative analysis and been used to estimate which countries offer more equal economic opportunity than others. Based on measures that describe movements among income quintiles and correlations between fathers' and sons' incomes, perceptions of mobility and equal opportunity have been framed by what might be termed the "iron law of specificity."[29] This is the tendency for the specification of a number, such as the percent of children who are born in the bottom income quintile and rise to the top quintile in their adult years, to forge a literal substitute for the substantive meaning of economic mobility and equal opportunity—appropriating the vocabulary of righteousness in the process. The issue here involves more than academic hair-splitting about how the age of fathers, the number of years over which incomes are averaged and the use of alternative measures impact the calculation of economic mobility. The question is, even if the exact same procedures are used to compute mobility rates in different countries, how meaningful are numerical comparisons of the results? This is a crucial matter. People's beliefs about mobility and equal opportunity have consequences for public morale and confidence in the fairness of the capitalist market. Because the average citizen has no data at hand to assess the degree of opportunity and mobility here and abroad, these beliefs are influenced by what they read and hear in the media and are told by political leaders.

Although there was a time when scholars were ridiculed by their colleagues as "popularizers" if their work commanded an audience with the public-at-large, today media attention does not so readily elicit opprobrium.[30] Indeed, there is a premium to be had for making the headlines. Selecting papers for the coveted first-days presentations at the annual conference of the National Bureau of Economic Research, award-winning economist David Card freely admits, "I choose papers that are going to be written up in the mainstream press."[31] Some features of economic life, such as equality and social mobility, are normally of interest to the media, particularly when they are neatly summarized with numbers that express where the United States stands on these value-laden qualities compared to other countries. And the media's interest is really peaked if these numbers suggest that the United States has fallen behind everybody else, which is often the message conveyed. Therefore, it is important to clarify what these numbers signify.

International comparisons measuring the relation between parents' and children's incomes disregard the fact that in some countries the ladder of economic mobility is much longer than in others and the rungs are much further apart. Consider, for example, the mobility of a child from a poor family in Country A, where the median disposable household income is $30,000, to that of a child raised in an equally low-income household in Country B, where the median income is $20,000. To reach the middle of the income ladder in Country A, the child must climb 50 percent higher than the one in Country B if both start from zero. From a starting point where both of their family household incomes are $10,000, the child in Country A has to climb twice as high to reach the middle of the income distribution. When the income ladders vary in length, it takes a greater increase over a father's income to move up a rung into another income quintile on the longer ladder—and the US income ladder is among the highest in the wealthy countries.

Contrary to those who conflate measures of income mobility with degrees of equal opportunity, Christophe Jencks and Laura Tach argue that the rate of intergenerational economic mobility "is not a good indicator of how close a society has come to equalizing opportunity. Measuring equality of opportunity requires data on *why* successful parents tend to have successful children."[32] The prevailing assumption that the statistical assessments of mobility signify equality of opportunity not only ignores the underlying dynamics of individual mobility, it discounts the diverse features of the political and cultural landscapes from which the estimates were derived. Consider, for example, some of the differences between Sweden and the United States. Gosta Esping-Andersen finds that years of education, cognitive performance, and work experience have a much smaller impact on earnings in Sweden than in the United States. He explains that in Sweden "earnings are far less related to any observable human attribute. This is hardly surprising considering Sweden's uniquely compressed wage structure."[33] In an extreme case, if everyone earned an equal amount of money, none of the differences in their inherited abilities, performance, or parental investments would correlate with their incomes. Then one is forced to ask: How were each citizen's economic rewards aligned to their contributions to society?

In the Swedish example the compressed wage structure is due to the government's greater controls on earnings than in the United States, which operate indirectly through higher rates of taxation and directly by setting wages for about 38 percent of the Swedish labor force that works in the public sector (as compared to 16 percent for the United States).[34] A relatively compressed wage structure functions not so much to level the playing field on which individuals advance according to their abilities and performance as to level economic outcomes of the game. Although it is often observed that Sweden has a higher rate of mobility than the United States, the Harvard-Berkeley study findings on intergenerational rates of mobility shed considerable doubt on this claim.[35] To the extent that Sweden's rates of social mobility are actually higher than those of the United States, it could be that smaller differences in Swedish incomes leave less room for parental influences to have measurable effects, at the same time making it easier to move up and down the ladder (as well as making this mobility less consequential in terms of absolute monetary gains achieved).

The parenthetical mention of absolute monetary gains is a reminder that the standard measures of intergenerational mobility define progress in terms of one household's economic advancement relative to others. This is the progressive mindset, discussed earlier, that reckons most people care less about the absolute level of their income than how much they possess or have gained relative to others; the "others" being a category generally delimited by national boundaries. But the average citizen is typically unaware of whether the intergenerational income elasticity index figure for the United States has gone up or down. Indeed, most people have never heard of it. However, they have a keen appreciation for an existential measure of economic progress. That is, most adults are cognizant of whether their material standard of living is better than that experienced as a child under their parents' roof. Rather than comparing how one's income changes relative to others all across the country, the absolute measure of mobility strikes much closer to home, examining an individual's changing level of prosperity over time. This is how people outside of academia tend to judge their economic progress.

According to the Brookings Institution study of economic mobility, 67 percent of Americans born in 1968 had higher levels of real family income in 1995–2002 than their parents had a generation earlier. The overall proportion of children who were better off than their parents increased to 81 percent when incomes were adjusted for family size; most of those who were not better off than their parents were born to families with the highest incomes. The median family income in the study's sample of native-born Americans rose from $55,000 to $71,000 between the two generations.[36] When broken down into upper and lower income groups, four out of five children from the bottom quintile of income distribution had higher family incomes than their parents and the median income for this group was twice as high as that of their parents. These were not all rags-to-riches stories. But beyond the increase in the median income reported in the Brookings analysis, findings from the Harvard-Berkeley study show that 9 percent of those born into the bottom quintile made the comparatively long climb by international criteria to the top 20 percent of the income distribution.[37] It is difficult to compare this scale of income mobility between, for example, Sweden and the United States, given the disparity in the height of their income ladders.

The median incomes recorded in the Brookings study were higher than the national measures, which appear over the same period in Census Bureau statistics. Analyzing a particular segment of the population, the Brookings sample focused on the absolute economic mobility of families with children, which excluded the elderly, very young adults, and immigrants. The economic mobility of immigrants is of particular interest in that it conveys a general sense of how well newcomers fare in the much vaunted "land of opportunity." Also, first- and second-generation immigrants currently constitute one-fourth of the US population and are projected to account for 37 percent by 2050.

According to the Pew Research Center's analysis of Census Bureau data, the 20 million adult children of immigrants are appreciably better off than their parents and have achieved a socioeconomic profile, which mirrors that of the general population.[38] Although the second-generation immigrants have surpassed their parents on all of the socioeconomic indicators in Table 7.1, it is important to bear in mind that this is a heterogeneous body composed in the main of diverse groups from Latin America and Southeast Asia.[39] While

TABLE 7.1

Absolute Mobility for Children of Immigrants

	Immigrant Generation	Their Adult US-Born Children	US Population
Median household income	45,800	58,100	58,200
% of college graduation	29	36	31
Rate of homeownership	51	64	65
% under the federal poverty line	18	11	13

Source: 2012 data from Pew Research Center analysis of Current Population surveys, Integrated Public Use Microdata Series (IPUMS) file. Reported in Pew Research Center, *Second-Generation Americans: A Portrait of the Adult Children of Immigrants* (Washington, D.C.: Pew Research Center, 2013), p. 7. Income data are for three-person households. http://www.pewsocialtrends.org/files/2013/02/FINAL_immigrant_generations_report_2-7-13.pdf

on average having done better than their parents, these regional groups have not all done equally well. Among the noticeable differences between them, Asian Americans arrived with more academic training and have attained higher levels of household income and education. The 2012 median income for second-generation Asian Americans, for example, was $67,500 compared to $48,400 for Hispanic Americans. Nevertheless, the figure for second-generation Hispanic Americans is within the range of US middle-class incomes, and among the top 9 percent of incomes throughout the world.[40]

The best evidence to date indicates that the US rate of relative mobility measured by how much of the difference between children's income is associated with the difference between their parents' income has not change over at least the last three decades. But mobility rates tell us very little about real standards of living—or how ordinary citizens would assess differences between their absolute and relative mobility. Even if their relative rate of mobility had declined in the recent decades, how many citizens would be inclined to forego the healthy increase in their standard of living to curb the rising prosperity of others? Progressives emphasize the vague psychological discomfort of relative deprivation, inequality by another name, which may be felt when people compare how much their income changes between generations to how much others gain or lose. This view of economic mobility discounts the tangible material comfort of an absolute gain in one's standard of living, regardless of how the neighbors are doing. In a society of abundance, the benefits of absolute mobility leave many citizens immune to the presumed psychological sting of relative deprivation.

Universalism

8

Taxing and Spending

Since the birth of the welfare state, progressives and conservatives have struggled with the question: Who should be eligible for public aid? Their responses informed the classic debate over the doctrines of universalism and selectivity.[1] Conservatives prefer that benefits be distributed selectively on the principle that social welfare programs should concentrate mainly on people lacking the resources to cope with economic, psychological, and physical distress. In contrast, universalism is a cornerstone of progressive policy, upholding the principle that the state should provide a full array of social services and cash transfers to all citizens, rich and poor alike. The universal–selective dichotomy, of course, is an ideal type that simplifies the alternative choices regarding eligibility for various welfare benefits.[2] But within this framework, the Swedish welfare state is widely regarded as a shining example that approximates the universal ideal by providing children's allowances, guaranteed old-age pensions, day care services, paid parental leave, medical care, and other benefits throughout the life cycle to all citizens regardless of their economic circumstances. As the Swedish Social Democratic Party would have it, every citizen is welcome at the table of the "people's home."

At the turn of the twenty-first century, however, the cumulative costs of cradle-to-grave social welfare benefits, the requirements of an aging population, and intensified global competition have generated fiscal pressures to limit social spending by concentrating on citizens who cannot afford the necessities of daily life. The aging demographics alone are daunting. Between 2014 and 2060, Europe's dependency ratio is expected to double, at which point every ten workers will be supporting almost six retirees. And that is assuming the workforce will be supplemented by more than 1 million immigrants a year. Closer to home, government spending on medical benefits in the United States is projected to climb by 60 percent over the next decade.[3] Thus, it comes as no surprise that major international organizations such as the World Bank, the International Monetary Fund, and the OECD recommend targeting welfare benefits to those most in need.[4] Although the ideal of universalism still commands fidelity, in practice, social policy reforms in Sweden and many other countries are introducing greater selectivity. Just how much greater and the extent to which this shift undermines the universal disposition of the Swedish welfare state are matters on which judgments differ. Thus, scholarly deliberations have variously described this shift as a flight from universalism, a drift toward means testing and a refinement of the universal approach so slight as to be imperceptible.[5]

If not exactly thriving in practice, the progressive ideal of universalism remains alive and well in theory. One reason is that providing benefits for everyone is seen as an effective way to avoid the division of society into opposing groups of givers and receivers. Those who disagree with this approach ask: Why should the state distribute scarce resources from the public coffers to a majority of citizens who really do not need them? Robert Goodin and Julian LeGrand find this "not merely wasteful—it is actually counterproductive."[6] Attempting to hoist progressives on their own petard, the opponents suggest that giving public aid to everyone undermines the redistribution of financial benefits to the poor and as such fails to advance economic equality. But as the Swedish political scientist Bo Rothstein points out, this need not be the case. With the right formula of taxing and spending, governments can easily insure that universal benefits will be redistributive.

According to Rothstein, it is a straightforward matter of arithmetic, as shown in Table 8.1.[7] For the sake of illustration, the numbers in Table 8.1 assume that the universal provisions of welfare benefits in cash and subsidized services amount to a transfer that averages $24,000 per household in each of the income quintiles and that their income is being taxed at a flat rate of 40 percent; after paying the tax and receiving the transfer, households in the top income bracket end up with less in their pockets and those in the bottom bracket end up with more; a similar pattern of gain and loss, though not as high, occurs for those in the upper-middle-income and lower-middle-income brackets.[8]

The amount of redistribution would have been even larger if the $24,000 transferred to every household was based on a progressive income tax, rather than the 40 percent flat rate. However, this is a static portrayal of annual taxes

TABLE 8.1
Universal Policy: Taxing and Spending

Group	Average Income	Tax 40%	Transfers	Income after Tax and Transfer
A: 20%	100,000	40,000	24,000	84,000
B: 20%	80,000	32,000	24,000	72,000
C: 20%	60,000	24,000	24,000	60,000
D: 20%	40,000	16,000	24,000	48,000
E: 20%	20,000	8,000	24,000	36,000
		120,000	120,000	

and transfers, which per force disregards the impact of economic mobility. Over the years many of the households will move up and down among the income brackets, decreasing the cumulative redistributive effects during a lifetime.

In this simplified model, after taxes and universal transfers the poorest households gain on average $16,000, those in the lower-middle-income group gain $8,000, the middle-income group breaks even; and the two upper-income groups take a loss. Overall, the numbers show that $120,000 of income must be collected in taxes for each $24,000 that is redistributed from the upper to the lower income groups. Thus, the redistribution achieved through universal benefits involves a considerable churning of private incomes; the government collects taxes with one hand and returns them with the other, and most of the money goes right back into the pockets from which it came. The middle-income group, for example, pays $24,000 in taxes, which is then returned to them in the form of public social welfare benefits. Universalism creates the appearance that everybody is getting something from the State, purportedly forging a sense of unity. According to Rothstein, one reason for the government to move all this money around is that "if you tax the rich and give to the poor, the rich will not accept higher taxes."[9]

Selective policy, of course, could deliver the identical benefits to the low-income groups while lowering everyone's taxes. That is, by targeting welfare transfers only to those most in need, the exact same net redistribution can be achieved with the upper income groups paying considerably less in taxes and those households in the bottom 60 percent of the income distribution paying no taxes at all. As shown in Table 8.2, redistribution through selective policy eliminates the churning of taxes and transfers. The choice between these approaches brings to mind the aphorism about taxation as the art of plucking the goose to get the most feathers with the least hissing. Would the rich prefer to have their government take $40,000 and then return $24,000 or just quietly pay the $16,000 in taxes and be done with it?

TABLE 8.2
Selective Policy: Taxing and Spending

Group	Average Income	Tax	Transfers	Income after Tax and Transfer
A: 20%	100,000	16% (16,000)	0	84,000
B: 20%	80,000	10% (8,000)	0	72,000
C: 20%	60,000	0	0	60,000
D: 20%	40,000	0	8,000	48,000
E: 20%	20,000	0	16,000	36,000
		24,000	24,000	

To provide equivalent redistribution to low-income households, governments favoring universalism, typically the Scandinavian welfare states, must tax and spend a great deal more than those that support selective policies.[10] Thus, universalism automatically inflates the level of social welfare expenditures, creating an illusory sense of welfare effort and public generosity. When progressives talk about the redistribution of income, Irving Kristol tells us, "they rarely mean a simple redistribution among individuals—more often they mean a redistribution *to the state*, which will then take the proper egalitarian measures."[11] Behind the talk about equality lurks a hidden agenda to increase the spending power of the state.

Since Harold Wilensky's landmark study in the mid-1970s, the gross amount of money a country spends on social welfare as a percent of its gross domestic product (GDP) has been accepted by academics and the media as an authoritative measure of the magnitude of generosity and effort bestowed by modern welfare states.[12] Wilensky's analysis marked the United States as a "laggard" in its welfare effort compared to other wealthy nations.[13] Over the decades this observation was habitually confirmed in the academic literature and routinely publicized by the media.[14] Writing in *The Washington Post*, Spencer Rich found that "a growing body of evidence shows that compared with other prosperous developed nations, the United States has a less extensive system of government assistance to the old, the needy and the disabled."[15] A 2007 *New York Times* editorial notes that the United States is "almost the stingiest among industrial nations" when it comes to social welfare spending. In a rising tone the editorial goes on to charge that "long a moral outrage, this tightfisted approach to public needs is becoming an economic hardship."[16]

More Is Better

The prevailing assumption that the United States represents the least generous welfare state is based mainly on the Organization for Economic Cooperation and Development's (OECD) measure of Gross Public Social Expenditure—an index of its member governments' direct social spending as a percent of their GDPs. As late as 2014, a wide-ranging review of welfare state research notes, "Cash spending as a percentage of GDP is the most widely used measure of how much "effort" is being made to directly redistribute income."[17] Its popularity notwithstanding, the conventional interpretation of this index as a proxy for welfare effort and generosity is empirically inaccurate and logically confused. Basically, the calculation of expenditures ignores both a range of transfers that promote social welfare, which take place in addition to direct spending by government, and the extent to which governments "claw back" a sizeable portion of these transfers by taxing the benefits. The indiscriminate judgment about the tight-fistedness of the US welfare state drawn from this incomplete measure is an indictment based on what might be termed "blind empiricism."[18]

In response to the limitations of the Gross Public Expenditure index, various measures were formulated to capture a more accurate account of social expenditures. Among the earliest efforts to rectify the misleading appraisal of social spending, the Need, Expenditure, and Taxes Index proposed in the late 1980s took account of federal tax expenditures for social purposes along with an adjustment for the differential impact of taxes.[19] At that time, US tax expenditures related to social welfare objectives amounted to an estimated 39 percent of direct federal social expenditures.[20] These expenditures are revenue losses due to special deductions and exemptions in the tax code that are justified as serving public purposes, such as enhancing social welfare and strengthening the economy. Sometimes described as "indirect spending," these tax benefits included the mortgage interest deduction on owner-occupied homes, the exclusion of tax payments on employee health insurance, and the earned income tax credit.

The notion that the revenues foregone owing to deductions in the tax code were equivalent to government expenditures had been bandied about for decades. As far back as the 1920s, Arthur Pigou argued that in addition to the checks written directly by the government, special tax deductions and exemptions were a form of social transfer.[21] Not everyone agreed. Irving Kristol claimed that to think of special tax exemptions as transfers tacitly assumes that all income covered by the general provision of the tax law belongs by right to the government, and what government decides by exemption or qualification not to collect in taxes constitutes a subsidy.[22] It was not until the mid-1970s that data on tax expenditures were introduced as a regular component of the President's budget in the United States, which was among the first countries to collect this information.[23]

By the latter half of 1990s, the shortcomings of the Gross Public Social Expenditures index had become increasingly evident. As Willem Adema gently put it, "Observations on social expenditure levels across countries that do not account for private social benefits and the impact of the tax system are prone to be misleading."[24] Seeking a more accurate gauge, Adema and his colleagues at the OECD developed a comprehensive index of social spending known as the Net Total Social Expenditure.[25] Tax expenditures were not the only benefits added to this new index. It introduced a model of social accounting that incorporated the cumulative value of direct public social expenditures, tax expenditures, publicly mandated private expenditures, and voluntary private social expenditures; the sum of these benefits is then reduced by the cost of direct and indirect taxes on these benefits, which vary considerably among countries.[26] The voluntary private social expenditures, such as employee health and pension benefits, typically promoted by tax breaks, constitute a substantial part of the total account devoted to social expenditure. Finally, the inclusion of publicly mandated private expenditures recognizes that governments can create social transfers through their powers of regulation. That is, in addition to taxing and spending, governments generate financial support for social purposes by passing legislation that requires the private sector to provide social benefits such as employer payments for sickness and maternity leave.[27] Mandated private expenditures, however, can be difficult to distinguish. When George Osborne sought to cut Britain's welfare bill, for example, his budget reduced the working tax credit (a benefit similar to the US Earned Income Tax Credit) at the same that it raised the minimum wage. This shifted some of the costs of a social welfare benefit to the private sector, softening the financial impact on low-income workers.[28] But the effects of minimum wage legislation are not counted among the publicly mandate private expenditures.

There are considerable differences between where countries rank on the comprehensive index of Net Total Social Expenditure as a percent of GDP and their positions under the narrower yardstick of the Gross Public Social Expenditure index. A comparison of twenty-three major OECD countries, for example, reveals the United States jumps from the twentieth place on the gross expenditure index to the sixth place on the net measure.[29] In suggesting that a country's welfare effort or generosity is exemplified by the percent of its GDP devoted to social spending, these comparisons rely on a relative measure of proportionality rather than the actual dollars allocated per capita for welfare purposes. Applying the per capita metric to gross and net social expenditures controlled for the purchasing power of different currencies further reshuffles the rankings. As illustrated in Table 8.3, when the comparisons shift from percent of GDP to per capita spending for social purposes, the United States rises from fourteenth place among the twenty-three countries to the first place. Contrary to academic claims and op-ed musings, the conventional interpretation would have to score it as the most generous welfare state.

TABLE 8.3

Alternative Measures of Social Expenditure: How Denmark, Germany, the United States, and the Netherlands Rank among Twenty-Three OECD Countries

Country	Gross Public Soc. Exp. as % of GDP	Net Total Soc. Exp. as % of GDP	Gross Public Soc. Exp. Per Capita PPP	Net Total Soc. Exp. Per Capita PPP
Denmark	2	7	2	7
Germany	4	1	6	3
United States	20	6	14	1
Netherlands	11	8	10	6

GDP, gross domestic product; PPP, purchasing power parity among currencies.

Source: Adapted from Neil Gilbert, "The Least Generous Welfare State? A Case of Blind Empiricism," *Journal of Comparative Policy Analysis* 11, no. 3 (2009), Appendix 1.

Whether the United States is at the top or the bottom of these rankings, it is hard to know what the comparative measures of social spending actually represent beyond the different monetary sums and accounting methods on which they are based. Indeed, on face value the indices of social expenditure are virtually incomprehensible as substantive indicators of effort, generosity, protection, and well-being. This is because they are indifferent to need, which clouds any comparisons. The United States' unemployment rate in 2005, for example, was about 30 percent lower than the six-country average rate for France, Italy, Norway, Sweden, Finland, and Germany, all of which had a higher level of Gross Public Social Expenditure than the United States.[30] Does their higher level of social expenditure signify more generosity, greater welfare effort, heightened social protection—or is it just a surrogate for the public cost of higher unemployment?

Then there is the case of what was labeled the "Dutch disease." With close to 20 percent of the labor force out on disability or sick leave in 1990, the cost of disability benefits amounted to 7 percent of the Netherland's GDP. Their disability rate was among the highest in the developed world. Rather than a sign of special effort to address a huge incidence of authentic disability, an OECD study attributed this unusual expenditure to the disincentive to work created by a large benefit that replaced up to 70 percent of the last gross wage. Should this social expenditure be interpreted as the result of a liberal disability benefit that signified welfare generosity or one that created a higher level of spending than was warranted by inducing many people with physical aches and pains to apply for a lifetime benefit?[31]

Similar questions regarding what social spending signifies could be raised about the high ranking of the United States on the index of net social expenditure per capita. To what extent does this spending reflect greater needs in the United States to subsidize low-wage employment through Earned Income Tax Credits and to assist a relatively high proportion of single-parent families? How much of the welfare effort involves direct subsidies to the middle class, such as the homeowner's hefty mortgage interest deductions or the food stamp benefits going to 8 million recipients with incomes greater than 200 percent of the poverty level—more than $45,000 for a family of four.[32]

Without comparing the magnitude of social needs among countries, a Ouija board is required to interpret what different levels of social expenditure signify. An interpretation that attributes the virtues of generosity and effort to proportionately higher outlays, however, is not derived from the spiritual guidance of supernatural beliefs. It is guided by a progressive vision of the good society, which essentially assumes that where the amounts of taxing and public spending are concerned, the higher the proportion of the GDP the better. This assumption derives from the progressive belief that government is more just and benevolent than the market in allocating the national income produced under capitalism. Of course, neither is exempt from unsavory doings. But in general, merit, productivity, and the desire for individual gain are associated with market income, which the welfare state redistributes on the basis of need, compassion, and the desire for communal security. This explains, in part, why supporters of universalism are not inconvenienced by the fact that in providing social welfare benefits to all citizens, governments must lay claim to a larger proportion of the national income to produce the same transfers as could be achieved through selective policy that distributes benefits according to need.

Creed of Universalism: Stigma and Political Disadvantage

The progressive case for universalism, however, is explicitly formulated on the social and political consequences of this approach, rather than on the underlying preference for government to control the allocation of as much of the national income as possible. The long-standing arguments in support of the universal principle contend that it avoids stigma, costs less to administer, averts moral hazard, and, most of all, offers political assurances that social welfare programs will be widely supported because everyone receives benefits. All these arguments rely more on a firm base of rhetorical declaration than empirical evidence.

The claim that eligibility for social benefits based on financial need is stigmatizing has been voiced so often over the decades as to give the appearance of having stood the test of time.[33] Almost fifty years ago, Richard Titmuss, founding director of the Department of Social Administration at the London School of Economics, made the case that in contrast to the selective allocation of benefits, the principle of universalism would avoid "involving users in any humiliating loss of status, dignity or self-respect. There should be no sense of inferiority, pauperism, shame or stigma in the use of publicly provided services."[34] This censorious view of means testing endures.[35] Clearly, one can imagine tactless bureaucrats conducting abrasive interviews that would denigrate the self-worth of applicants or the embarrassment that might be felt by a father paying with food stamps in a supermarket under the gaze of other shoppers on line behind him. At the same time, however, college students applying for financial aid do not seem psychologically distressed by the means test. And many low-income workers fill out tax forms to claim the means-tested Earned Income Tax Credit without an apparent loss of self-respect.

The point is that a means test is not inherently demeaning. Its administration can be abusive or innocuous. And the social status of those applying for benefits is probably a lot more important to their sense of self-respect than the application process. A low-income father unable to support his family may feel a lack of self-worth even before arriving at the welfare office. In contrast, to be seen as poor and struggling is more a badge of character than a cause of embarrassment for privileged college students. But even for low-income welfare recipients, research fails to confirm the harsh psychological effects attributed to means-tested eligibility procedures during the 1960s and 1970s, a period before contemporary reforms have tempered the methods and stretched the scope of means testing.[36] A British survey of over one thousand people claiming welfare benefits in 2012 found that nearly 80 percent of the respondents reported no personal sense of stigma. The personal experience of an overwhelming majority of welfare recipients simply does not correspond with the imputed consequences of means testing.[37]

Whatever stigmatizing affects might have been connected to means testing when Richard Titmuss staked out the budding field of social policy, the landscape has changed along with the latitude of means-tested policies The so-called man in the house rule allowed for unannounced midnight visits by caseworkers to insure that welfare mothers were not living with an able-bodied man, which would make them ineligible for benefits; in 1968 it was deemed unconstitutional. Food stamps are now designed to look like a credit card. Welfare recipients are expected to work, which typifies, perhaps, the most significant break with the past. That is, the status of recipients has blurred as means-tested benefits are no longer concentrated on the poorest people who are not working; two of the largest means-tested welfare programs in the United States extend benefits to the middle class; food stamps serve millions of households with incomes over 200 percent of the poverty line, and the Earned Income Tax Credit assists couples with three children earning up to $53,267. With the eligibility guidelines stretched to encompass a substantial proportion of the population, including those with practically middle-class incomes, contemporary means-tested programs increasingly operate more to exclude upper income groups than to embrace only the non-employed indigent.[38]

Moving away from programs designed exclusively to serve people not in work, the changing course of means-tested benefits reduced what in earlier times was deemed a "moral hazard," another way of saying incentives for bad behavior, which in this case was the avoidance of paid employment. Between the US welfare reform of 1996 and the expansion of the Earned Income Tax Credit, two of the major means-tested programs in the United States are now seen as encouraging and rewarding work. Lending more than encouragement, the 1996 welfare reform required recipients to work and sweetened the demand by increasing the amount of earning they were allowed to retain without reducing the welfare benefit.[39] As an incentive to work, the Earned Income Tax Credit benefit is designed to increase as low-income earnings rise up to $13,650 for a family with two children, and then it slowly tapers off above earnings of $17,800. Over the last two decades, the trend toward coupling means-tested benefits with work-oriented incentives has gained momentum in many of the advanced welfare states.[40] This change is vividly expressed in the contemporary discourse on social policy. What was once commonly referred to in the textbooks as the welfare state objectives of "income maintenance" and "social protection" is now "wrapped in the elaborate rhetoric of social inclusion (in the labor force), empowerment (to earn wages), activation (to find a job), and responsibility (to take a job)."[41]

As for the administrative cost, means-tested benefits are generally more expensive to process than universal benefits. The former require making case-by-case distinctions among applicants on the basis of their financial resources; the latter do not. Individual screening demands greater time and effort than allocating benefits to everyone in a demographic category such as children, the elderly, and parents. But the extent of the extra effort depends largely on the type of means test employed, which may range from a declaration on an income tax form to a highly detailed process involving thorough documentation of assets and income, a closely monitored follow-up, and periodic benefit adjustments in response to the recipient's changing circumstances. Although the administrative costs of means-tested benefits are higher than universal transfers, limiting social benefits to those who cannot afford to pay is still much less expensive overall. The higher cost of universalism and its indifference to need does not deter support for this approach because from the progressive perspective more important political, social, and economic issues are at stake.

Universal social policies are believed to garner a political advantage for both the program benefits they deliver and the party in power dispensing these benefits. As Harry Hopkins, the settlement house social worker who became President Franklin D. Roosevelt's intimate adviser, was reported to have said, "We will tax and tax, and spend and spend, and elect and elect" (a remark which he categorically denied).[42] Beyond the political return that some associate with a more-is-better attitude toward government taxing and spending, the universal approach is held to guarantee a higher quality of social provisions than programs designed for only low-income groups, which are said to end up like their clients—in shabby quarters, with few resources and looking for a way out.

The mantra "programs for the poor are poor programs" exemplifies a standard belief held by supporters of universal preschool.[43] It sounds logical, but on reflection it is a bit too simplistic. One need look no further than the wide range of quality and disappointing results for low-income students in the kindergarten-to-12th grade system to conclude that universalism is hardly a guarantee of quality education, particularly for low-income students. Indeed, the "programs for the poor" mantra ignores the possibility that with universal entitlement the middle and upper classes are likely to be more effective than the poor in finding and consuming the highest quality of education that is available. As Richard Titmuss, one of the first and arguably greatest champions of universalism had to admit, after fifteen years of experience with the universal provisions of Britain's National Health Service, "the higher income groups make better use of the service; they tend to receive more specialist attention; they occupy more of the beds in better equipped and staffed hospitals; receive more elective surgery; have better maternity care; and are more likely to get psychiatric help and psychotherapy than low-income groups."[44] Still he could wax enthusiastically about some aspects of the universal health care system. Comparing his experience being treated for cancer with that of a young West Indian from Trinidad served in the same office, Titmuss observes, "His appointment was the same time as mine for radium treatment—10 o'clock every day. Sometimes he went in to the Theratron Room first; sometimes I did. What determined waiting was simply the vagaries of London traffic—not race, religion, color or class."[45]

The assumption that universalism creates a coalition of interests between the least well-off and the wealthier classes of taxpayers, which supports a high level of social welfare spending, rests on a one-sided line of reasoning. It is the side that says average taxpayers will accept higher taxes if they get some social benefits in return, which brings us back to the question that was earlier left hanging (in regard to the choices offered in Tables 8.1 and 8.2). That is, what if the choice was phrased in reverse, would the taxpayers prefer to forego the social benefit that the government decides to give them, if they could pay lower taxes as a result of selective transfers and keep the money in their pockets to spend as they wish? Phrased either way, these are abstract choices that presume a degree of fiscal transparency that would allow individuals to compare the costs of additional taxes and the derived value of social benefits, which is hardly available.

Speculation about the political advantage of universalism rests on a shaky line of reasoning that could benefit from the reinforcement of empirical evidence. In this regard, Bo Rothstein's example of how it was possible for universal benefits to be redistributive was amplified by the findings of two other well-known Swedish social scientists. Walter Korpi and Joakim Palme's research showed that redistribution was not only possible, but likely to be higher in welfare states that favored universal policies than in those which were more inclined to limit social benefits to the most needy. They described this counterintuitive result—the more benefits are targeted on the poor, the lower the level of redistribution—as "the paradox of redistribution."[46] In the familiar mode of comparative welfare state research, their findings were based on the correlation of two variables during one year for a small sample of eleven countries, which was anchored by Sweden at the high end of universalism and redistribution and the United States next to the bottom.

These findings did not go uncontested. Published in 1998, the paradox of redistribution was calculated on data from 1985. Since then, serious doubts have been raised by studies seeking to replicate the paradoxical findings with rigorous research designs that included larger samples, longitudinal analysis, and alternative measures of income. Lane Kenworthy reproduced the 1985 analysis using the same measurements and source of data over an extended period of time. He found that the positive relationship between the degree of universalism and the level of redistribution which appeared in 1985 began to fade after 1990 and essentially disappeared in 2000 and 2005, although Sweden continued to register the highest level of redistribution and the United States the lowest. Kenworthy concludes that although the premise that targeting social policy reduces political support is not unreasonable, "the experience of rich countries in recent decades suggests reasons to question it."[47]

Further reason for doubt is submitted in evidence from the United States, which demonstrates considerable similarities in the political fortunes of means-tested and universal social programs between 1980 and 2000.[48] Indeed, other findings on the US experience indicate that the exercise of political influence is more complex than assumed by analyses that extrapolate global preferences for overall spending from an academic classification of welfare states as more or less universal. The flow of influence in the political arena is highly regulated by the interplay of interest group preferences around particular issues. As mentioned earlier (Chapter 5), Gilen's study revealed that on a number of issues concerning benefits to low-income people, policies supported by social welfare interest groups prevailed over those favored by the general public.[49]

From a comparative perspective, the most persuasive evidence that universalism has no discernable impact on levels of redistribution comes from a wide-ranging and methodologically sophisticated study of twenty-five countries, including the eleven countries in the original 1985 study. In analyses using two different data sets and alternative definitions of income, Ive Marx and his colleagues found no clear relationship between universalism and redistribution across countries. On the contrary, they note that "for what it matters, targeting tends to be associated with higher levels of redistributive impact, especially when overall effort in terms of spending is high."[50]

Contemporary empirical analyses of the relationship between targeting and redistribution dispel the so-called paradox of redistribution—"the more we target benefits at the poor, the less likely we are to reduce poverty and inequality."[51] Yet after all is said and done, a persistent reservation casts a dark shadow of uncertainty over the entire body of comparative research on how social welfare spending affects the redistribution of income and the level of poverty. The standard approach to measuring the impact of social transfers on redistribution and poverty is based on estimating the difference between household incomes after social transfers and the income these households *would have had* in the absence of the social transfer. The problem is that there is no way to really know what the household income *would have been* if the social transfers did not exist.[52]

Does knowing they will be getting a public pension have any influence on when workers decide to retire or how much money they try to save for retirement? Does knowing that unemployment compensation will last for two years have any influence on when and how hard unemployed people start looking for another job?

Social transfers influence people's economic behavior. Thus, it is unrealistic to assume that market income would remain the same in the absence of the existing social transfers. Under current social policies, for example, the market incomes of many elderly people fall to zero when they retire; their financial resources are then replenished to varying degrees by transfer income from public pensions. Among the wealthy welfare states public pensions often account for more than 90 percent of the household income available to the retirement-age population. The pensions represent a substantial social expenditure that lifts many of the elderly out of poverty.

The question is what would happen in the absence of these transfers? Would the market income of the retired elderly still be zero? The answer is yes, according to the standard method of computing the redistributive impact of social transfers. This method requires accepting the counterfactual assumption that market incomes would be unaffected by the absence of the existing public pensions—the elderly would have no money, period. That might be true for some. Others might postpone retirement and keep working. It is also possible that with no public pensions due them many people would feel more of a necessity to save privately for their retirement. And they would have extra resources to purchase a private annuity with the salary savings from the elimination of payroll taxes typically used to finance public pensions. In this scenario, rather than a market income of zero, the retired elderly could be receiving a sizeable payout from capital investments. A credible estimate suggests that on reaching the age of retirement in 2008 a couple earning the average US income over their working life would have accumulated over $1.3 million if they had paid into a private account what otherwise would been have contributed to Social Security payroll taxes. If they had the misfortune to wait a year and retired just after the financial crisis in 2009, their private account would have declined by 37 percent to $855,175—still not a paltry sum.[53]

In assuming that the market income of the retired elderly would not change in the absence of public pensions, most studies exaggerate the degree of redistribution and poverty reduction that can be attributed to social transfers. This not only distorts the estimate in a given country; it creates a bias that discredits comparative analyses of countries that differ in the proportion of income that elderly households receive from public pensions. In Belgium, France, and Sweden, for example, public pensions account for over 90 percent of the total disposable income of the retirement-age population. For that reason alone social transfers appear to increase the redistribution of income and reduce the level of poverty in those countries much more than in the

United States, Canada, and Australia, where public pensions are 50 percent or less of the disposable income of the retired.[54]

Granting that comparative measures of the welfare state's economic impact are "biased due to the counterfactual underlying any such evaluation—that the welfare state has not affected the distribution of private income and that the differences in welfare state design across countries have had the same zero effect on private incomes," Peter Whiteford concludes that the amount of redistribution attributed to the welfare state in many countries is significantly less than reported.[55] Indeed, most researchers openly recognize this problem. Sometimes they attempt to cope with it by excluding the retired population from their analysis. This eliminates the largest social expenditure associated with modern welfare states, but it still does not resolve the question of how economic behavior might be influenced by social transfers to other groups such as the unemployed and people with disabilities. Another strategy is to report the results while admitting, not that the counterfactual problem actually destroys any confidence in the interpretation of comparative findings, but as academic convention dictates, noting it as a "limitation" of the research.[56] When these findings reach the media and the public at large, the numerical precision in which they are expressed masks the underlying uncertainty of what they represent.

There is no sound evidence for the claims that selectivity stigmatizes recipients of public benefits and universalism encourages political support resulting in a greater redistribution of income. Some would say that lack of proof is not disproof. Even in the absence of empirical validation, these ideas remain comfortably lodged within a belief system that favors giving government a greater role in distributing market income. In the end, the more-is-better attitude toward government control over the allocation of national income serves to extend the reach and cost of government without increasing public aid to the most disadvantaged. But the preference for universal social policy embraces more than strengthening the role of the state vis-à-vis the market. Over the last few decades progressive proposals for the development of universal preschool programs in the United States foreshadow an increasing role of the state in the traditional functions of family life.

9

From Cradle to Grave

Universal day care is the final stretch on the road of "cradle-to-grave" coverage, which characterized Edward Bellamy's utopian welfare state.[1] Coined by Bellamy in 1888, this phrase conveys the modern ambitions of progressive policymakers vividly expressed in *The Life of Julia*, a slide show broadcast during the 2012 presidential election. Following the imaginary life of an ordinary American woman from childhood to retirement, Ross Douthat describes the journey as a "sweeping vision of government's place in society, in which the individual depends on the state at every stage of life and no decision—personal, educational, entrepreneurial, sexual—can be contemplated without the promise that it will be somehow subsidized by Washington."[2]

By extending the long arm of the state into the early years of childrearing, the universal provision of preschool care embodies two objectives that are high on the modern progressive agenda: raising female labor force participation rates and leveling the inherited benefits that children born into well-off families derive from parental socialization. The prevailing assumptions are that universal day care will increase the economic independence and gender equality of mothers with young children and advance the social mobility of children from disadvantaged families. To realize these aims, both the market and the state are called upon to supply the caring and household production once performed owing to mutual obligation and affection within the domestic sphere of family life.

A critical examination of these views suggests that in two-earner families with preschool children the financial benefits and economic independence gained by mothers (or fathers) shifting their labor from the household to the market are illusory in many, if not most, cases.[3] Although paid employment may liberate spouses from financial reliance on their partners, this independence comes at the cost of obedience to the discipline of the market imposed by bosses, supervisors, and customers.[4] These are strangers over whom paid employees have hardly any of the interpersonal power that accompanies the affection, commitments, and customary bonds of family life. Along with personal submission to the demands of the workplace, the two-earner household must contend with greater dependence on the market to perform the quotidian functions of household management and parental duty. In 2013 almost half of every dollar Americans spent on food was consumed in restaurants, compared to thirty-five cents in 1992.[5] And even when food is purchased for the home, the meals often come ready-made. What was once unpaid work is regularly outsourced to restaurants, gardeners, party planners, cleaning services, laundries, handymen, shopping services, child care providers, dog walkers, tutors, bookkeepers, and life organizers.

With this commodification of household services, the gardeners, party planners, cleaners, tutors, and caregivers are on the two-earner-family's payroll, while the second earner is now working largely to support these staff—they are all chained to the market. As the cash value of household production and care is established, it heightens social awareness of just how much a stay-at-home mother's unpaid labor is worth. Authoritative opinions suggest nonpaid family work accounts for at least half of a society's economic activity.[6] More detailed estimates have been drawn from annual surveys of how much time per week 15,000 mothers spend on their ten most time-consuming jobs. Applying data on hourly wages for these jobs in 2014, the findings place the annual value of a stay-at-home mother's work at $118,905. This is about $40,000 more than the value of unpaid labor furnished by mothers who are employed full-time.[7] These women continue to bear the brunt of household production and child care, although they devote less time to this work than stay-at-home mothers.[8] Some of the reduction in time allotted to housework by employed mothers in two-earner families is compensated for by fathers, who have increased the number of weekly hours spent on unpaid labor; the rest of the work is outsourced to the market or involves discretionary household chores that no longer get done.[9]

Whether or not the estimated difference in the value of household labor performed by stay-at-home and employed mothers is entirely on the mark, when both parents are employed, there is clearly a significant expense generated by the reduction in unpaid labor dedicated to meeting family needs. This expense, of course, varies by family composition and over the life course. In the United States, the expense is staggering for young families with preschool children. There is no getting around the labor-intensive requirements of caring for young children. At the University of California in Berkeley, a public institution, the cost of day care for children from infancy to school age averages more than $20,000 per year. California's median female income for full-time workers is $40,144.[10] A lower quality of child care can be purchased for less. But even at half the price, the arithmetic is troubling for a two-income family with two preschool children wherein the mother earns the median income or less. And the day care charges are only part of the costs. After subtracting work-related expenses, taxes, and payments for the various tasks outsourced to the market, the net gain derived from a second income is hard to discern. Hence, progressive proposals for universal day care provide a much needed government subsidy in order to make the shift of a mother's labor from household work to paid employment financially worthwhile for low to middle wage earners with young children. For those in better paid occupations—doctors, lawyers, professors, media personalities, and corporate executives—subsidized universal care is more of a bonus that raises the already higher level of material consumption afforded by their second income.

If the state would fund an average of anywhere from $15,000 to $20,000 per capita for high-quality out-of-home childhood care, why not offer a similar, perhaps slightly reduced, subsidy to parents who would rather perform this work at home? Parental child care can readily be deemed the functional equivalent of gainful employment. Consider the mother who drops her two children off at a public day care center and then drives to her job at a different preschool facility, where she is paid to mind other people's children. Although some might argue that the care given in public centers is the more efficient (if not warm-hearted) alternative, the savings are not self-evident. The labor-intensive demand of child care work limits the extent to which an increase in the low ratio of caregivers to children can reduce the direct costs of public care without undermining the safety and quality of this service. On the other side of the ledger, home care by parents eliminates all the costs associated with building and maintaining a public child care facility along with the administrative overhead.[11]

Offering the choice of a subsidized public service or cash for parental care affords equal treatment both to those who prefer to devote more time to domestic life and care during the early stages of childrearing and those who value an early start on paid employment, which may benefit their prospects of reaching the top of the corporate ladder. But the room up there is limited—most people spend their lives laboring on the middle rungs of their fields. Although the choice to devote five to seven years to child care and household management curtails some career options, as the life span has lengthened, seven years at home would leave more than thirty years to invest in paid employment—enough time to exhaust the alleged joys of work for many people. Indeed, in most of the advanced industrialized world, the joys are such that workers tend to withdraw from the labor force well below the official age for receiving a full old-age pension.[12]

Since 1990 a number of countries with universal child care provisions, including Norway, Finland, Sweden, Denmark, and Germany, have offered families the choice between subsidized services and a cash benefit for those who do not enroll their children in the public programs.[13] The per capita cash benefits to stay-at-home parents are quite modest in comparison to the public subsidies for child care centers. Still, in every instance progressive parties on the Left have supported the universal provision of public care and opposed offering the choice of cash for care as an alternative benefit.

Because the cash-for-care benefit is taken mainly by mothers, it is seen as reinforcing the traditional division of labor in family life, inhibiting women's independence and undermining gender equality in the market.[14] These concerns tend to be expressed most vocally by an influential body of professionals who think, talk, and write for a living—professors, journalists, foundation officers, think-tank scholars, and media commentators. As a high-status group with well-paying jobs that are divorced from the conventional 9-to-5 discipline of everyday work, their reasoning about the financial gains and personal independence achieved by transferring a mother's labor to the market is self-referential. It reflects more the labor of those for whom "doing lunch" in a pleasant restaurant is considered work rather than the toil of waitresses, cooks, dishwashers, truck drivers, and cleaners who make that working lunch possible. One might argue that in advocating the shift of household labor to the market, progressive efforts to promote gender equality have trumped concerns about alleviating social class differences and in the process advanced the interests of capitalism.

In contrast to promoting female labor force participation, which resonates with the ambitions and experiences of professional elites, universal day care is also advanced as a program to offset the social and cultural inheritance of children from privileged families. As an empirical argument for its effectiveness in reducing the advantages of social class, Gosta Esping-Andersen calculates that Nordic countries display a greater degree of cognitive equality than the United States. Noting the uniformity and high pedagogical standards of universal care, he forthrightly claims that "the uneven distribution of cultural capital among families is greatly neutralized in the Nordic countries, simply because much of the cognitive stimulus has been shifted from the parents to centers *that do not replicate social class differences.*"[15] This view is often expressed as a reason against offering the option of cash-for-care benefits since less-educated low-income earners, including many immigrant mothers, are highly represented among those who choose to stay at home, while their children are among those likely to benefit most from absorbing the language and cultural norms communicated in public day care.[16]

Many parents in the United State would recoil at the idea of universal child care as a mechanism through which the state aims to neutralize the family's impact on the cognitive development of their offspring. In part, this reflects an adverse perception of the current performance of the public educational system, which casts a shadow on its prospects to deliver a high quality of care to preschoolers from all walks of life.[17] Reservations about universal day care cannot be disassociated from the large expenditures and disappointing outcomes of public education for older children. Despite the fourth highest level of spending on education (averaging about $12,000 per capita) among thirty-four of the wealthiest industrial democracies, the United States ranks twenty-seventh in math, twentieth in science, and seventeenth in reading on the OECD's international student assessment of scholastic performance.[18]

Closing the Developmental Gap?

Of course, even during the foundational stages of human development, universal day care would not entirely override the influences of family life. After all, the children continue to spend their evenings, weekends, and vacations with their parents. And the force of biological endowments cannot be discounted. But to whatever degree universal day care may neutralize the social and cognitive impact of parental interactions so as to give disadvantaged children a more equal start in life, there is an unspoken question of how this shifting balance of influence from parents to child care centers affects the development of children who come from middle- and upper-middle-class families. The communal day care experience is supposed to benefit all children. Otherwise why should middle-class families participate? Thus, it should not only enrich the social and cognitive skills of participants from well-to-do families, but in order to close the developmental gap between the classes, it would have to make an even greater impact on the children from disadvantaged families.

That is a tall order, which a considerable body of research has failed to substantiate. Admittedly, the study of nonmaternal care is methodologically challenging and socially sensitive. Just as working mothers are troubled by findings that imply child development may be stunted in out-of-home care, stay-at-home mothers are irked by findings that suggest children thrive more in day care settings than at home. Concluding that day care "typically does no harm," the bland findings of initial studies in the early 1980s gave no offense to either side.[19] A second wave of research, based largely on survey methods, was launched in the 1990s by a team of twenty-five researchers from ten universities. Following a sample of 1,364 children from birth through age seven in ten vicinities across the United States, this large-scale investigation generated a voluminous body of empirical work analyzing the quality of care and a wide range of developmental outcomes.[20] The findings were mixed and muffled by a host of qualifications. On one hand, they revealed that the likelihood of behavioral problems showing up in kindergarten rose consistently with the number of hours per week spent in day care, regardless of the quality of the service.[21] But the behavioral problems associated with extended day care were no longer evident by the third grade, as the children eventually mellowed out. On the other hand, the findings showed an overall gain in academic skills linked to high-quality child care, which were sustained through the third grade.[22] But these gains were modest. Other large-sample studies also found that attending child care was associated with modest gains in pre-reading and math skills.[23]

Starting in 2002, the Head Start Impact Study launched a third wave of child care research based on an experimental design that included more than 4,500 three-and-four-year-old children in 383 Head Start centers across the country. It was arguably the most rigorous and comprehensive assessment to date—and the academic outcomes were undoubtedly the most disappointing. At the end of the first Head Start year, there was firm evidence that the three-year-old program participants scored significantly higher than children in the control group on eight out of twenty-three cognitive outcomes and the four-year-olds did so on seven of the twenty-three cognitive measures. But these promising results quickly faded out by the first grade. By the end of the third grade the initial gains of Head Start students had vanished to the point that significant difference between the program participants and the control group appeared on only two outcomes, and these cancelled each other out. The four-year-old Head Start cohort scored a little higher on one of the reading tests, and the three-year-old cohort had a slightly lower promotion rate than the non–Head Start students.[24]

Although the overall results of the Head Start research are discouraging, those promoting the universal day care agenda can find reasons to persevere. Additional combing of the data reveals that the national averages conceal large variations in the effects of different Head Start centers as well as their impact on subgroups of children from diverse backgrounds.[25] Finding these variations in program outcomes fuels the argument that universal preschool can work in the right conditions and that the inadequate outcomes on the national level reflect a lack of sufficient funding to create these conditions. Proponents also assert the possibility of a "sleeper effect" that will trigger positive results sometime in the future, a line of reasoning that has the momentary advantage of being quite difficult to disprove.[26] But even in the generously funded Perry Preschool and Abecedarian programs, which after almost half a century still lend hope to the promise of early child care, the long-term beneficial outcomes came nowhere near to closing the educational and socioeconomic achievement gaps between children from the lower and middle classes.

In light of all the evidence, it is hard to envision how children from the most disadvantaged families would benefit by making child care programs *universally* available. Indeed, the Head Start findings raise a serious question about the social and educational value of a large-scale national program focusing on children just from low-income (but not necessarily impoverished) families, claims about "sleeper effects" and funding deficiencies notwithstanding. Parenthetically, it is worth noting that between 35 and 50 percent of Head Start participants are not poor, according to the official definition of poverty.[27]

To sum up, universalism in general serves to enlarge the economic and social spheres of state influence through taxing and spending aimed at delivering social welfare benefits as widely as possible. In the specific case of child care, it amplifies public beneficence and responsibility in the private realm of domestic activity during the early years of childhood, a critical juncture in the course of family life. Contrary to the prevailing assumptions, however, universal coverage of publicly supervised child care would fail to make a tangible impact on the social mobility of disadvantaged children and do little to promote the economic independence and well-being of most mothers who are not in the elite occupations. In the absence of these outcomes, proponents of universal child care appear to be persuaded more by the progressive penchant for increasing the dominion of the state vis-à-vis the family and the market than by empirical confirmation of any benefits derived by mothers and children.

Surely there is an argument to be made that out-of-home care programs are advisable, if not essential, for children living in severely deprived circumstances. By definition a preschooler is better off spending eight hours a day supervised by nurturing adults in a safe stimulating environment than in a home where her emotional and intellectual needs are being neglected. But this argument lends no logical support or empirical basis for the *universal* provision of child care. When ideology trumps evidence, neither the progressive inclination to increase government influence nor the conservative inclination to limit it is sufficient to inspire sensible thought about the role of government in promoting the good society.

The Social Security Crisis

While progressives want to increase spending on a universal system of public care for children, at the other end of the life cycle the universal program of Social Security faces a crushing long-term deficit. A cornerstone of President Roosevelt's New Deal, this program provides the major source of income for most retirees. When Roosevelt signed the Social Security Act in 1935, the average life expectancy of 61.7 years was 3 years below the standard age of retirement. It looked like a financially sound deal. By 2013, however, life expectancy in the United States had climbed to 78.8 years.[28] The higher rates of infant mortality in 1935 accounted for some of this seventeen-year difference in life expectancy. In fact, for those who reached the age of 65 there was only about a four-year difference between the remaining life expectancy in 1935 and 2013. But the percent of the male population over 18 years old that survived to age 65 in 2013 was almost double the adult survival rate in 1935.[29] Not only are more people living longer but families are having fewer children today. The result is a rapidly aging society. In 1940 about 6.8 percent of the population was over 65 years of age; by 2050 those over 65 will account for 20 percent of the population.

Add it all up and the demographic shift has a significant impact on the Social Security program's fiscal capacity to meet its benefit obligations, which are financed on a pay-as-you-go basis. That means that the Social Security taxes collected from those now working go to pay for the pensions of current retirees. This arrangement worked well in 1950 when there were 16.5 workers contributing taxes for each beneficiary. Although the amount coming in would generate a surplus, the ratio was rapidly declining. By 2015 just 2.8 workers were supporting each beneficiary. That ratio cannot sustain the pension payments stipulated by Social Security's defined benefit plan.[30]

Old-age pensions are typically organized as defined benefit or defined contribution plans. In the latter, the amount of money received at retirement depends entirely on how much each worker contributed to their own account and the returns on their investments. In contrast, the level of retirement income provided by Social Security is based on a defined benefit plan under which the government promises to pay retired workers a specific amount of money. The defined benefit is calculated using a formula that includes the pensioner's age and earnings history. The final amount is adjusted to allow for a degree of redistribution, which distinguishes this program as *social* insurance. That is, Social Security benefits replace a larger proportion of the average earnings of low-income workers than of high-income workers; the program also provides a supplemental dependent's allowance, which grants spouses an additional 50 percent of the primary wage earner's retirement benefit.[31]

Although it has a sturdy ring, the *defined benefit* is not a contractual guarantee. What Congress defines, it can redefine. Indeed, over the last fifty years adjustments have been made in the amount of retirement income and the degree of redistribution generated by Social Security. Since the late 1970s Social Security reforms have increased financial contributions to the system by raising the employer-employee tax rate along with the taxable-earnings base. And other measures have reduced the overall amount of benefits by lifting the retirement age from 65 to 67 years and imposing an income tax on pension benefits for retirees with a modest amount of income from other sources.[32] Yet in 2010 annual outlays for the program exceeded annual revenues credited to the Social Security trust funds. Despite the various efforts to maintain the program's solvency, by 2015 the Social Security Trust Funds' Board of Trustees estimated that continuing to provide benefits under the current formula will result in a staggering deficit of $9.4 trillion over the next 75 years. For the time being the current level of pension benefits has been sustained by spending down the surplus that had accrued in earlier times. This short-term fix cannot resolve the immense deficit looming. The trust fund reserves will be depleted in 2035, at which point the program would be able to pay only 77 percent of scheduled benefits.[33]

The problem is serious, but not critical. A variety of measures are available to restore Social Security's fiscal balance. To do so in one fell swoop would require an immediate and permanent 21.1 percent increase in revenues or an immediate and permanent 16.4 percent reduction in scheduled benefits, or some mix therein.[34] Such abrupt actions would be politically challenging, to say the least. Of course, many incremental adjustments are possible. The Congressional Budget Office identifies thirty-six policy options that in various combinations could provide long-term financial stability for Social Security. These proposals include measures to modify cost-of-living increases, change the monthly benefit formula, lift the retirement age, revise the tax on earnings, alter spousal benefits, and introduce a poverty-related minimum.[35] Whatever the choice of policies, the solution to Social Security's shortfall requires shifting resources from a shrinking proportion of workers to a growing proportion of retirees, which ultimately comes down to raising taxes or reducing benefits.

Despite the prospects of a future reduction in Social Security benefits, some authorities argue that the retirement crisis is not as acute as it appears.[36] On the whole, today's elderly are better off financially and much less dependent on Social Security than when the program started. Between 1977 and 2007, workers' participation in employer-sponsored retirement plans grew more than twice as fast as the working-age population. These private plans cover 86 million people or about one-half of the working-age population. Over three-quarters of these schemes are defined contribution plans owned and managed by the employees, making them shareholders in the financial marketplace.[37] Additionally, 80 percent of the elderly own their homes, the median value of which is $170,000, and 55 percent of the ownership is free and clear.[38] Thus, many of their children stand to inherit, if not fortunes, significant sums, which would supplement the next generations' retirement income from Social Security.[39]

Public Support for Private Responsibility

Still, the fiscal challenge of an aging society demands some adjustments, if for no other reason than to assure that the erosion of Social Security benefits does not deny a decent retirement income to those with the least resources. Amid the economic abundance of the twenty-first century, it is likely that public officials will address the deficit by tweaking taxes and benefits in order to keep the existing arrangements intact. But is it necessary for the government to promise *every* retiree a specific wage-replacement rate, when so many possess other income and assets? In so doing, US policymakers would relinquish a compelling opportunity to rethink the conventional approach to Social Security. The Swedish parliament seized this opportunity in 1998,

passing legislation that transformed their pension system from a defined benefit to a defined contribution plan. For those seeking to balance revenues and
payments in a retirement system where benefits are determined more by the
individual's responsibility to work and save than by political negotiations, the
Swedish approach deserves a closer look.

The Swedish pension reform combines three sources of retirement
income: a basic account, which is funded by a notional defined contribution
plan that is publicly managed; a premium account, which is fully funded by
a privately managed defined contribution plan; and a guaranteed minimum
benefit, paid out of general revenues. Under the notionally defined contribution scheme, the employer and employee share the cost of pension credits
valued at 16 percent of the worker's earnings; these credits are allocated
to the insured worker's basic account, which is publicly managed. This is
a *notional* contribution because although the 16 percent payment is credited to the worker's account, the money actually goes to fund the pensions
of those presently retired who were covered by the previous pay-as you-go
plan. Under the new system, upon retirement the workers' annual benefits
are calculated by dividing the balance in their notional accounts by the average years of life expectancy remaining for their birth cohort, adjusted
annually by a rate of interest. Thus, while the notional defined contribution
plan operates on a pay-as-you-go basis, it mimics a fully funded individual
plan.[40] That is, each worker's retirement income is based essentially on what
he or she contributed plus interest, which is indexed to the growth in average income.

To preserve the plan's financial stability without changing the contribution rate, a balancing mechanism is built into the indexed rate of return. This
mechanism is set to automatically reduce the rate return if the pension's li-
abilities become greater than its assets. Thus, political influences are limited
as budgetary strains are routinely allayed by accounting rules rather than
through stakeholder negotiations.[41]

Although the 1998 pension reform was supported by five political parties representing more than 85 percent of the Swedish voters, it remains hotly
debated.[42] Karl-Gustav Scherman, former director-general of the Swedish
National Social Insurance Board, maintains that the automatic balancing
mechanism is profoundly undemocratic, leaving no room "for any other
social goals or for a political monitoring of the generational contract in the
future."[43] In a similar vein, Jan Hagberg argues that the new system aban-
doned the Swedish concept of social solidarity, traditionally associated with
pensions that generate a progressive redistribution of income among retirees.
The progressive ideal has been supplanted by the cost-benefit principle of *actuarial* solidarity, "which ensures that, for all individuals and cohorts, there
is a constant relationship between the current value of contributions and the

pension received. A 'direct pipeline to one's own wallet' was the phrase that was frequently used to convey the essence of the new system."[44]

The new system, however, does promote a limited degree of redistribution based on criteria other than income. Thus, for example, the state grants annual pension credits for the unpaid child care work of stay-at-home parents. In addition, the unisex average life-expectancy tables used to calculate pension benefits redistribute income between those pensioners who live longer than the average for their cohort and those whose life span is below the average. This redistribution by age, however, does not necessarily advance egalitarian objectives. To the extent that wealthy people tend to live longer than those with less income and women tend to live longer than men, the unisex life expectancy table creates a redistribution of income that favors women and the wealthy over low-income men.

Under the new system, benefits from the basic retirement account are supplemented by income from the premium account. This defined contribution plan is privately managed and fully funded by taxes, amounting to 2.5 percent of the workers' earnings. Unlike the publicly managed basic account, here the contributions are invested by individual workers in a mutual fund of their choosing, selected from a list of funds vetted by the Swedish Pension Authority. The rate of return on the premium accounts depends on what the financial markets yield. Upon retirement these private funds are converted to lifetime annuities. In a curious contrast to the Swedish experience, the fate of similar proposals for the partial privatization of Social Security contributions in the United States have encountered firm resistance—as too radical a departure from public responsibility for social protection.[45]

Finally, for citizens who have no work history or a very low pension from the combined value of the basic and premium accounts, the new system provides a guaranteed minimum income payable at age 65. This means-tested benefit is financed from general revenues, creating a distinct break in the link between benefits and contributions characterized by the other plans. In 2014, the minimum annual income for a single pensioner was 94,572 Kronor ($11,763).[46]

Before drawing any conclusions about the Swedish pension reform, we must bear in mind that it is still in a transitional period, with many current participants receiving benefits from both the old and the new systems. Moreover, engulfed by a global recession, the new system weathered a financial meltdown during the early years of implementation. When the automatic balancing mechanism was triggered for the first time in 2010, the accounting rules mandated a sudden drop of 4.6 percent in the average pension.[47] Political pressures generated by the prospects of such a precipitous decline led to a modification of the rules, which allowed for gradually phasing in benefit reductions over a three-year period. Thus, some adjustments have already been made in the original design. Still, as it currently operates, the new system restrains political meddling, directly rewards individual determination to work and save for retirement, recognizes the utility of means-tested benefits for assisting only those most in need, and supports investments in the private market. Although the 1998 reform has yet to stand the test of time, it is a thought-provoking alternative to the conventional progressive model of universal social insurance.

Conclusion

10

The Social Compass of Progressive Conservatism

The opening pages of this book described Tony Judt's concerns about the future of social democracy, which ended with an appeal for progressives to ponder the questions: What is a good society and what can the state do well? In this closing section, we come full circle to reflect on these questions. My analysis of the progressive tendency to inflate the magnitude and existential consequences of poverty, inequality, and waning social mobility in the United States is not meant to leave a Pollyannaish impression of having achieved the good society in which life is just fine for everybody—and there is little left for government to do.

Opinions differ, of course, about the makings of the good society and the role of the state in its construction. Within the parameters of progressive conservatism, government plays an active role as both a counterforce to the market distribution of resources and a guardian of traditional values. Although I characterize this approach as progressive conservatism, it is not difficult to imagine that partisans on either side of the aisle may find that label unsatisfactory.[1] As for the requisites of the good society, within the larger democratic context of individual freedom and prosperity, at a minimum it provides for the material well-being of its most disadvantaged members, cultivates the social and emotional development of children in family life, and imbues citizenship with a shared sense of communal rights and duties. Although over the centuries visionaries have drafted detailed plans of the good society, an elaborate utopian landscape is not in keeping with the social compass of progressive-conservative policies, which tend to be incremental, empirically grounded, and in most cases means tested. To demonstrate this approach to social policy, let us examine a few measures that suggest how progressive conservatism may advance the good society.

Certainly, it is hard to construct a version of the good society in which the state does not afford an adequate level of care and material comfort for its neediest citizens, who are without other support. The issue that arises in prosperous societies involves distinguishing the relatively few who suffer the material deprivations of poverty. As noted earlier, in the United States, a large proportion of the people officially defined as poor own homes, cars, air conditioners, computers, and many other essentials, the sum of which is not tantamount to material deprivation. And many are poor only for a brief period of time. The chronic poor, a group highly impacted by multiple disorders—mental illness, addiction, abuse, cognitive disabilities, and physical infirmities—represent a relatively small fraction of those identified by the official standard. The serious needs of the chronic poor are of a different order from the material wants of the increasing number of households with incomes well above the official poverty line, which are receiving the major share of social welfare transfers.

These transfers are going to households with incomes far above the federal poverty line, in part, because the eligibility level for many income-tested social welfare benefits has been rising to the point that it extends into the middle class. Thus, for example, among the ten largest programs for low-income people, Medicaid eligibility goes up to an income as high as $92,152 and the Earned Income Tax Credit reaches households with incomes up to $53,267.[2] And there are other programs under which recipients may earn from 200 to 400 percent of the official poverty guideline.[3] The door of income-tested eligibility for social benefits has inadvertently opened even further due to the dramatic growth in cohabitation, which climbed from 6 to 12 percent of all US couples between 1995 and 2014.[4] Several income-tested programs, such as the Earned Income Tax Credit and the Additional Child Care Tax Credit, do not include the income of cohabiters in determining the applicant's eligibility; other programs such as Medicaid, Section 8 Housing Vouchers, and public assistance (in most states) do not count the income of nonparent cohabiters.[5] This allows an unemployed mother to qualify for various income-tested benefits while sharing resources in a cohabiting relationship with a partner whose income would make their household otherwise ineligible for benefits if they were joined in wedlock.

Lifting the bar on eligibility for income-tested public benefits reduces the share of social welfare transfers received by those at the very bottom of the income distribution. And their slice of the transfers is further reduced when universal benefits, such as Social Security, are included. In fact, over the period from 1979 to 2007 the overall share of public benefits received by households in the lowest-income quintile declined from 54 to 36 percent of all transfer payments, while the share accruing to those in the top two income quintiles rose from 17 to 25 percent.[6] Although those in the lower income brackets receive the largest proportion of the benefits, their share is diminishing and these payments represent only direct social transfers. This calculation of benefits excludes indirect social transfers, such as home mortgage interest deductions and the Child Care Tax Credit, that are delivered through tax expenditures, which heavily favor families in the higher income brackets.[7]

However it is figured, the regressive trend raises some misgivings about the role of government as an effective counterforce to the market by offering communal security in the midst of an economic order that rewards individual drive and competition. Although an increasing portion of the transfers flow to those already in the lap of material comfort, the chronic poor remain roughing it on the city streets from New York to San Francisco, a visible reminder that the good society has yet to arrive.

Proposals to broaden eligibility and expand universal social welfare programs draw our attention to the issue of how much more government should be spending and away from the question of how well what is already being spent alleviates the privations of those most in need. Despite appeals for universal benefits, efforts to advance the good society are better served by increasing the use of the means test on public benefits currently consumed by households in the upper income brackets. To this end, a comprehensive approach would simplify social transfers by collapsing most of the eighty programs offering income-tested benefits into a single payment with a uniform level of eligibility that narrows the band of income to which it applies and avoids creating disincentives to work.[8] The United Kingdom has started moving in this direction with a fundamental overhaul of its welfare system, which replaced six separate means-tested benefits with a single payment known as the Universal Credit.[9] Concentrating public expenditures on where they will achieve the greatest good in delivering social care and material comfort would allow the poorest beneficiaries to get more than they currently receive. In the midst of material abundance, the good society can well afford to provide honorable dependence to those people who for various reasons are incapable of participating in the market economy.

The good society, however, is more than just a place that protects its members from the ruin of poverty and disease. It is a social landscape that cultivates family life as the seedbed of human development. The bonds of family life form children's first sense of human connection and shape their habits, dispositions, and moral values. These bonds between parents and children are nurtured in the home, not in the commercial market or the public day care center. And they are unraveling to an unprecedented degree in many OECD countries, where the fertility rates have fallen so low as to threaten demographic suicide.[10]

In the United States between 1980 and 2012, the proportion of women in their forties who had never married tripled from 4.8 percent to 13.8 percent; as the rates of marriage have declined, the divorce rate has leveled off at somewhere between 40 to 50 percent, and about 40 percent of children are born outside of marriage.[11] Although the amount of cohabitation has increased, these arrangements usually create a delicate bond that is more readily dissolved than marriage and harder to document. There are some who welcome this erosion of traditional family life as another creative disruption of postmodern society—one that breaches the oppressive confines of bour-geois domesticity. But most public voices from the Right and the Left decry the fragmentation and instability of family for its devastating effects on children and the community at large. Few express it better than Daniel Moynihan, when he wrote: "From the wild Irish slums of the nineteenth-century Eastern seaboard, to the riot-torn suburbs of Los Angeles, there is one unmistak-able lesson in American history: a community that allows a large number of young men to grow up in broken families, dominated by women, never acquiring any stable relationship to male authority, never acquiring any set of rational expectations about the future—that community asks for and gets chaos. Crime, violence, unrest, disorder . . . that is not only to be expected; it is very near to inevitable. And it is richly deserved."[12] Of course, there are many one-parent families that do a heroic job of raising healthy, secure, and successful children. However, as Mitch Pearlstein puts it, "two parent fami-lies offer no guarantees when it comes to kids doing well—just much better odds."[13]

Over the next generation, the instability of family life may be self-correcting to some degree as marriage and procreation are increasingly being postponed until the late twenties. Starting families later in life allows young adults more time to mature and gain clarity on what they are looking for in a partner. Yet it seems as likely that the instability of family life may become ever more normalized through serial monogamy, cohabitation, and the hookup culture, with children increasingly being raised by single parents, step parents, and cohabiting partners.[14] Examining the evolution of human relationships, Stephanie Coontz concludes that "we can never reinstate mar-riage as the primary source of commitment and caregiving in the modern world."[15]

In any case, practically speaking, there are limits to what government in a democratic society can do to affect individual decisions that would stabilize and reinforce the family unit. Human affairs are hard to change. Conventional remedies of more and better paying jobs and universal child care, so-called family-friendly policies, do little to strengthen the commitments of family life, let alone insure sympathetic and skillful caregiving for children.[16] If there are no nostrums, however, there are some preventive measures that can make a profound difference in the lives of young children, particularly those from severely disadvantaged families. Based upon experimental studies, a sizeable body of evidence accumulated over three decades confirms the positive ef-fects of home visiting by trained nurses on children of low-income mothers. The findings demonstrate that these efforts to enhance the quality of mater-nal functioning have long-term beneficial impacts on academic achievement, law-abiding behavior, and mental health of the children in families served.[17]

A national program that delivered in-home nursing services to all fami-lies with newborn children residing in the 20 percent of census tracts with the lowest incomes in every state would bolster the competence of maternal care and sustain family life as the sanctuary of human development in the poorest communities. Unlike public child care that substitutes the state for the family, home-visiting services reinforce the bonds between parents and children by shoring up the family's role in the social, emotional, and moral development of their newborn members. But even the best home-visiting services are no panacea for the fraction of dysfunctional households that are unable to satisfy the developmental needs of their children. Given a viable alternative, these children are better off away from home for most of their waking hours. In these instances, the home-visiting services would perform a screening function that helped to identify the extreme cases which require enriched services for preschool children, such as intensive full-day, out-of-home care by highly qualified professionals.

Welfare state transfers aimed at alleviating the material hardships of the chronic poor and home-nursing services targeted to low-income census tracts throughout the country exemplify progressive conservatism's means-tested approach to redistributive policies. These measures seek to compensate for the deprivation suffered by those most in need. But the good society would be incomplete, even with enriched socialization in family life and the redistribution of material benefits allowing the chronic poor to achieve a decent standard of living. Beyond material comfort and familial well-being, there is a social dimension of the good society, which speaks to a human desire for belonging—the quest for community. The good society kindles a sense of social solidarity that unites life in the public sphere. Regarding the government's role in this endeavor, progressive advocates of universalism argue that making everyone a recipient of welfare benefits creates a sort of social glue. Beneficiaries are not divided into groups of givers and receivers—the rich and poor are, so to speak, all eating at the same table of the welfare state. However any social transfer of resources ultimately involves those that give more than they receive. Although most people recognize this, means testing just makes that transfer more transparent.[18] And, of course, these recipients are not all seated around face to face at the state table; they are at home getting pension and family support checks in the mail or sending their children to a nearby day care center. Only in the most abstract sense can one begin to imagine that universal benefits create an integrative bond or shared experience that conveys a sense of belonging to a common enterprise, which connects individuals from different groups in society.

Deliberations about the way universalism may advance social cohesion typically revolve around how much the welfare state should give to whom. Instead, progressive conservativism is inclined to resist universal handouts by government and endorse the social bonds formed in fulfilling the universal obligations of citizenship. This represents a sense of belonging created among members of the community through their mutual contributions to the commonweal. It is the call to unity through service powerfully conveyed in President Kennedy's memorable challenge to his fellow Americans "ask not what your country can do for you—ask what you can do for your country." Shortly after Kennedy's 1961 inauguration, the Peace Corps was formed, followed in 1965 by the Volunteers in Service to America program that was later incorporated into AmeriCorps, under the Clinton administration.[19] The idea of national service appeals to many people on the Right and the Left of the political spectrum. Both of the 2008 presidential candidates, John McCain and Barack Obama, favored the expansion of national service programs. Hoping to connect volunteers to communities which were in need of assistance, Obama called on young Americans "to step into the currents of history."[20] McCain proposed expansion of the existing programs so that every young person who wanted to serve would have a chance to do so. He saw national service as an opportunity for young people to invest their time and energy in a meaningful public cause.[21]

Although the current voluntary programs remain geared primarily to middle-class college graduates, if we try hard enough, they could be seen as the precursor for a mandatory national service that would enroll all young adults between 18 and 21 years of age. Providing a common experience of public service for youth from all classes, such a universal program would lend credence to the value of engaged citizenship. It would also serve as a crucible for democratic intermingling of young adults whose paths in life otherwise might never cross, enlisting them shoulder to shoulder in a public cause that transcends the pervasive self-interest of market capitalism. Contributing their energies to civic duties such as disaster relief, environmental protection, infrastructure renewal, community development, patrolling national parks, tutoring disadvantaged children, and assisting the elderly, national service could become a unifying modern rite of passage for young people on the road to adulthood. Practically speaking, a year or two in national service would ease the unemployment rate among young adults, provide medical assistance and remedial services for those in need of health care, and leave plenty of time to complete courtship, marriage, and procreation by what is now the average age for such milestones. If such a scheme ever made it to the legislative drawing board, however, policymakers would need to bear in mind that, as Robert Nisbet warned, the rise of totalitarianism can be set in motion when one's sense of belonging is vested more in the state than in local associations and primary groups.[22] This observation suggests that the design of a national service program would benefit from a public–private partnership between governmental and civic organizations which sought to create an espirit de corps among national service participants linked to diverse spheres of activity.

In the modern era of abundance it is not too much to imagine crafting policies that consolidate social spending, afford a decent standard of living for the chronic poor, promote effective parental functioning and quality care for children from disadvantaged families, and reinforce a sense of public purpose and unity through national service. Although a utopian society that eradicates the material excesses of capitalism and mollifies the intellectual zeal of institutionalized discontent is beyond the compass of progressive conservatism, the rudiments of the good society are well within its reach.

NOTES

Chapter 1

1. Tony Judt, "What Is Living and What Is Dead in Social Democracy?" *New York Review of Books* (December 17, 2009), pp. 86–96.

2. Tony Judt died on August 6, 2010, four months after the meeting.

3. Judt, op. cit., p. 92.

4. Daniel Bell, *The End of Ideology* (New York: Free Press, 1960), p. 402.

5. Ibid., p. 405.

6. Gunnar Myrdal, *Beyond the Welfare State* (New Haven, CT: Yale University Press, 1960), p. 73.

7. These figures on public social expenditures are drawn from data reported by the OECD in *Social Expenditures 1960–1990: Problems of Growth and Control* (Paris: OECD, 1985); W. Adema, P. Fron, and M. Ladaique (2011), "Is the European Welfare State Really More Expensive? Indicators on Social Spending, 1980–2012"; and "A Manual to the OECD Social Expenditure Database (SOCX)," OECD Social, Employment and Migration Working Papers, No. 124, OECD Publishing. http://dx.doi.org/10.1787/5kg2d2d4pbf0-en. The 19 countries include Canada, France, Germany, Japan, Italy, the United States, the United Kingdom, Australia, Austria, Belgium, Denmark, Finland, Greece, Ireland, Netherlands, New Zealand, Norway, Sweden, and Switzerland.

8. For a detailed analysis of these developments, see Neil Gilbert, *Transformation of the Welfare State: The Silent Surrender of Public Responsibility* (New York: Oxford University Press, 2004) and Neil Gilbert and Rebecca Van Voorhis, eds., *Changing Patterns of Social Protection* (New Brunswick, NJ: Transaction Publications, 2003).

9. Tony Eardley, "New Relations of Welfare in the Contracting State: The Marketisation of Services for the Unemployed in Australia," Social Policy Research Center Discussion Paper 79. SPRC, University of New South Wales (1997); Adalbert Evers and Ivan Svetlik, eds., *Balancing Pluralism: New Welfare Mixes for the Elderly* (Aldershot, England: Avebury, 1993); Brinton Milward and Keith Provan, "The Hollow State: Private Provision of Public Service," in Helen Ingram and Steven Rathgeb Smith, *Public Policy for Democracy* (Washington, D.C.: The Brookings Institution, 1993), pp. 222–237; Richard Weatherley, "From Entitlement to Contract: Reshaping the Welfare State in Australia," *Journal of Sociology and Social Welfare* 3, no. 3 (1994): 153–173. The distinction between the Keynesian Welfare State and the Schumpeterian Workfare State contrasts John Maynard Keynes's ideas about the merits of state intervention in the market with Joseph Schumpeter's views on the fiscal limits of taxation beyond which the state would sabotage innovative activity and entrepreneurial drive. B. Jessop, "From Keynesian Welfare to the Schumpeterian Workfare State," in R. Burrows and B. Loader (eds.), *Towards a Post-Fordist Welfare State?* (London: Routledge, 1994); Jacob Torfing, "From the Keynesian Welfare State to a Schumpeterian Workfare Regime—the Offensive Neo-Statist Case of

Denmark," Paper presented at the 9th International Conference on Socio-Economics, Montreal, Canada, July 5–7, 1997.

10. Adalbert Evers and Anne-Marie Guillemard (eds.), *Social Policy and Citizenship: The Changing Landscape* (New York: Oxford University Press, 2012); Neil Gilbert, op. cit.; Neil Gilbert and Barbara Gilbert, *The Enabling State: Modern Welfare Capitalism in America* (New York: Oxford University Press, 1989).

11. As it turns out, this stereotype was based on a real welfare recipient. See Josh Levin, "The Welfare Queen," *Slate*, December 19, 2013. http://www.slate.com/articles/news_and_politics/history/2013/12/linda_taylor_welfare_queen_ronald_reagan_made_her_a_notorious_american_villain.html, accessed on January 12, 2015.

12. Suzanne Daley, "Danes Rethink a Welfare State Ample to a Fault," *The New York Times*, August 20, 2013.

13. OECD, *Economic Survey: Netherlands* (Paris: OECD, 1991).

14. Richard Stevenson, "Swedes Facing Rigors of Welfare Cuts," *New York Times* (March 14, 1993).

15. Bo Rothstein, "Dead and Alive in Social Democracy," Talk given at the conference "What Is Living and What Is Dead in Social Democracy," organized by Tony Judt at New York University on April 9–10, 2010. This was the introductory talk for the last day of discussions, which addressed the theme of "What is to be done?"

16. Pew Research Center for the People & the Press, "A Clear Rejection of the Status Quo, No Consensus about Future Policies: GOP Wins Big Despite Party's Low Favorability," November 3, 2010, http://pweresearch.org/pubs/1789/2010-mid-term-elections-exit-poll-analysis. This was in sharp contrast to public attitudes in the midst of the Great Depression when opinion surveys showed the vast majority of Americans supported increased public spending. Jodie T. Allen, Pew Research Center, *How a Different America Responded to the Great Depression*, December 14, 2010.

17. Adema, Fron and Ladiaque, op. cit., p.41.

18. Differentiating liberals from conservatives, Barry Goldwater observes that while conservatives see man as an economic and spiritual creature, liberals, "in the name of a concern for 'human beings'—regard the satisfaction of economic wants as the dominant mission of society." Barry Goldwater, *The Conscience of a Conservative* (Washington, D.C.: Regnery Publishing, 1990), p. 18. http://thf_media.s3.amazonaws.com/2011/pdf/PresEssay2004.pdf, accessed on January 20, 2015.

19. Joseph Schumpeter, *Capitalism, Socialism and Democracy*, 3rd ed. (New York: Harper and Row [1942], 1950), p. 83.

20. Lionel Robbins, "The Economic Functions of the State in English Classical Political Economy," in Edmund Phelps, ed., *Private Wants and Public Needs* (New York: W.W. Norton, 1962), pp. 96–101. Robbins notes that Adam Smith's agenda embraced education and public health functions of government.

21. Jeremy Bentham, *The Works of Jeremy Bentham,* published under the Superintendence of his Executor, John Bowring (Edinburgh: William Tait, 1838–1843). 11 vols. Vol. 9, Chapter IX: Ministers Collectively. http://oll.libertyfund.org/title/1999/132010, accessed on June 19, 2012.

22. Friedrich Hayek, *The Road to Serfdom* (Chicago: University of Chicago Press, 1944), p. 120. Hayek shared his Nobel Prize with Gunnar Myrdal, op. cit., whose competing

views about the relationship between the market and the state fostered the twentieth-century development of the Swedish social democratic welfare state.

23. Anthony Atkinson, "Top Incomes in the United Kingdom over the Twentieth Century," University of Oxford Discussion Paper in Economic History and Social Security, No. 43 (January 2002).

24. Milton Friedman, *Capitalism and Freedom* (Chicago: University of Chicago Press, 1962).

25. Torben M. Andersen and Joydeep Bhattacharya, "On Myopia as Rationale for Social Security," *Economic Theory* 47, no. 1 (2011): 135–158.

26. Milton Friedman, op. cit.

27. Social Security Administration, *Annual Statistical Supplement, 2005,* table 9.G1. http://www.ssa.gov/policy/docs/statcomps/supplement/2005/9g.html, accessed on June 16, 2012.

28. Charles Murray, *In Our Hands: A Plan to Replace the Welfare State* (Washington D.C.: AEI Press, 2006). Murray's guaranteed income is slightly above the 2006 official poverty line for a single person and would be about $7,000 above the poverty threshold for two adults; Friedman's proposal was $400 below the 1962 poverty threshold.

29. Daniel P. Moynihan, *The Politics of a Guaranteed Income: The Nixon Administration and the Family Assistance Plan* (New York: Random House, 1973).

30. Robert Theobald, *Free Men and Free Markets* (New York: C.N. Potter, 1963); Bruce Ackerman and Anne Alstott, *The Stakeholder Society* (New Haven, CT: Yale University Press, 1999); Philippe Van Parijs, *Real Freedom for All* (New York: Oxford University Press, 1995). Since 1986 the Basic Income Earth Network has been advocating for the adoption of a guaranteed income on many fronts. For details, see bien@basicincome.org.

31. Albert Hirschman, *The Passions and the Interests* (Princeton, NJ: Princeton University Press, 1977).

32. According to Freud, the sublimation of instincts through the practice of intellectual activity yielded finer satisfactions than those derived from indulging one's primary instinctual impulses. However, he deemed the pleasure of sublimated activity relatively mild compared to instinctual gratifications. One might conclude that the sublimated pleasures of success on the market were not quite as intense as putting one's enemies to rest on the battlefield. Sigmund Freud, *Civilization and Its Discontents*, James Strachey, trans. and ed. (New York: Norton, 1961), pp. 26–27.

33. Max Weber, *The Protestant Ethic and the Spirit of Capitalism*, Talcott Parsons trans. (New York: Scribner, 1958).

34. Daniel Bell, op. cit., p. 21.

35. Judt, op. cit., pp. 94–96.

36. Gordon M. Fisher, *From Hunter to Orshansky: An Overview of (Unofficial) Poverty Lines in the United States from 1904 to 1965* (Washington, D.C.: US Census Bureau). http://www.census.gov/hhes/povmeas/publications/povthres/fisher4.html#N_21_, accessed on September 1, 2012.

Chapter 2

1. Howard Glennerster, John Hills, David Piachaud, and Jo Webb, *One Hundred Years of Poverty and Policy* (York: Joseph Rowntree Foundation, 2004), p. 19; Booth

distinguished eight classes, among whom the bottom four suffered deprivation. He found that 30.7 percent of the London families were in poverty. T. Simey and M. B. Simey, *Charles Booth, Social Scientist* (London: Oxford University Press, 1960).

2. Robert Hunter, *Poverty: Social Conscience in the Progressive Era*, ed. Peter d'A Jones (New York: Harper Torch Books, 1965; originally published by Macmillan, 1904).

3. Jacob Riis, *The Battle with the Slum* (London: Macmillan, 1902).

4. Michael Harrington, *The Other America: Poverty in the United States* (New York: Macmillan, 1962), p. 45.

5. Frank Riessman and Arlene Hannah, "The Poverty Movement," *Columbia University Forum* (Fall 1963), p. 29. Numerous publications followed over the next few years, including six major anthologies: two entitled "Poverty in America," two examined "Poverty in (Amid) Affluence," one presented "Poverty as a Public Issue," and another offered "New Perspectives on Poverty." Neil Gilbert, *Capitalism and the Welfare State* (New Haven, CT: Yale University Press, 1983), p. 58.

6. John Kenneth Galbraith, *The Affluent Society* (New York: Mentor Books, 1963), p. 250.

7. Alvin Hansen, "Standards and Values in a Rich Society," in Edmund Phelps, ed., *Private Wants and Public Needs* (New York: W.W. Norton, 1962), p. 1. Hansen's chapter in this work first appeared in his 1957 book, *The American Economy.*

8. Galbraith, op. cit., p. 252.

9. Although he mentions that a compassionate affluent society would provide those in need a guaranteed minimum income essential to live in dignity and comfort, this notion was dismissed as politically infeasible and problematic when applied to poverty among people suffering from alcoholism and mental illness. Ibid., p. 255.

10. H. G. Wells, *Anticipations of the Reaction of Mechanical and Scientific Progress: Upon Human Life and Thought* (Mineola, NY: Dover Publications, 1999), p. 45.

11. Vance Packard, *The Hidden Persuaders* (New York: McKay, 1957).

12. For an analysis of how advertising has been fine-tuned by modern technology, see Martin Lindstrom, *Brandwashed: Tricks Companies Use to Manipulate Our Minds and Persuade Us to Buy* (New York: Crown Business, 2011).

13. "A Genius Departs," *The Economist*, October 8, 2011, p. 82.

14. Friedrich Hayek, "The Non Sequitur of the 'Dependence Effect,'" in Edmund Phelps, ed., *Private Wants and Public Needs* (New York: W.W. Norton, 1965); Friedrich Hayek, *The Road to Serfdom* (Chicago: University of Chicago Press, 1944).

15. Neil Gilbert, *Transformation of the Welfare State: The Silent Surrender of Public Responsibility* (New York: Oxford University Press, 2004).

16. This conservative estimate is based on the official calculation of median income, which is adjusted according to the Consumer Price Index Research Series (CPI-U-RS). http://www.census.gov/hhes/www/income/data/historical/household/2010/H06AR_2010.xls The CPI-U-RS is a controversial measure often charged with understating the real increase in household income. An alternative calculation reveals a substantially greater rise in the median income. For details, see Bruce Meyer and James Sullivan, "American Mobility," *Commentary* 133, no. 3 (March 2012): 30–34. According to other data also adjusted by the CPI-U-RS, between 1958 and 2010 the average income per tax unit increased by 66 percent. See Emmanuel Saez, http://eml.berkeley.edu/~saez/#income

17. Employee Benefit Research Institute, "Finance of Employee Benefits, 1960–2003," *Facts from EBRI* (January 2005); Bureau of Labor Statistics, *Employer Costs for Employee*

Compensation Historical Listing March 2004—September 2012, ftp://ftp.bls.gov/pub/special.requests/ocwc/ect/ececqrtn.pdf, accessed on December 15, 2012. These figures exclude paid leave.

18. Neil Gilbert, "Accounting for Employee Benefits: Issues of Measurement, Valuations and Social Equivalencies," in Douglas Besharov and Kenneth Couch eds., *Counting the Poor: New Thinking About European Poverty Measures and Lessons for the United States* (New York: Oxford University Press, 2012).

19. Editorial, "The Recession's Awful Impact," *The New York Times*, September 16, 2010.

20. Sabrina Tavernise, "Soaring Poverty Casts Spotlight on 'Lost Decade,'" *The New York Times*, September 13, 2011.

21. Peter Edelman, *So Rich, So Poor: Why It's So Hard to End Poverty in America* (New York: The New Press, 2012), p. xiv.

22. Charles Blow, "Hard-Knock (Hardly Acknowledged) Life," *The New York Times*, January 28, 2011.

23. White House, January 20, 2015. *President Obama's State of the Union Address—Remarks as Prepared for Delivery*, https://medium.com/@WhiteHouse/president-obamas-state-of-the-union-address-remarks-as-prepared-for-delivery-55f9825449b2

24. Thomas Corbett, "The Rise and Fall of Poverty as a Policy Issue," *Focus* 30, no. 2 (Fall/Winter 2013/2014): 3–9.

25. Mollie Orshansky, "Children of the Poor," *Social Security Bulletin* 26, no. 7 (1963): 3–13; a little later she refined the measure to included poverty in all families, not just those with children; see Mollie Orshansky, "Counting the Poor: Another Look at the Poverty Threshold," *Social Security Bulletin* 28, no. 1 (1965): 3–29.

26. Rebecca Blank, "How to Improve Poverty Measurement in the United States," Presidential Address to the Association for Public Policy Analysis and Management at their annual conference November 8–12, 2007, Washington, D.C., p. 8.

27. Sheldon Danziger, "The Mismeasure of Poverty," *The New York Times*, September 17, 2013.

28. Christopher Jencks, "The War on Poverty: Was It Lost?" *The New York Review of Books*, April 2, 2015.

29. Constance Citro and Robert Michaels, *Measuring Poverty: A New Approach* (Washington, D.C.: National Academy Press, 1995).

30. Blank, op. cit., p. 21.

31. Citro and Michaels, op. cit., p. 385.

32. Kathleen Short, "The Research Supplemental Poverty Measure: 2010," *Current Population Reports*, US Census Bureau, November 2011.

33. The organization's name was changed to AARP in 1999, because it sought to broaden the base of membership to elderly, but not necessarily retired people. According to Ann Jenkins, president of the AARP Foundation, "These numbers only reinforce the conversations we at AARP Foundation have with struggling people age 50+ every day. Older Americans are struggling to make ends meet." Becky Squires, "Health Care Costs Pushed More Seniors Into Poverty in 2011," AARP Foundation (November 27, 2012), http://www.aarp.org/aarp-foundation/our-work/income/info-2012/poverty-in-america.html

34. Richard Fry, D'Vera Cohn, Gretchen Livingston, and Paul Taylor, *The Rising Age Gap in Economic Well-Being* (Washington, D.C.: Pew Research Center), November 7, 2011.

35. Rakesh Kochhar, Richard Fry, and Paul Taylor, *Wealth Gaps Rise to Record Highs Between Whites, Blacks and Hispanics Twenty-to-One*, Pew Research Center's Social & Demographic Trends, July 26, 2011, http://pewresearch.org/pubs/2069/housing-bubble-subprime-mortgages-hispanics-blacks-household-wealth-disparity

36. Douglas Besharov and Neil Gilbert, "Marriage Penalties in the Modern Social Welfare State," *R Street Policy Study* no. 40 (September 2015).

37. For a review of the supplemental measure, see Interagency Technical Working Group on Developing a Supplemental Poverty Measure, "Observations from the Interagency Technical Working Group on Developing a Supplemental Poverty Measure," March 2010, http://www.census.gov/hhes/www/povmeas/SPM-TWGObservationsw.pdf, accessed June 13, 2010; also see K. Short, "'Who Is Poor?' A New Look with the Supplemental Poverty Measure" (Washington, D.C.: US Census Bureau, 2011); T. Garner and K. Short, "Creating a Consistent Poverty Measure over Time Using NAS Procedures: 1996–2005. BLS Working Paper No. 417, US Bureau of Labor Statistics (Washington, D.C.: Government Printing Office, 2008); David Johnson, "Progress Toward Improving the U.S. Poverty Measure: Developing the New Supplemental Poverty Measure," *Focus* 27, no. 2 (Winter 2010): 1–3.

38. Steven Pressman and Robert Scott III, "Consumer Debt and Poverty Measurement," *Focus* 27, no. 1 (Summer 2010): 9–12.

39. Consumer Expenditure Survey, US Bureau of Labor Statistics, 2011, http://www.bls.gov/cex/2010/Standard/quintile.pdf, accessed March 1, 2012.

40. Nicholas Eberstadt, "The Mismeasure of Poverty," *Policy Review*, August 1, 2006.

41. Bruce Meyer and James Sullivan, "Identifying the Disadvantaged: Official Poverty, Consumption Poverty and the New Supplemental Poverty Measure," *Journal of Economic Perspectives* 26, no. 3 (Summer 2012): 111–136.

42. Karen Spar, *Federal Benefits and Services for People with Low Income: Programs Policy and Spending FY2008–FY2009* (February 15, 2011), Congressional Research Office Report R41625, January 31, 2011.

43. David Johnson, "Measuring Consumption and Consumption Poverty: Possibilities and Issues," paper prepared for "Reconsidering the Federal Poverty Measure" American Enterprise Institute, November 18, 2004; also see Eberstadt, op. cit.

44. Bruce D. Meyer, Wallace K. C. Mok, and James X. Sullivan, "The Under-Reporting of Transfers in Household Surveys: Its Nature and Consequences," NBER Working Paper No. 15181 (July 2009).

45. Meyer and Sullivan, op. cit.

46. In a study of welfare recipients in Illinois between 1988 and 1990, Edin and Jencks found that almost 80 percent of their sample worked (in both legal and illegal activities) without reporting their income. Kathryn Edin and Christopher Jencks, "Welfare" in Christopher Jencks, *Rethinking Social Policy* (Cambridge, MA: Harvard University Press, 1992), pp. 204–236. Other studies reveal significant employment rates, though not quite as high as in the Edin and Jencks research. For example, Maureen Marcenko and Jay Fagan, "Welfare to Work: What Are the Obstacles," *Journal of Sociology and Social Welfare* 70, no. 3 (1996): 113–131, report 27 percent; Dave O'Neill and June O' Neill, *Lessons for Welfare Reform: An Analysis of the AFDC Caseload and Past Welfare-to-Work Programs* (Kalamazoo, MI: W.E. Upjohn Institute for Employment Research, 1997) report 49.4 percent; and Kathleen Harris, "Work and Welfare Among Single Mothers in Poverty,"

American Journal of Sociology 99, no. 2 (1993): 317–353, reports 51 percent. Kathryn Edin and Laura Lein, "Work, Welfare, and Single Mothers' Economic Survival Strategies," *American Sociological Review* 62, no. 2 (1997): 253–266, provide further evidence of unreported work ranging from 32 to 52 percent of welfare mothers in four cities.

47. Charles Murray, *Losing Ground: American Social Policy, 1950–1980* (New York: Basic Books, 1984).

48. For discussion of concerns about the poverty trap in relation to various groups, see Jonathon Bradshaw and Jane Miller, "Lone-Parent Families in the U.K.: Challenges to Social Policy," *International Social Security Review* 43, no. 4 (1990): 446–459; Alain Euzeby, "Unemployment Compensation and Unemployment in Industrialized Market Economy Countries," *International Social Security Review* 41, no. 1 (1988): 3–24 ; and OECD, *The Future of Social Protection* (Paris: OECD, 1988).

49. OECD, *Shaping Structural Change: The Role of Women* (Paris: OECD, 1991).

50. Sudipto Banerjee, "Intra-family Cash Transfers in Older American Households," *Issue Brief No. 415* (Employee Benefit Research Institute, June 2015).

51. David Johnson, op. cit.

52. Meyer and Sullivan, op. cit.

53. US Energy Information Administration, "Residential Energy Consumption Survey (RECS) Data Tables 2009," Table HC9.2, http://www.eia.gov/consumption/residential/data/2009/index.cfm, accessed October 9, 2011; American Housing Survey National Tables: 2009 Using Census 2000-Based Weighting, http://www.census.gov/housing/ahs/data/ahs2009, accessed October 7, 2011.

54. Story from BBC NEWS: http://news.bbc.co.uk/go/pr/fr/-/2/hi/uk_news/magazine/8201900.stm, accessed October 8, 2011.

55. US Energy Information Administration, "Residential Energy Consumption Survey (RECS) Data Tables 2009," Table HC5.5, HC7.5, HC 3.5. http://www.eia.gov/consumption/residential/data/2009/index.cfm, accessed October 9, 2011; American Housing Survey National Tables: 2009 Using Census 2000-based Weighting; http://www.census.gov/housing/ahs/data/ahs2009. html, accessed October 7, 2011.

56. Robert Rector and Rachel Sheffield, "Air Conditioning, Cable TV, and an Xbox: What Is Poverty in the United States?" *Backgrounder* no. 2575, July 18, 2011, published by the Heritage Foundation.

57. Katrina vanden Heuvel, "Colbert Challenges the Poverty Deniers," http://www.thenation.com/blog162421/colbert-challenges-poverty-deniers?, accessed September 25, 2011.

58. Adam Smith [1776], *An Enquiry into the Nature and Causes of the Wealth of Nations*, Book 5, chapter 2, p. 148. http://www.econlib.org/library/Smith/smWN21.html#B.V, Ch. 2, "Of the Sources of the General or Public Revenue of the Society."

59. Pew Research Center, "Luxury or Necessity? Things We Can't Live Without: The List Has Grown in the Past Decade," 2006. http://pewresearch.org

60. These students were not residing with relatives. Alemayehu Bishaw, *Examining the Effect of Off-Campus College Students on Poverty Rates* (Washington, D.C.: US Census Bureau, Social Economic and Housing Statistics Division, May 1, 2013). http://www.census.gov/hhes/www/poverty/publications/bishaw/bishawSEHSD201317.pdf, accessed January 15, 2015.

61. Mark Rank, *One Nation Underprivileged: Why American Poverty Affects Us All* (New York: Oxford University Press, 2004). The figures were calculated based on annual incomes, which tend to overstate the actual time living in poverty. For example, a high school graduate who remains unemployed for six months and then starts a job at $18,000 salary will register an annual income of $9,000, which is below the poverty line, even though for half the year his earnings were well above the line.

62. Rank offers this interpretation. Ibid.

63. Mark Rank, Thomas Hirschl, and Kirk Foster, *Chasing the American Dream: Understanding What Shapes Our Fortunes* (New York: Oxford University Press, 2014), p. 97.

64. Ibid., p. 192.

65. Nicholas Eberstadt, op. cit.

66. R. J. Anderson, "Dynamics of Economic Well-Being: Poverty 2004–2006," *Current Population Reports* P70–123, March 2011.

67. Carmen DeNavas-Walt, Bernadette Proctor, and Jessica Smith, US Census Bureau Current Population Reports, P60–239, *Income, Poverty, and Health Insurance Coverage in the United States: 2010* (Washington, D.C.: US Government Printing Office, 2011).

68. Linda Levine, "The Increase in Unemployment Since 2007: Is It Cyclical or Structural?" *Congressional Research Service Report for Congress*, January 24, 2013.

69. According to a study conducted through the Columbia University Population Research Center, since 1973 about 5 percent of the population has lived in "deep poverty," defined as those with income less than 50 percent of the poverty line. Christopher Wimer, Liana Fox, Irv Garfinkel, Neeraj Kaushal, and Jane Waldfogel, "Trends in Poverty with an Anchored Supplemental Poverty Measure," CPRC Working Paper No. 13-02, https://courseworks.columbia.edu/access/content/group/c5a1ef92-c03c-4d88-0018ea43dd3cc5db/Articles/Fox_Waging%20War%20on%20Poverty_dec13.pdf, accessed January 23, 2015.

Chapter 3

1. Neil Gilbert, *Welfare Justice: Restoring Social Equity* (New Haven, CT: Yale University Press, 1995), pp. 96–98; Robert Rosenheck, Linda Frisman, and Wesley Kasprow, "Improving Access to Disability Benefits Among Homeless Persons With Mental Illness: An Agency-Specific Approach to Services Integration," *American Journal of Public Health* 89, no. 4 (April 1999): 525; Ezra Susser, Elmer L. Struening, and Sarah Conover, "Psychiatric Problems in Homeless Men Lifetime Psychosis, Substance Use, and Current Distress in New Arrivals at New York City Shelters," *Archives of General Psychiatry* 46, no. 9 (1989): 845–850. US Department of Housing and Urban Development Office of Community Planning and Development, *The 2008 Annual Homeless Assessment Report* (July 2009), identified about 40 percent of the homeless sampled as disabled. This study focused on homeless people in shelters and transition housing and the data on disability status were missing in 22 percent of the sample.

2. Nicholas Eberstadt, "The Mismeasure of Poverty," *Policy Review*, August 1, 2006; Carmen DeNavas-Walt, Bernadette Proctor, and Jessica Smith, US Census Bureau Current Population Reports, P60–239, *Income, Poverty, and Health Insurance Coverage in the United States: 2010* (Washington, D.C.: US Government Printing Office, 2011).;

Joan Rodgers and John L. Rodgers, "Chronic Poverty in the United States," *Journal of Human Resources* 28, no. 1 (1993): 25–54, estimated that chronic poverty accounted for one-third of those officially designated as poor in 1987; Patricia Ruggles, *Drawing the Line—Alternative Poverty Measures and Their Implications for Public Policy* (Washington, D.C.: The Urban Institute Press, 1990); Bruce Headey, Peter Krause, and Gert G. Wagner, "Poverty Redefined as Low Consumption and Low Wealth, Not Just Low Income: Psychological Consequences in Australia and Germany," in Douglas J. Besharov and Kenneth A. Couch, eds., *Counting the Poor: New Thinking about European Poverty Measures and Lessons for the United States* (New York: Oxford University Press, 2012), pp. 363–388.

3. In 2011, close to 7 million people received disability benefits under the means-tested SSI program, which averaged approximately $500 per month. An additional 7.5 million people received disability benefits under the SSDI program, which averaged $1,100 per month. All of the people in these groups may not experience chronic poverty. But with mean benefits of SSI well below the official poverty line and the mean benefits of SSDI just slightly over that line, there would be significant overlap between these disabled beneficiaries and the chronic poor. "Monthly Statistics," *Social Security Bulletin* 71, no. 4 (2011).

4. John Kenneth Galbraith, *The Affluent Society* (New York: Mentor Books, 1963), p. 254.

5. John K. Galbraith, *The Affluent Society*, 40th anniversary edition (New York: Houghton Mifflin, 1998), p. 238.

6. Ibid., p. 240.

7. Carmen DeNavas-Walt, Bernadette D. Proctor, and Cheryl Hill Lee, US Census Bureau, Current Population Reports, P60-231, *Income, Poverty, and Health Insurance Coverage in the United States: 2005* (Washington, D.C: US Government Printing Office, 2006).

8. *Economic Report of the President*, February 2012, Table B-29, p. 353. Data adjusted in constant dollars using Bureau of Labor Statistics CPI calculator.

9. Karen Spar, *Cash and Noncash Benefits for Persons with Limited Income: Eligibility Rules, Recipient and Expenditure Data*, FY 2002–2004, Congressional Research Service Report RL 33340 (March 27, 2006).

10. This one-year increase in spending was due largely to the economic stimulus from the American Recovery and Reinvestment Act enacted in February 2009. Karen Spar, *Federal Benefits and Services for People with Low Income: Programs Policy and Spending FY2008–FY2009* (February 15, 2011), Congressional Research Office Report R41625, January 31, 2011.

11. Robert Moffitt, "The Great Recession and the Social Safety Net," *The Annals of the American Academy of Political and Social Science* 650 (November 2013): 143–166. He notes that this was mainly due to the Earned Income Tax Credit program, which benefitted low-income workers.

12. The US Department of Housing and Urban Development Office of Community Planning and Development, *The 2011 Point-in-Time Estimates of Homelessness: Supplement to the Annual Homeless Assessment Report* (December 2011).

13. SNAP Monthly Data, http://www.fins.usda.gov/pd/34SNAPmonthly.htm, accessed December 1, 2011.

14. Rather than speak of "hunger," the US Department of Agriculture employs the concept of "food insecurity." According to the USDA, 5.76 percent of US households were classified as having "very low food security" in 2013; this was a condition under which "eating patterns of one or more household members were disrupted and their food intake reduced, at least some time during the year, because they could not afford enough food." http://www.ers.usda.gov/topics/food-nutrition-assistance/food-security-in-the-us/key-statistics-graphics.aspx#verylow

15. Researchers from the US Department of Agriculture found that when measured on the basis of edible weight or average proportion size, grains, vegetables, fruits, and dairy foods are less expensive than food high in saturated fats and added sugar. See Andrea Carlson and Elizabeth Frazao, *Are Healthy Foods Really More Expensive? It Depends on How You Measure the Price.* EIB-96, US Department of Agriculture, Economic Research Service, May 2012. A RAND Corporation study reports that there is no relationship between the diet and the availability of supermarkets, fast food, and other grocery stores near schools and residential neighborhoods. Ann Ruppeng and Roland Sturm, "School and Residential Neighborhood Food Environment and Diet Among California Youth," *American Journal of Preventive Medicine* 42, no. 2 (February 2012): 129–135.

16. Drew Desilver, "Obesity and Poverty Don't Always Go Together," *Pew Research Center* (November 13, 2013); Roland Strum, "Obesity and Poverty in America: Time and Demographic Trends," http://depts.washington.edu/uwcphn/news/summits/poverty_obesity/sturm_pov.pdf

17. Center for Disease Control and Prevention. http://www.cdc.gov/obesity/data/trends.html

18. Dana Gunders, "Wasted: How America Is Losing Up to 40 Percent of Its Food from Farm to Fork to Landfill," Natural Resources Defense Council Issue paper, August 2012 IP:12-06-B.

19. "The Big Picture," *The Economist*, December 7, 2012.

20. Laurence Chandy and Geoffrey Gertz, *Poverty in Numbers: The Changing State of Global Poverty from 2005 to 2015* (Washington, D.C.: Brookings Institution 2011).

21. This was made possible largely by the explosive productivity in capitalist societies in modern times. Brad DeLong estimates that between 5000 B.C. and 1800 A.D. the GDP worldwide barely rose from $130 to $250 per capita (in constant 2000 US dollars). Two hundred years later, in comparison, the worldwide GDP per capita averaged $8,175. Brad DeLong, *Macroeconomics* (New York: McGraw Hill, 2002).

22. Romina Boarini and Marco Mira d'Ercole, "Measures of Material Deprivation in OECD Countries," OECD Social, Employment and Migration Working Papers, No. 37 (August 2006). http://dx.doi.org/10.1787/866767270205

23. Neil Gilbert, "Realities and Mythologies of Rape " *Society* (May/June 1992); Neil Gilbert, "The Phantom Epidemic of Sexual Assault," *The Public Interest.* (Spring 1991), 54–65; Neil Gilbert, "Advocacy Research and Social Policy," in Michael Tonry (ed.) *Crime and Justice: A Review of Research* (Chicago: University of Chicago Press, 1997). Among other issues, 73 percent of the students categorized as rape victims according to the advocacy researcher's awkward and vaguely worded definition, did not think they had been raped; 42 percent of these women had sex again with the man who supposedly raped them.

24. FBI, *Crime in the United States, 2014.* https://www.fbi.gov/about-us/cjis/ucr/crime-in-the-u.s/2014/crime-in-the-u.s.-2014/tables/table-1

25. Sofi Sinozich and Lynn Langton, *Rape and Sexual Assault Victimization Among College-Age Females, 1995–2013* (Washington, D.C.: US Department of Justice, Bureau of Justice Statistics, December 2014).

26. David Cantor, Bonnie Fisher, Susan Chibnall, Reanne Townsend, Hyunshik Lee, Carol Bruce, and Gail Thomas, *Report on the AAU Campus Climate Survey on Sexual Assault and Sexual Misconduct* Prepared by Westat for The Association of American Universities (Sept.21, 2015). https://www.aau.edu/uploadedFiles/AAU_Publications/AAU_ Reports/Sexual_Assault_Campus_Survey/AAU_Campus_Climate_Survey_12_14_ 15.pdf, accessed March 7, 2016. This study involved a web-based survey with a response rate of only 19.3 percent. The vast majority of respondents indicated that they never reported the incident of "sexual assault" because they 'did not think it was serious enough." Curiously when asked: "How likely do you think it is that you will experience sexual assault or sexual misconduct on campus?" only 8 percent of the women thought that it was "very" or "extremely" likely – even though according to the survey 25 percent already had been victims. Despite these incongruities and the unrepresentative sample, the media rushed to headline the sensational findings. See, for example, Richard Perez-Pena, "1 in 4 Women Experience Sex Assault on Campus," The *New York Times* September 22, 2015, p.A17. Similar coverage was given by the *Washington Post, The Huffington Post* and *Slate*, to name only a few.

27. Although poor and minority women are much more likely to be victims of rape than middle-class college students, their communities receive less attention and support from rape counseling centers and prevention programs. This is highlighted in the award-winning series by Nara Schoenberg and Sam Roe, "Rape: The Making of an Epidemic," *The Toledo Blade*, October 10–12, 1993.

28. Rebecca Blank, *It Takes a Nation* (New York: Russell Sage Foundation, 1997).

29. Douglas Besharov, "Testimony Before the U.S. House of Representatives Committee on Agriculture," February 25, 2015.

30. Irving Kristol, "Taxes, Poverty and Equality," *The Public Interest* 37 (Fall 1974), p. 28.

31. Joel Best, "Promoting Bad Statistics," *Society* 38, no. 3 (March/April 2001): 10–15.

32. Neil Gilbert. "Advocacy Research and Social Policy," op.cit.

33. Richard Horton and Selina Lo, "Nutrition: A Quintessential Sustainable Development Goal," *The Lancet* (June 6, 2013). http://dx.doi.org/10.1016/S0140-6736(13)61100-9. In the United States, .09 percent of households with children reported a child experiencing hunger at least once during the year. Besharov, op. cit.

34. Neil Gilbert, "European Measures of Poverty and Social Exclusion: Material Deprivation, Consumption and Satisfaction," *Journal of Policy Analysis and Management* 28, no. 4 (2009): 738–744.

35. Bruce Headey, Peter Krause, and Gert G. Wagner, op. cit.

36. EU Council of Ministers (2008). "Joint Report on Social Protection and Social Inclusion 2009" (together with supporting document and country profiles), Office for Official Publications of the European Communities, Luxembourg. http://ec.europa.eu/ employment_social/spsi/joint_reports_en.htm#2009.

37. Eric Marlier, Bea Cantillon, Brian Nolan, Karel Van den Bosch, and Tim Van Rie, "Developing and Learning from EU Measures of Social Inclusion" in Douglas J. Besharov and Kenneth A. Couch, eds., op. cit., pp. 297–342.

38. International Institute for Labour Studies, *Social Exclusion and Anti-Poverty Strategies* (Geneva: International Labour Organization, 1996).

39. Eric Marlier, Bea Cantillon, Brian Nolan, Karel Van den Bosch, and Tim Van Rie, op. cit.; Orsolya Lelkes and Katrin Gasior, "Income Poverty and Social Exclusion in the EU: Situation in 2008 and Trends," *Policy Brief: January 2012* (Vienna: European Centre for Social Welfare Policy and Research, 2012).

40. The specific measures for the indicators of housing and child well-being are in the process of being developed. Eric Marlier, Bea Cantillon, Brian Nolan, Karel Van den Bosch, and Tim Van Rie, op. cit.

41. Neil Gilbert, "European Measures of Poverty and Social Exclusion: Material Deprivation, Consumption and Satisfaction," op. cit.

42. Ibid.

43. Brian Nolan and Christopher Whelan, "Using Non-Monetary Deprivation Indicators to Analyze Poverty and Social Exclusion: Lessons from Europe?" *Journal of Policy Analysis and Management* 29, no. 2 (Spring 2010): 305–325.

44. "Income Inequality: Who Exactly Are the 1%?" *The Economist*, January 21, 2012, p. 31.

45. For example, see Richard Layard, *Happiness: Lessons from a New Science* (New York: Penguin Books, 2005); Derek Bok, *The Politics of Happiness* (Princeton, NJ: Princeton University Press, 2010); Richard Easterlin, "Does Economic Growth Improve the Human Lot? Some Empirical Evidence." Paul A. David and Melvin W. Reder, eds., *Nations and Households in Economic Growth: Essays in Honor of Moses Abramovitz* (New York: Academic Press, Inc. 1974); Easterlin, R. A., McVey, L. A., Switek, M., Sawangfa, O., Zweig, J. S. "The Happiness-Income Paradox Revisited," *Proceedings of the National Academy of Sciences* 107, no. 52 (2010): 22463–22468; Amitai Etzioni, "Politics and Culture in an Age of Austerity," *International Journal of Politics, Culture, and Society* (March 2014) http://ssrn.com/abstract=2405098, accessed January 5, 2015; John F. Helliwell, Richard Layard, and Jeffrey Sachs (eds.), *World Happiness Report 2015* (New York: Earth Institute, 2015).

46. Daniel Kahneman and Jason Riis, "Living and Thinking about It: Two Perspectives on Life," in F. Huppert, N. Baylis, and B. Keverne (eds.), *The Science of Well-Being* (Oxford: Oxford University Press, 2005).

47. Daniel Kahneman and Angus Deaton, "High Income Improves Evaluation of Life but Not Emotional Well Being," *Proceedings of the National Academy of Sciences* (August 4, 2010), http://www.pnas.org/content/107/38/16489.full, accessed on October 3, 2015.

48. Tyler Cowen, "The Inequality That Matters," *The American Interest* (January/ February 2011).

49. Frank Newport, "Americans Prioritize Economy over Reducing Wealth Gap," Gallop Report, December 16, 2011. http://www.gallup.com/poll/151568/Americans-Prioritize-Growing-Economy-Reducing-Wealth-Gap.aspx, accessed January 23, 2012.

50. Jodie Allen. "How a Different America Responded to the Great Depression," PewResearch Center Publications (December 14, 2010). http://www.pewresearch.org/2010/12/14/how-a-different-america-responded-to-the-great-depression/

51. Vivekinan Ashok, Ilyana Kuziemko, and Ebonya Washington, "Support for Redistribution in an Age of Rising Inequality: New Stylized Facts and Some Tentative

Explanations," Brookings Papers on Economic Activity Conference Draft, March 19–20, 2015. http://www.brookings.edu/~/media/projects/bpea/spring-2015/2015a_ashok. pdf. The researchers examined responses to three different questions, which tapped support for redistribution. Although there was no increase in the demand for redistribution, there were substantial differences among demographic groups. Interestingly, the elderly and African Americans were among those who showed the most movement against income redistribution.

52. Alexis de Tocqueville, *Democracy in America* [1835] (New York: Washington Square Press edition, 1965), p. 29.

53. John Rawls, *A Theory of Justice* (Cambridge, MA: Harvard University Press, 1971), pp. 60–79. Although an increase in inequality that is to everyone's advantage would be acceptable, he notes that when the differences between rich and poor are excessive, the distribution falls short of the best arrangement—though no precise measure of "excessive" is offered.

54. Sam Tanenhaus, "Will the Tea Get Cold?" *New York Review of Books*, March 8, 2012, p. 7.

55. OECD (2011), *Society at a Glance 2011—OECD Social Indicators* (www.oecd.org/els/social/indicators/SAG); Eurostat data: http://appsso.eurostat.ec.europa.eu/nui/submitModifiedQuery.do, accessed January 23, 2012.

56. Galbraith, *The Affluent Society* (1963), p. 72.

57. A brief recession in 1957 was followed by the decade from 1959 to 1969 during which the unemployment rate averaged 4.8 percent. Table B–42, Civilian unemployment rate, 1959–2005. http://www.gpoaccess.gov/eop/2006/B42.xls

58. The White House, Office of the Press Secretary, "Remarks by the President on Economic Growth and Deficit Reduction," September 19, 2011.

59. Amitai Etzioni, "The New Normal," *Sociological Forum* 26, no. 4 (December 2011): 779–789.

60. Albert Hirschman, *Shifting Involvements: Private Interest and Public Action* (Princeton, NJ: Princeton University Press, 1982), p. 49. Hirschman contends that there is a cycle of collective behavior that alternates between periods of involvement concentrated in the public and private spheres of life. According to this thesis, these involvements shift as citizens eventually come to experience disappointments in the pursuit of satisfactions in each sphere. Hence, disappointments with the satisfactions generated by private consumption give rise to a new concentration of energy on public concerns.

61. According to calculations by Emmanuel Saez, the average family income was $1,505 in 1930 compared $52,619 in 2013 (in constant dollars, excluding taxes and transfers). Data were taken from the Saez website, http://eml.berkeley.edu/~saez/#income, accessed January 25, 2015. The average family size declined from 4.11 in 1930 to 2.54 in 2013.

62. Liz Alderman, "In France, New Review of 35-Hour Workweek," *The New York Times*. http://www.nytimes.com/2014/11/27/business/international/france-has-second-thoughts-on-its-35-hour-workweek.html

63. John Maynard Keynes, *Essays in Persuasion, Economic Possibilities for Our Grandchildren* (New York: W.W. Norton, 1963), p. 362.

Chapter 4

1. William Wordsworth, "My Heart Leaps Up When I Behold" (1802), in G. B. Harrison, ed., *Major British Writers II* (enlarged edition) (New York: Harcourt, Brace and Company, 1954), p. 91.

2. Karl Marx, *Das Kapital*, Friedrich Engels, ed., Vol. 1 (Gateway edition) (Chicago: Henry Regnery Co., 1959), pp. 33–34.

3. Edward Bellamy, *Looking Backward* (New York: New American Library of World Literature, 1960), p. 75.Originally published in 1888, this work was one of the three best-selling novels of its time.

4. Ibid., p. 95.

5. Aristotle, *The Politics* (Modern Library Edition) (New York: Random House, 1943), pp. 260–263.

6. Gregory Vlastos, "Justice and Equality," in Richard Brandt, ed., *Social Justice* (Englewood Cliffs, NJ: Prentice-Hall, 1962), p. 32.

7. President Obama, "Remarks by the President at a Campaign Event in Roanoke, Virginia," The White House, Office of the Press Secretary, July 13, 2012. https://www.whitehouse.gov/the-press-office/2012/07/13/remarks-president-campaign-event-roanoke-virginia

8. Robert Nozick, *Anarchy, State and Utopia* (New York: Basic Books, 1974).

9. President Obama, "State of the Union 2012 Address," January 24, 2012. Estimates suggest that the proposed minimum tax on millionaires would have yielded an additional $30 to $40 billion in federal tax revenue. Although not a trivial sum, it would have made a relatively small dent in the $1.3 trillion deficit in 2011. As a reference point, the $30 billion would have been enough to cover the National Institute of Health's 2012 budget. Michelle Hirsch, "Obama's Tax Plan: $30 B More from Millionaires," *The Fiscal Times*, January 27, 2012. http://www.thefiscaltimes.com/Articles/2012/01/27/Obamas-Tax-Plan-30B-More-from-Millionaires.aspx#page1

10. *The Economist*, "French Taxes: Another Absurdity," April 2013, p. 60.

11. See, for example, the online exchange "Getting the Question Right in Debates over Income Inequality: A Response to Garfinkel and Smeeding," Richard Burkhauser and Jeff Larrimore, Cornell University, Joint Committee on Taxation, October 20, 2011; Timothy M. Smeeding and Irwin Garfinkel, 2011, "Getting the Question and the Data Right in Debates about Changes in 'Real Income' and Income Inequality: A Response to Burkhauser, Larrimore and Simon." http://www.russellsage.org/blog Accessed 2/21/12; also see Richard Burkhauser, Jeff Larrimore, and Kosali Simon, "A 'Second Opinion' on the Economic Health of the American Middle Class," *National Tax Journal* 65, no. 1 (March 2012): 7–32. Winner of the 2012 Richard Musgrave Prize for the best paper published in the *National Tax Journal*; winner of the 2013 Addington Prize in Measurement from the Fraser Institute.

12. Michael Forster et.al., *Divided We Stand: Why Inequality Keeps Rising* (Paris: OECD, 2011).

13. OECD, Income Distribution Database. http://www.oecd.org/social/income-distribution-database.htm, accessed January 29, 2015.

14. US Bureau of Economic Analysis, *Real Personal Income for States and Metropolitan Areas, 2008–2012*, April 24, 2014, http://www.bea.gov/newsreleases/regional/rpp/rpp_newsrelease.htm, accessed February 13, 2015.

15. Nicholas Barr, *The Economics of the Welfare State* (Stanford, CA: Stanford University Press, 1993).The distribution clause in Rawls's second principle holds that inequality is acceptable as long as it is arranged so that everyone benefits. The second principle also stipulates that these inequalities must be attached to positions and offices open to all. John Rawls, *A Theory of Justice* (Cambridge, MA: Harvard University Press, 1971), p. 60.

16. The US Census Bureau, for example, offers four alternative definitions of income that draw upon combinations of earned income, property income, government cash transfers, government in-kind transfer, the imputed value of capital gains and rental income, and deductions of imputed work expenses, federal and state taxes, and means-tested government transfers. US Census Bureau, *The Effect of Taxes and Transfers on Income and Poverty in the United States: 2005*, PG 60–232 (Washington D.C.: Government Printing Office, 2007); Michael Forster et. al., op. cit., p. 227.

17. Thus, for example, Census Bureau data from the Current Population Survey allow for the calculation of income based on households rather than tax units, which must be used when data are drawn from the Internal Revenue Service. Because households that may contain more than one tax unit benefit from the economies of scale, Gini coefficients based on these sources of data yield different results. Richard Burkhauser, "Presidential Address Evaluating the Questions That Alternative Policy Success Measures Answer," *Journal of Policy Analysis and Management* 30, no. 2 (Spring 2011): 205–215.

18. United Nations Economic Commission for Europe, *Canberra Group Handbook on Household Income Statistics*, 2nd ed. (Geneva: United Nations, 2011).

19. See, for example, Thomas Piketty and Emmanuel Saez, "Income Inequality in the United States," *The Quarterly Journal of Economics* CXVII:1 (February 2003), p. 5; Michael Forster et. al., op. cit., p. 227; OECD, *Growing Unequal: Income Distribution and Poverty in OECD Countries* (Paris: OECD, 2008).

20. US Census Bureau, *The Effect of Taxes and Transfers on Income and Poverty in the United States: 2005*, PG 60–232 (Washington, D.C.: Government Printing Office, 2007). In addition to summing the income from various sources, this definition involves the subtraction of imputed costs of work-related expenses except for child care.

21. OECD, "Household Disposable Income," in *OECD Factbook 2013: Economic, Environmental and Social Statistics* (Paris: OECD, 2013). http://dx.doi.org/10.1787/factbook-2013-23-en, accessed February 9, 2014.

22. Joint Committee on Taxation, *Overview of the Definition of Income Used by the Staff of the Joint Committee on Taxation in Distributional Analyses* (JCX-15-12), February 8, 2012.

23. Thornstein Veblen, *The Theory of the Leisure Class* (New York: Mentor Books edition, 1953; first published 1899). In a different vein, Veblen described the economic plight of the scholarly class, as a group whose social status required a level of conspicuous consumption associated with a "higher social grade than their pecuniary grade should warrant" (p. 87).

24. One of my leisure time activities involves monthly participation in a book club devoted to reading works related to child and family policy, whose members represent faculty from half a dozen departments at U.C. Berkeley. None of us consider this work, but reading is one of the activities that faculty get paid to do.

25. William Dale Crist, "Saving Public Colleges and Universities: An Urgent Call to Political Action," *The NEA 2005 Almanac of Higher Education* (Washington, D.C.: NEA, 2005). Gary Becker invoked "psychic income" to explain why in modern times women would choose to have children, even though it is an event that can be counted on to deplete the family's economic resources. The altruistic behavior of families is seen as exchanging the emotional pleasures of psychic income for material benefits of hard cash. Gary Becker, *A Treatise on the Family* (Cambridge, MA: Harvard University Press, 1981). This view highlights the conceptual difficulty of deciding whether to treat parents' time spent with children as leisure or work. In dealing with this issue, the analyses of time-use surveys examined the impact of time spent in child care both as work or leisure. Mark Aguiar and Erik Hurst, "Measuring Trends in Leisure: The Allocation of Time over Five Decades," *The Quarterly Journal of Economics* 122, no. 3 (2007): 969–1006.

26. Mark Aguiar and Erik Hurst, op. cit.; OECD, *Society at a Glance: OECD Social Indicators* (Paris: OECD, 2009).

27. Juliet Schor, *The Overworked American: The Unexpected Decline of Leisure* (New York: Basic Books, 1992); Arlie Russell Hochschild, *The Time Bind: When Work Becomes Home and Home Becomes Work* (New York: Macmillan, 2001).

28. Steve Lohr, "For Impatient Web Users, an Eye Blink Is Just Too Long to Wait," *The New York Times* (March 2012), p. A1. The research cited was based on self-reports. The accuracy of user perceptions of time in seconds is open to question. Alexander Podelko, "How Response Times Impact Business," in Stoyan Stefanov ed., *Web Performance Daybook*, vol. 2 (Sebastopol, CA: O Reilly Media, 2012).

29. Arlie Hochschild with Anne Machung, *The Second Shift: Working Parents and the Revolution at Home* (New York: Viking Penguin, 1989).

30. Neil Gilbert, *A Mother's Work: How Feminism, the Market and Policy Shape Family Life* (New Haven, CT: Yale University Press, 2008).

31. Daphne Lofquist, Terry Lugaila, Martin O'Connell, and Sarah Feliz, *Households and Families: 2010*, 2010 Census Briefs, April 2012, https://www.census.gov/prod/cen2010/briefs/c2010br-14.pdf, accessed on February 23, 2014. In 1960 families averaged 3.65 members compared to the average family size of 3.14 in 2010. Between 1971 and 2010 the percent of clothes dryers in all households increased from 44.5 percent to 75 percent; dishwashers increased from 19 to 64 percent and microwaves from less than 1 percent to 73 percent. US Census Bureau, *Current Housing Reports, Series H150/09, American Housing Survey for the United States: 2009* (Washington, DC: US Government Printing Office, 2011); W. Michael Cox and Richard Alm, *By Our Own Bootstraps: Economic Opportunity & the Dynamics of Income Distribution*, Federal Reserve Bank of Dallas Annual Report 1995.

32. Mark Aguiar and Erik Hurst, "Measuring Trends in Leisure," op. cit.

33. Aguiar and Hurst estimate that at the average market wage, the overall increase in leisure between 1965 and 2003 would be equivalent to 8 to 9 percent of the GDP in 2003. Mark Aguiar and Erik Hurst, "Measuring Trends in Leisure: The Allocation of Time over Five Decades," Federal Reserve Bank of Boston Working Paper No. 06-2 (January 2006). (Their estimate of the monetized value of leisure time presented in this working paper was not included in the *Quarterly Journal of Economics* article based on this work.)

34. Both of these approaches have been criticized for equating one's earnings with the value of leisure time, which implies that leisure time is inherently more valuable to

high-wage earners than low-wage earners. Pedram Sendi and Werner Brouwer, "Leisure Time in Economic Evaluation: Theoretical and Practical Considerations," *Expert Review of Pharmacoeconomics & Outcomes Research* 4, no. 1 (2004): 1–3.

35. A detailed analysis of the thirty-one operational definitions of the components of household income and their associated measurement issues can be found in United Nations Economic Commission for Europe, *Canberra Group Handbook on Household Income Statistics*, 2nd ed. (Geneva: United Nations, 2011); also see Joint Committee on Taxation, *Overview of the Definition of Income Used by the Staff of the Joint Committee on Taxation in Distributional Analyses* (JCX-15-12), February 8, 2012.

36. Philip Armour, Richard V. Burkhauser, and Jeff Larrimore, "Deconstructing Income and Income Inequality Measures: A Crosswalk from Market Income to Comprehensive Income," *American Economic Review* 103 (May 2013): 173–177. Timothy M. Smeeding and Jeffrey P. Thompson, "Recent Trends in the Distribution of Income: Labor, Wealth and More Complete Measures of Well Being," Working Paper 225, Political Economy Research Institute, University of Massachusetts, Amherst (June 2010), http://tinyurl.com/qd8qrxx

37. The Gini coefficient for the United States based on market income in 2010 was .499 compared to .380 when based on disposable household income. OECD Income Distribution Database at http://www.oecd.org/social/societyataglance.htm., accessed on March 6, 2014; OECD (2011), *Society at a Glance 2011—OECD Social Indicators*.

38. In 2010 among the thirty-four member countries of the OECD, the United States had the fourth highest level of inequality measured by disposable household income and the eleventh highest level measured by market income. http://www.oecd.org.social-income-distribution-database.htm, accessed on March 6, 2017.

39. These income figures are for 2007. Michael Forster et al., op. cit.; OECD, *Society at a Glance 2011* (Paris: OECD, 2011).

40. William Frankena, "The Concept of Social Justice," in Richard Brandt, ed., *Social Justice* (Englewood Cliffs, NJ: Prentice-Hall, 1962), p. 23.

41. Pew Research Center, *Partisan Polarization Surges in Bush, Obama Years: Trends in American Values: 1987–2012*, June 4, 2012, http://www.people-press.org/2012/06/04/partisan-polarization-surges-in-bush-obama-years/

42. Thomas Piketty and Emmanuel Saez, "Income Inequality in the United States," *The Quarterly Journal of Economics* CXVII:1 (February 2003). Among the numerous references to this work in the media, *The Washington Post* blog recognized their U-shaped curve of inequality as the "graph of the year." http://www.washingtonpost.com/blogs/wonkblog/wp/2013/12/31/emmanuel-saez-and-thomas-pikettys-graph-of-the-year/

43. Philip Armour, Richard V. Burkhauser, and Jeff Larrimore, op. cit.

44. Richard Burkhauser, "Presidential Address Evaluating," op.cit.

45. Philip Armour, Richard V. Burkhauser, and Jeff Larrimore, op. cit. The government transfers included here involve both cash and in-kind benefits, specifically food stamps, housing subsidies, and school lunches but not the value of employer- and government-provided health insurance. For an analysis of the income growth when cash transfers and health insurance are included, but not in-kind benefits, see Richard Burkhauser, Jeff Larrimore, and Kosali Simon, op. cit.

46. Congressional Budget Office, *The Distribution of Household Income and Federal Taxes 2008 and 2009* (Washington, D.C.: Government Printing Office, 2012). The major

components of income included here differ from those recommended by the Canberra Group mainly in regard to capital gains, which the Canberra guidelines exclude from the measure of household income in favor of their treatment as changes in net worth.

47. Congressional Budget Office, *The Distribution of Household Income and Federal Taxes, 2010* (Washington D.C.: Government Printing Office, December 2013).

48. Further analysis of the CBO data indicates that slowest gains were made by those in the middle and lower middle income groups. Gary Burtless, "Income Growth and Income Inequality: The Facts May Surprise You," *Brookings Institution Opinions*, January 14, 2014. http://www.brookings.edu/research/opinions/2014/01/06-income-gains-and-inequality-burtless

49. Philip Armour, Richard V. Burkhauser, and Jeff Larrimore, op. cit. Due to lack of comparable data over the 1979–2007 period, the income measures including accrued capital gains were for the period from 1989 to 2007 during which the household income of the bottom quintile climbed by almost 15 percent compared to a 1.6 percent gain registered by the top quintile.

50. Congressional Budget Office, *The Distribution of Household Income and Federal Taxes, 2010* (Washington, D.C.: Government Printing Office, December 2013), http://www.cbo.gov/sites/default/files/cbofiles/attachments/44604-AverageTaxRates.pdf, accessed February 17, 2014.

51. Richard Burkhauser and Jeff Larrimore, "Correspondence: The One Percent," *Journal of Economic Perspectives* 28, no. 1 (Winter 2014): 245–246.

52. When accrued gains from housing are excluded from the measure, between 1989 and 2007 the mean income of the bottom quintile increased by 32.2 percent compared to 12.8 percent in the highest bracket. Philip Armour, Richard V. Burkhauser, and Jeff Larrimore, op. cit.

53. US Treasury Department, *Income Mobility in the U.S. From 1996 to 2005* (Washington, D.C.: Government Printing Office, November 13, 2007). A similar rate of mobility was reported for those in the bottom quintile from 1986 to 1996. Unlike the CBO measure, these findings are based on pretax market income plus cash but not tax-exempt or in-kind transfer. Also the unit of analysis is not adjusted for household size.

54. Kathryn Shelton and Richard McKenzie, "Why the 'Rich' Can Get Rich Faster Than the Poor," National Center for Policy Analysis, *Policy Report 358*, July 10, 2014. http://www.ncpa.org/pub/st358 accessed 2/6/15.

55. Diana Furchtgott-Roth, "The Myth of Increasing Income Inequality," *Issues 2012*, 2 (March 2012) http://www.manhattan-institute.org/html/ir_2.htm, accessed February 6, 2015.

56. The rate of married adults in the United States declined from 62 percent in 1980 to 51 percent in 2012. Those who did marry tended to be more highly educated than the unmarried population. Richard Fry, "New Census Data Show More Americans Are Tying the Knot, but Mostly It's the College-Educated." Pew Research Center, February 6, 2014, http://www.pewresearch.org/fact-tank/2014/02/06/new-census-data-show-more-americans-are-tying-the-knot-but-mostly-its-the-college-educated/, accessed February 6, 2015.

57. W. Bradford Wilcox, Robert I. Lerman, *For Richer, for Poorer: How Family Structures Economic Success in America*. AEI and Institute for Family Studies, October 28, 2014. http://www.aei.org/wp-content/uploads/2014/10/IFS-ForRicherForPoorer Final_Web.pdf, accessed February 7, 2015.

58. Congressional Budget Office, *The Distribution of Household Income and Federal Taxes, 2010* (Washington, D.C.: Government Printing Office, December 2013). http://www.cbo.gov/sites/default/files/cbofiles/attachments/44604-AverageTaxRates.pdf, accessed February 17, 2014.

59. Facundo Alvaredo, Anthony B. Atkinson, Thomas Piketty, and Emmanuel Saez, "The Top 1 Percent in International and Historical Perspective," *Journal of Economic Perspectives*, 27, no. 3 (2013): 320. For analyses that focuses on market income, also see Thomas Piketty and Emmanuel Saez, "Income Inequality in the United States, 1913–1998," *The Quarterly Journal of Economics* 118, no. 1 (February 2003): 1–39 ; Emmanuel Saez, "Striking It Richer: The Evolution of Top Incomes in the United States," *Pathways Magazine* (Winter 2008): 6–7. The difference between the CBO estimate that the top 1 percent of households netted 15 percent of all pretax income and the Alvaredo et al. estimate of 20 percent is accounted for by the fact that the CBO data focused on income adjusted for household size and included government transfer, whereas the 20 percent estimate is based on tax units and excludes transfers.

60. Richard Burkhauser, Shuaizhang Feng, Stephen P. Jenkins, and Jeff Larrimore, "Recent Trends in Top Income Shares in the USA: Reconciling Estimates from March CPS and IRS Tax Return Data," NBER Working Paper No. 15320 (September 2009); Robert Gordon, "Misperceptions about the Magnitude and Timing of Changes in American Income Inequality." NBER Working Paper No. 15351 (September 2009). http://www.nber.org/papers/w15351

61. Kyle Pomerleau, "Summary of Latest Federal Income Tax Data," *Fiscal Fact* 408 (December 18, 2013). http://taxfoundation.org/article/summary-latest-federal-income-tax-data, accessed March 24, 2014. These figures represent adjusted gross income. The average income in the top 1 percent was $1,013,100 in 2010. Congressional Budget Office, *The Distribution of Household Income and Federal Taxes, 2010* (Washington, D.C.: Government Printing Office, December 2013). http://www.cbo.gov/sites/default/files/cbofiles/attach-ments/44604-AverageTaxRates.pdf, accessed February 17, 2014.

62. Peter Eavis, "Invasion of the Supersalaries," *The New York Times*, April 13, 2014, p. BU1.

63. Michael McCann, "In Lawsuit Minor Leaguers Charge They Are Members of 'Working Poor,'" *Sports Illustrated* (February 12, 2014), http://sportsillustrated.cnn.com/mlb/news/20140212/minor-league-baseball-players-lawsuit/#ixzz2x1Ofg8L5

64. Josh Gerstein, "What Obama Didn't Say in His State of the Union," *Politico*, January 21, 2015. http://www.politico.com/story/2015/01/obama-sotu-2015-whats-left-out-114440.html, accessed February 8, 2015.

65. Alan Wolfe, *One Nation, After All: What Americans Really Think About God, Country, Family, Racism, Welfare, Immigration, Homosexuality, Work, The Right, The Left and Each Other* (New York: Penguin Books, 1998).

66. Andrew Dugan, "Americans Most Likely to Say They Belong to the Middle Class," *Gallup Politics*, November 30, 2012. http://www.gallup.com/poll/159029/americans-likely-say-belong-middle-class.aspx

67. Dionne Searcey and Robert Gebeloffjan, "Middle Class Shrinks Further as More Fall Out Instead of Climbing Up," *The New York Times*, January 25, 2015, http://www.nytimes.com/2015/01/26/business/economy/middle-class-shrinks-further-as-more-fall-out-instead-of-climbing-up.html, accessed February 8, 2015; Rakesh Kochhar

and Richard Fry, "America's 'Middle' Holds Its Ground after the Great Recession," *Pew Research Center, Fact Tank*, February 4, 2015. http://www.pewresearch.org/fact-tank/2015/02/04/americas-middle-holds-its-ground-after-the-great-recession/

68. OECD, *Society at a Glance 2014: OECD Social Indicators* (Paris: OECD, 2014). http://www.keepeek.com/Digital-Asset-Management/oecd/social-issues-migration-health/society-at-a-glance-2014/household-income_soc_glance-2014-7-en#page1, accessed February 7, 2015.

69. Tyler Cowen, "Income Inequality Is Not Rising Globally. It's Falling," *The Upshot, The New York Times*, July 19, 2014. http://www.nytimes.com/2014/07/20/upshot/income-inequality-is-not-rising-globally-its-falling-.html?_r=0, accessed February 9, 2015.

70. Special tax deductions and exemptions were identified as a form of government transfer in Arthur Pigou's classic text *Economics of Welfare* in the 1920s and later classified as fiscal welfare by Richard Titmuss, the founding director of the Department of Social Administration at the London School of Economics. In the mid-1970s Stanley Surrey labeled these transfers as "tax expenditures." As a result of Surrey's work, Congress ordered a national accounting of tax expenditures in 1974. For a discussion of this development, see Richard Titmuss, *Essays on the "Welfare State"* (London: Unwin University Books, 1958); Stanley Surrey, *Pathways to Tax Reform* (Cambridge, MA: Harvard University Press, 1973) and Richard Goode, "The Economic Definition of Income," in Joseph Pechman ed., *Comprehensive Income Taxation* (Washington, D.C.: Brookings Institution, 1977).

71. Congressional Budget Office, *The Distribution of Major Tax Expenditures in the Individual Income Tax System* (Washington, D.C.: Government Printing Office, May 2013). Due to the decline in housing prices, the tax expenditure on mortgage interest deductions was 25 percent lower in 2013 than in 2006. Had housing prices remained at the 2006 level, the tax expenditure in 2013 would have been around $105 billion.

72. Peter Peterson, "Entitlement Reform: The Way to Eliminate the Deficit," *New York Review of Books* 41, no. 7, pp. 39–47.

73. Andrew Hanson, Ike Brannon, and Zackary Hawley, "Rethinking Tax Benefits for Home Owners," *National Affairs* (Spring 2014), pp. 40–54. At more than 2,500 square feet, the average home purchased in 2013 was 40 percent larger than the average size of homes bought in 1980.

74. Abhijit V Banerjee and Esther Duflo, "Inequality and Growth: What Can the Data Say?" *Journal of Economic Growth* 8, no. 3 (September 2003): 267–299.

75. Congressional Budget Office, The Effects of a Minimum-Wage Increase on Employment and Family Income (February 2014), http://www.cbo.gov/publication/44995. The CBO estimates suggest that families with income below the federal poverty line would receive only 19 percent of the total increase in wages, while 29 percent would go to those families earning more than three times the poverty threshold.

76. Aparna Mathur, Sita Slavov, and Michael Strain, "Should the Top Marginal Income Tax Rate Be 73 Percent?" *Tax Notes*, November 19, 2012.

77. Even before the advent of capitalism, the marketplace was not entirely without checks and balances. The ruins of Pompeii contain a stall that served as an ancient equivalent of the bureau of weights and measures, which inhibited tradesmen from putting too much of their thumb on the scales. Vermont Royster, "'Regulation' Isn't a Dirty Word," *The Wall Street Journal*, September 9, 1987, p. 36.

78. Barry Schwartz, "Capitalism, the Market, 'the Underclass,' and the Future," *Society* 37, no. 1 (November/December 1999), p. 37.

79. Joesph Stiglitz, *The Price of Inequality* (New York: Penguin Books, 2012), p. 51.

80. The quote is from a speech by President Obama, which was reaffirmed in public comments by Senate Majority Leader Harry Reid. See White House Press Office, "Remarks by the President on Economic Mobility," THEARC, Washington, D.C., December 4, 2013, http://www.whitehouse.gov/the-press-office/2013/12/04/remarks-president-economic-mobility; Susan Jones, "Harry Reid: 'No Greater Challenge . . . Than Income Inequality,'" CNN News.com, December 20, 2013. http://cnsnews.com/news/article/susan-jones/harry-reid-no-greater-challengethan-income-inequality

81. Consider the progressive disturbance over the inequality of pay between men and women, who now earn eighty-eight cents to the dollar for men. That relatively small difference might be due to unfair treatment of women or the possibility that women have different preferences for fields of work or even higher levels of commitment to family life versus work than men.

Chapter 5

1. Stanley Rothman, Neil Nevitte, and S. Robert Lichter, "Politics and Professional Advancement," *Academic Questions* 18, no. 2 (June 2005): 71–84; Tim Groseclose, *Left Turn: How Liberal Media Bias Distorts the American Mind* (New York: St. Martin's Press, 2011); S. Robert Lichter, Stanley Rothman, and Linda S. Lichter, *The Media Elite* (Bethesda, MD: Adler and Adler, 1986).

2. Joseph Stiglitz, *The Price of Inequality* (New York: Penguin Books, 2012).

3. Richard Wilkinson and Kate Pickett, *The Spirit Level: Why Greater Equality Makes Societies Stronger* (New York: Bloomsbury Press, 2010).

4. Roy Hattersley, "Last Among Equals," *New Statesman*, March 26, 2009.

5. Editorial, "The Spirit Level: Spooking the Right," *The Guardian*, July 26, 2010. In responding to the most potent critique brought against the study's research methods, the editorial notes that this critique "pays no heed to the wider literature, going back decades, that has linked ill health with *poverty.*" This conflation of poverty with inequality misses the book's central point, which is that its findings refer to inequality, not poverty.

6. Nicholas Kristof, "Equality, a True Soul Food," *The New York Times*, January 2, 2011, p. WK10.

7. John Carey, "The Spirit Level: Why More Equal Societies Almost Always Do Better," *The Sunday Times*, March 8, 2009.

8. There is some evidence for a relationship between stress and poverty in low- and middle-income countries. See, for example, Crick Lund et al., "Poverty and Common Mental Disorders in Low and Middle Income Countries: A Systematic Review," *Social Science & Medicine* 71, no. 3 (August 2010): 517–528.

9. Chronic stress has been linked to a variety of poor health and psychosocial outcomes. See, for example, Stanislav V. Kasl, "Stress and Health," *Annual Review of Public Health* 5 (May 1984): 319–341; Virginia Hill Rice, *Handbook of Stress, Coping, and Health: Implications for Nursing Research Theory, and Practice*, 2nd ed. (Thousand Oaks, CA: Sage, 2012); William R. Lovallo, *Stress and Health: Biological and Psychological Interactions*, 2nd ed. (Thousand Oaks, CA: Sage, 2005).

10. Wilkinson and Pickett, op. cit., p. 43.

11. Ibid.

12. Vladimir Gimpelson and Daniel Treisman, "Misperceiving Inequality," National Bureau of Economic Research Working Paper No. 21174 (May 2015), http://www.nber.org/papers/w21174, accessed on July 1, 2015.

13. Richard Layard, *Happiness: Lessons from a New Science* (New York: Penguin Books, 2005), p. 44.

14. Pamela Villarreal, "How Much Are Teachers Really Paid? A Nationwide Analysis of Teacher Pay" (Dallas, TX: National Center for Policy Analysis, September 2014). http://www.ncpa.org/pdfs/2014_Teacher_Pay_Report-NCPA_MacIver.pdf, accessed February 14, 2015.

15. In 2012 Japan's suicide rate was 50 percent higher than that of the United States and three times as high as the United Kingdom, both countries with significantly higher levels of income inequality. World Health Organization, *Preventing Suicide: A Global Imperative* (Geneva: WHO, 2014); James Arnold, "Japanese Office Stress at Record Levels," *BBC News World Edition*, http://news.bbc.co.uk/2/hi/business/2006132.stm, accessed January 3, 2015.

16. Compared to the United States, for example, Japanese parents are four times more likely to report that their children are under too much academic pressure. Richard Wike and Juliana Horowitz, *Parental Pressure on Students Pew Research Center Global Attitudes Project*, August 24, 2006, http://www.pewglobal.org/2006/08/24/parental-pressure-on-students/, accessed January 5, 2015.

17. And almost half of those not in a relationship with the opposite sex are not even interested in dating. National Institute of Population and Social Security Research: The Fourteenth Japanese National Fertility Survey in 2010, "Attitudes Toward Marriage and Family among Japanese Singles," November 2011; http://www.ipss.go.jp/sitead/index_english/nfs14/Nfs14_Singles_Eng.pdf, accessed January 3, 2015.

18. World Bank Poverty Reduction and Economic Management Unit African Region, *Kenya Economic Update June 2013* (Kenya: World Bank, 2013), http://www.worldbank.org/content/dam/Worldbank/document/Africa/Kenya/kenya-economic-update-june-2013.pdf, accessed January 5, 2015.

19. Although the average effect of the treatment on cortisol levels was not significant, the findings did show that cortisol levels were significantly lower in households receiving lump-sum allotments than monthly installments and that households receiving the larger transfers($1,525) had significantly lower levels of cortisol than those receiving the small transfer ($404). Johannes Haushofer and Jeremy Shapiro, "Household Response to Income Changes: Evidence from an Unconditional Cash Transfer Program in Kenya" (November 15, 2013).

20. If anything, the authors report that the spillover effects were generally in the positive direction, though not statistically significant. Ibid., p. 23.

21. Daniel Patrick Moynihan, "Defining Deviancy Down," *The American Scholar* 62, no. 1 (Winter 1993): 17–30.

22. Technically referred to as a regression line, it is calculated to minimize the sum of the squared vertical distances from each data point.

23. Peter Saunders, *Beware False Prophets: Equality, the Good Society and the Spirit Level* (London: Policy Exchange, 2010). This is an exacting methodological critique of the statistical analysis reported in *The Spirit Level*. Saunders shows that throughout this

study, the analyses consistently overlook the problem of outliers and routinely ignore the potentially powerful impact of cultural and historical differences among the limited number of countries in the sample. His close examination shows that, in the vast majority of cases, *The Spirit Level*'s statistical findings reflected spurious correlations.

24. Ibid.,106–107. Saunders presents this demonstration more as an example of how to formulate statistical measures to suit an argument than as an objective analysis of the relationship between inequality and the Social Misery Index.

25. Sources of data: OECD Stat Extracts. "Income Distribution and Poverty," http://stats.oecd.org/, accessed August 24, 2014, and United Nations Economic Commission for Europe Statistical Database, http://w3.unece.org/pxweb/dialog/varval.asp?ma=02_GEFHAdoFertility_r&path=./database/STAT/30-GE/02-Families_households/&lang=1&ti=Adolescent+fertility, accessed August 27, 2014.

26. Alternative explanations can be devised when data do not fit the inequality storyline. One might argue, for instance, that the introduction of advanced birth control techniques occurred in some countries more rapidly than others. One study suggests that access to improved contraceptives and educational opportunities for women may have influenced the decline of teen birthrates in the United States and other OECD countries. However, the authors note that proving these relationships was a difficult proposition. In any event, the impact of economic inequality is not considered consequential. Melisa Kearney and Phillip Levine, "Teen Births Are Falling: What's Going On?" *Policy Brief*, March 2014 (Washington, D.C.: The Brookings Institution).

27. Wilkinson and Pickett, op. cit., pp. 81–85.

28. Richard Wilkinson and Kate Pickett, "Income Inequality and Population Health: A Review and Explanation of the Evidence," *Social Science and Medicine* 62 (2006): 1768–1784.

29. Ken Judge, Jo-Ann Mulligan, and Michaela Benzeval, "The Relationship Between Income Inequality and Population Health," *Social Science and Medicine* 46 (1998): 567–579. They note that the analysis employs alternative measures of the relationship between income inequality, infant mortality, and life expectancy based on the most authoritative data available.

30. J. Lynch, G. D. Smith, S. Harper, M. Hillemeier, N. Ross, G. Kaplan, and M. Wolfson, "Is Income Inequality a Determinant of Population Health? Part 1. A Systematic Review," *Milbank Quarterly* 82, no. 1 (2004): 5–99. The ninety-eight studies in this review account for the majority of the studies in the review conducted by Wilkinson and Pickett, "Income Inequality," op. cit.

31. Andrew Leigh, Christopher Jencks, and Timothy Smeeding, "Health and Economic Inequality," in Wiemer Salverda, Brian Nolan, and Timothy Smeeding, eds., *The Oxford Handbook of Economic Inequality* (Oxford: Oxford University Press, 2011), pp. 384–405.

32. J. Lynch, G. D. Smith, S. Harper, and M. Hillemeier, "Is Income Inequality a Determinant of Population Health? Part 2. U.S. National and Regional Trends in Income Inequality and Age- and Cause-Specific Mortality," *Milbank Quarterly* 82, no. 2 (2004): 355–400.

33. Johan P Mackenbach, "Income Inequality and Population Health: Evidence Favouring a Negative Correlation Between Income Inequality and Life Expectancy Has Disappeared," *British Medical Journal* 324 (January 5, 2002): 1–2.

34. Angus Deaton and Darren Lubotsky, "Income Inequality and Mortality in U.S. Cities: Weighing the Evidence, A Response to Ash," *Social Science and Medicine* 68 (2009): 1914–1917; Angus Deaton and Darren Lubotsky, "Mortality, Inequality and Race in American Cities and States," *Social Science and Medicine* 56 (2003): 1139–1153; Ken Judge, Jo-Ann Mulligan, and Michaela Benzeval, op. cit.; A.Wagstaff and E. van Doorslaer, "Income Inequality and Health: What Does the Literature Tell Us?" *Annual Revue of Public Health* 21 (2000): 543–567.

35. Leigh, Jencks, and Smeeding, op. cit.

36. See, for example, Stiglitz, op. cit., and Lawrence Lessig, *Republic, Lost: How Money Corrupts Congress—And a Plan to Stop It* (New York: Twelve, 2011).

37. James Madison, "The Structure of the Government Must Furnish the Proper Checks and Balances Between the Different Departments," *The Federalist No. 51*, February 6, 1788. (There is some question as to whether No. 51 was authored by Madison or Hamilton.) http://thomas.loc.gov/home/histdox/fedpapers.html, accessed January 12, 2015.

38. J. F. "Why American Elections Cost So Much," *The Economist explains*, February 9, 2014.http://www.economist.com/blogs/economist-explains/2014/02/economist-explains-4, accessed January 13, 2015.

39. Spending went from $3.082 to $6.285 billion. Data are from opensecrets at https://www.opensecrets.org/lobby/.

40. Michael Tomasky, "The Billionaire Brothers Take on the US," *The New York Review of Books*, June 19, 2014, pp. 22–24.

41. Willie Brown, "Let Koch Brothers Roll—They're Likely to Lose Big," *San Francisco Chronicle*, February 1, 2015, p. D1.

42. Katia Savchuk, "Billionaire Tom Steyer on Money in Politics, Spending $74 M on the Election," *Forbes*, http://www.forbes.com/sites/katiasavchuk/2014/11/03/billionaire-tom-steyer-on-money-in-politics-spending-74-m-on-the-election/, accessed November 3, 2014.

43. Joseph Postell, "Both Sides of the Table," *Claremont Review of Books* (Fall 2014): 47–49.

44. Data are from opensecrets at https://www.opensecrets.org/lobby/

45. The American Association of Retired Persons formally changed its name to AARP, broadening its membership base to include elderly persons who did not consider themselves retired. http://www.aarp.org/about-aarp/?intcmp=FTR-LINKS-WWA-ABOUT

46. Daniel Kessler, "Real Medicare Reform," *National Affairs* 13 (Fall 2012): 77–94. Sometimes, however, the enormous income received from AARP's business interests, particularly lending its stamp of approval to commercial insurers, may shape its orientation to policy reforms more than concerns for constituent interests. In 2014, AARP spent about $900,000 on lobbying. Opensecrets, op. cit.

47. See, for example, Floyd Hunter, *Community Power Structure* (Chapel Hill: University of North Carolina Press, 1953) and August Hollingshead, *Elmtown's Youth* (New York: Science Editions, 1961); Hollingshead reports that upper class families' control of the major political parties on the township and county levels "results in the formulation of conservative policies and the election of officials who act in the capacity of agents for class I interests" (p . 86).

48. Nelson Polsby, *Community Power and Political Theory* (New Haven, CT: Yale University Press, 1963), p. 3.

49. Ibid., pp. 8–10.

50. Martin Gilens, *Affluence and Influence: Economic Inequality and Political Power in America* (Princeton, NJ: Princeton University Press. Kindle Edition, 2012). Three income groups—low, middle and high—were defined focusing on respondents whose incomes were at the 10th percentile, 50th percentile, and 90th percentile.

51. The period during the Johnson administration, from 1963 to 1969, was the only other time in which the level of political inequality was as low as in the 2001–2006 years. But that was because the overall level of political responsiveness to the policy preferences expressed by citizens was itself very low with regard to all income levels. Ibid.

52. Kathryn Shelton and Richard McKenzie, "Why the 'Rich' Can Get Rich Faster Than the Poor," National Center for Policy Analysis, Policy Report 358, July 10, 2014, http://www.ncpa.org/pub/st358, accessed February 6, 2015.

53. American Political Science Association Task Force on Inequality and American Democracy, "American Democracy in an Age of Rising Inequality," *Perspectives on Politics* 2, no. 4 (December 2004), p. 662.

54. James Buchanan, "Public Choice: Politics Without Romance," *Policy* 19, no. 3 (Spring 2003), p. 15.

55. Madison, op. cit.

56. For a discussion of the potential of the Internet age to disrupt political hierarchies, see Naill Ferguson, "Networks and Hierarchies," *The American Interest* 6 (July/August 2014): 16–24.

57. Lane Kenworthy, *Egalitarian Capitalism: Jobs, Income and Growth in Affluent Countries* (New York: Russell Sage Foundation, 2004); Scott Winship, "Does Inequality Harm the Economy?" *National Affairs* 15 (Spring 2013): 33–49.

58. Alberto Alesina and Dani Rodrik, "Distributive Politics and Economic Growth," *The Quarterly Journal of Economics* 109, no. 2 (1994): 465–490.

59. Emile Durkheim, *The Division of Labor in Society*, trans. George Simpson (New York: Free Press, 1933) (English translation of *De la Division du Travail Social*, first published in 1893).

60. Durkheim initially thought that the "mechanical" form of social solidarity based on homogeneity would be displaced by what he termed "organic solidarity," which stemmed not from social uniformity but from the interdependence of complementary roles under the division of labor in modern society. However, as Robert Nisbet points out, on further reflection, Durkheim was doubtful that organic solidarity would replace the fundamental elements of mechanical solidarity as the core of social cohesion. In the preface to the second edition of *The Division of Labor in Society*, he stressed the continuing need for social and moral homogeneity as the foundation of a solidarity that contributes harmony and order to modern society. Robert Nisbet, *Emile Durkheim* (Englewood Cliffs, NJ: Prentice Hall, 1965).

61. A test of the egalitarian ethos began in 2015 as waves of immigrants from the Middle East were arriving on the shores of small, relatively homogenous Western European countries.

62. Alejandro Portes and Julia Sensenbrenner, "Embeddedness and Immigration: Notes on the Social Determination of Economic Action," in Mary Brinton and Victor Nee, eds., *The New Institutionalism in Sociology* (New York: Russell Sage Foundation, 1998), p. 140; the mixed effects of solidarity are also found among extended

families in traditional societies. See E. Wayne Nafizger, "The Effect of the Nigerian Extended Family on Entrepreneurial Activity," *Economic Development and Cultural Change* 18, no. 1 (October 1969): 25–33.

63. Lewis Coser, *The Functions of Social Conflict* (New York: The Free Press, 1956).

64. One study notes that although between 1972 and 1992 the percent of high school graduates entering college increased in every quartile, the gap between the rate of college entrance in the bottom and top quartiles also increased. Christopher Jencks, Ann Owens, Tracey Shollenberger, and Queenie Zhu, "How Has Rising Economic Inequality Affected Children's Educational Outcomes?" (August 14, 2010), unpublished paper. http://www.hks.harvard.edu/inequality/Seminar/Papers/Jencks11.pdf, accessed March 5, 2015.

65. Eugene Steuerle, "Do Incentives Affect Behavior? Would an Economist Know?" *Tax Notes* (April 3, 2006), p. 95.

66. David Dollar, "United States-China Two-Way Direct Investment: Opportunities and Challenges," The Brookings Institution (January 2015), http://www.brookings.edu/blogs/up-front/posts/2015/02/26-investment-between-us-and-china-dollar, accessed March 3, 2015.

67. For an analysis tracing the different phases of globalization back to the turn of the twentieth century, see Stephan Leibfried and Elmar Rieger, "Conflict over Germany's Competitiveness: Exiting from the Global Economy?" Occasional Paper, Center for German European Studies, University of California, Berkeley, 1995.

68. Investment Company Institute, *2014 Investment Company Factbook* (Washington D.C.: Investment Company Institute, 2014), http://www.icifactbook.org/fb_ch6.html#individual; Richard Nadler, "The Rise of Worker Capitalism," *Policy Analysis* 359 (November 1, 1999): 1–27; for another view of globalization as more of a new form than a modern phase of capitalism, see Jeremy Rifkin, *The End of Work: The Decline of the Global Labor Force and the Dawn of the Post-Market Era* (New York: G. P. Putnam, 1995).

69. Federico Cingano, " Trends in Income Inequality and Its Impact on Economic Growth," OECD Social, Employment, and Migration Working Papers, No. 163 (Paris: OECD Publishing, 2014), http://dx.doi.org/10.1787/5jxrjncwxv6j-en

70. Dan Andrews, Christopher Jencks, and Andrew Leigh. "Do Rising Top Incomes Lift All Boats?" *B. E. Journal of Economic Analysis & Policy* 11, no. 1 (2011):article 6.

71. Lane Kenworthy, op. cit., p. 66. Inequality was defined by the Gini coefficient and economic growth measured by changes in per-capita GDP.

72. Andrews, Jencks, and Leigh, op. cit. Inequality was defined by changes in the share of pretax income received by the richest 10 percent and 1 percent; economic growth was measured by a five-year moving average of GDP.

73. Even Marx observed that crude communism was an expression of envy and the desire to level everything down. Karl Marx, *Early Writings*, trans. Rodney Livingstone and Gregor Benton (London: Penguin Books, 1992), p. 346.

74. Sara Solnick and David Hemenway, "Is More Always Better? A Survey on Positional Concerns," *Journal of Economic Behavior and Organization* 37, no. 3 (November 1998): 373–383.

75. Richard Layard, op. cit., p. 42.

76. For example, Gilles Saint-Paul, *The Tyranny of Utility: Behavioral Social Science and the Rise of Paternalism* (Princeton, NJ: Princeton University Press, 2011), p. 53, notes "the majority prefer the first option." Daniel Abebe and Jonathan S. Masur, "International

Agreements, Internal Heterogeneity and Climate Change: The 'Two Chinas' Problem," *Virginia Journal of International Law* 50, no. 2 (2010), p. 325, observe the findings show "that most people prefer higher relative income to higher absolute income."

77. Amos Tversky and Dale Griffen, "Endowment and Contrast in Judgments of Well-Being," *Subjective Well-Being*, eds. Fritz Strack, Michael Argyle, and Norbert Schwarz (Oxford: Pergamon Press, 1991), pp. 101–119.

78. Gary Charness and Matthew Rabin, "Understanding Social Preferences with Simple Tests," *Quarterly Journal of Economics* 117, no. 3 (2002): 817–869. In the Berkeley lab 100 units of money equaled $1.00; in the Barcelona lab 100 units equaled 100 pesetas (around 70 cents). An even larger percent of players (69 percent) chose not to reduce the difference in payoff when the choice was between being paid 400 units of lab money and having another player also receive 400 units or being paid 400 lab units and having another player receive 750 units. This is one of various studies analyzing social preferences, which find subjects making sacrifices that increase inequality to help others.

79. Joseph Epstein, *Envy* (New York: Oxford University Press, 2003), p. 20. There is good reason for this question; one of the foremost essayists of our time, Epstein has been compared with Ruskin and Arnold and Wilde as "a shining example of how essay writing and criticism aspire to equal footing with imaginative literature." William Giraldi, "On Joseph Epstein," *The New Criterion* (May 2014), https://www.newcriterion.com/articles.cfm/On-Joseph-Epstein-7888?Clip=1

80. Ibid., p. 26.

81. Joseph Schumpeter, *Capitalism, Socialism and Democracy* (New York: Harper Torchbooks, 1942), p. 147. Robert Nozick describes this group as "wordsmith intellectuals" in "Why Do Intellectuals Oppose Capitalism?" *Cato Policy Report* (January/February 1998):1, 9–11.

82. Ibid. p. 152.

83. Ibid., p. 147.

84. Nathan Glazer, "Neoconservatives from the Start," *The Public Interest* (Spring 2005): 12–17.

85. Irving Kristol, *Two Cheers for Capitalism* (New York: Basic Books, 1978), p. 165.

86. Robert Nozick, op. cit.

87. Thorstein Veblen, *The Theory of the Leisure Class* (New York: Mentor Books, 1912), p. 87.

88. Ludwig Von Mises, *The Anti-Capitalistic Mentality* (Indianapolis: Liberty Fund Inc., 2006, first published in 1956).

89. For an entertaining description of the intellectual class afflicted by SID (status-income disequilibrium), see David Brooks, *Bobos in Paradise: The New Upper Class and How They Got There* (New York: Simon and Schuster, 2000), pp. 178–185.

90. Nozick, op. cit., notes that intellectuals want society to be more like a school, the environment in which they shined so brightly.

91. Joseph Epstein, op. cit., p. 81.

Chatper 6

1. President Obama, "Remarks by the President on Economic Mobility," December 4, 2013, The White House, Office of the Press Secretary, https://www.whitehouse.gov/

the-press-office/2013/12/04/remarks-president-economic-mobility, accessed March 17, 2015.

2. The Editorial Board, "The President on Inequality," *The New York Times*, December 4, 2013.

3. Lake Wobegon is a weekly topic of amusement on Keillor's well-known Public Radio show "A Prairie Home Companion."

4. Kathryn Shelton and Richard McKenzie, "Why the 'Rich' Can Get Rich Faster Than the Poor," National Center for Policy Analysis, Policy Report 358, July 10, 2014. http://www.ncpa.org/pub/st358, accessed February 6, 2015. US Census Bureau, *Current Population Survey, 2011 Annual Social and Economic Supplement*, Table HINC-05: Percent Distribution of Households, by Selected Characteristics Within Income Quintile and Top 5 Percent in 2010; Table HINC-01: Selected Characteristics of Households, by Total Money Income in 2010. http://www.census.gov/hhes/www/cpstables/032011/hhinc/toc.htm, accessed February 6, 2015.

5. Jacob Hacker, *The Great Risk Shift* (New York: Oxford University Press, 2006), p. 25. The finding on "loss aversion" was among the corpus of work by Kahneman and Tversky that challenged the prevailing assumption of microeconomics and launched the discipline of behavioral economics, for which the psychologist Kahneman was awarded the Noble Prize. For a lively overview of this work, see Daniel Kahneman, *Thinking, Fast and Slow* (London: Penguin Books, 2012).

6. Robert Reich, "People Are Paid What They Are Worth—Or Are They?" *San Francisco Chronicle* (April 5, 2105), p. F8.

7. For example, the Gallup poll reports a decline in the public perception that the average person has plenty of opportunity to get ahead from 81 percent in 1998 to 52 percent in 2013. Andrew Dugan and Frank Newport, "In U.S., Fewer Believe 'Plenty of Opportunity' to Get Ahead" (October 25, 2013), http://www.gallup.com/poll/165584/fewer-believe-plenty-opportunity-ahead.aspx, accessed March 31, 2015; Rana Foroohar, "What Ever Happened to Upward Mobility," *Time Magazine* 34, no. 3 (November 14, 2011), claims that "the numbers support the idea that for most people, it's harder to get ahead than it's ever been in the postwar era."

8. Raj Chetty, Nathaniel Hendren, Patrick Kline, Emmanuel Saez, and Nicholas Turner, "Is the United States Still a Land of Opportunity? Recent Trends in Intergenerational Mobility," National Bureau of Economic Research Working Paper No. 19844 (January 2014). Earlier studies with smaller samples have yielded mixed evidence on social mobility. For example, Daniel Aaronson and Bhashkar Mazumder, "Intergenerational Economic Mobility in the U.S., 1940 to 2000," FRB Chicago Working Paper No. 2005-12 (December 2005), report finding a decline in mobility after 1980, which they suggest was a return to an historical norm. This study is based on 6 million observations and does not directly link parent and child incomes. In contrast, Chul-In Lee and Gary Solon, "Trends in Intergenerational Income Mobility," National Bureau of Economic Research Working Paper No. 12007 (January 2006), found no change in intergenerational mobility in an analysis of children born to 5,000 families between 1952 and 1975, which were surveyed in the Panel Study of Income Dynamics.

9. These measures included the correlation between the percentile ranks of parent and child incomes, transitions among income quintiles, and the correlation between the natural logarithm of the sons' and fathers' incomes.

10. College attendance rates were linked to parent income using IRS 1098-T forms.

11. Among those born in 1971, a 10 percentile increase in where their parents' income ranked relative to other parents of the children in their cohort was associated with a 2.34 percentile increase in the children's income rank relative to other children, which was almost the same as the association between the cohort of children who were born in 1986 and their parents. For those born in 1986, a 10 percentile increase in their parents' income rank was associated with a 2.65 percentile increase in the child's income rank. These findings refer to the children's income at age 26. The slight increase (0.31 percent) between 1971 and 1986 in the association between the parent and child's rank in the income distribution reveals that the percentile rank of children born in 1986 was tied just a little more closely to the parent's rank than for those born in 1971, which represents an insignificant decline in intergenerational mobility

12. The gap narrowed for both men and women. The quality of colleges attended showed a similar result.

13. Chetty, Hendren, Kline, Saez, and Turner, op. cit, p. 10. The other studies referred to here are as follows: Thomas Hertz, "Trends in the Intergenerational Elasticity of Family Income in the United States," *Industrial Relations: A Journal of Economy and Society* 46, no. 1 (2007): 22–50, and Lee and Solon, op. cit.

14. Deirdre Bloome, "Income Inequality and Intergenerational Income Mobility in the United States," *Social Forces* 93, no. 3 (2015): 1047–1080.

15. Raj Chetty, Nathaniel Hendren, Patrick Kline, and Emmanuel Saez, "Where Is the Land of Opportunity? The Geography of Intergenerational Mobility in the United States," National Bureau of Economic Research Working Paper No. 19843 (January 2014). The geographic districts are formally described as commuting zones, aggregations of counties that are similar to metro areas. The study focused on 709 commuting zones, which had at least 250 children in the 1980–1982 core sample.

16. When mobility was measured by the correlation between children's and parents' income percentile ranks, Los Angeles, California, had the weakest relationship, which represents the highest level of income mobility; here a 10 percent increase in parents' income rank is associated with a 2.31 percent increase in their children's rank; in contrast, Cincinnati, Ohio, had the strongest relationship with a 10 percent increase in parents' income rank associated with a 4.29 percent increase in their children's income rank. The stronger the relationship, the more closely the link between the child's and the parent's percentile rank in the income distribution; hence, the lower the level of intergenerational mobility. Ibid., Table IV.

17. Other characteristics examined in this study included local public goods and tax policies, access to higher education, migration and networks, and local labor market conditions.

18. The measure of income inequality that was used excluded the top 1 percent in the income distribution.

19. In a similar vein, the correlation between race and mobility disappears when the percent of single-parent families is introduced into the equation, which, as the authors observe, "demonstrates the tremendous explanatory power of the single-parent measure." Ibid., p. 38.

20. Alan B. Krueger, "The Rise and Consequences of Inequality in the United States," presented at the Center for American Progress (January 12, 2012). The graph displayed

the same questionable analysis of two variable relationships weighted at one end by four Scandinavian countries that was critically examined in the review of Wilkinson and Pickett's study (see Chapter 5), except that the Gatsby curve was based on an even smaller sample of ten countries.

21. Chetty, Hendren, Kline, and Saez, op. cit., and Bloome, op. cit.

22. Gretchen Livingston, *The Rise of Single Fathers*, Pew Research Center Report (July 2, 2013), http://www.pewsocialtrends.org/2013/07/02/the-rise-of-single-fathers/ , accessed April 4, 2015.

23. Peter D. Brandon, "Trends over Time in the Educational Attainments of Single Mothers," Institute for Research on Poverty Discussion Paper no. 1023-93, Institute for Research on Poverty University of Wisconsin-Madison October 1993.

24. Between 1960 and 2011 the educational attainment of some college or more among mothers with infants increased from 18 percent to 66 percent. Gretchen Livingston and D'Vera Cohen, *Record Share of New Mothers Are College Educated: Long-Term Trend Accelerates Since Recession*, Pew Research Report (May 10, 2013). http://www.pewsocialtrends.org/2013/05/10/record-share-of-new-mothers-are-college-educated/, accessed April 4, 2015.

25. US Department of Education, National Center for Education Statistics, *Digest of Educational Statistics*, Table 104.20, https://nces.ed.gov/programs/digest/d13/tables/dt13_104.20.asp, accessed April 5, 2015.

26. Betty Hart and Todd R. Risley, *Meaningful Differences in the Everyday Experiences of Young American Children* (Baltimore, MD: Brookes Publishing, 1995).

27. Robert D. Putnam, Carl B. Frederick, and Kaisa Snellman, "Growing Class Gaps in Social Connectedness among American Youth, 1975–2009," Harvard Kennedy School of Government, The Saguaro Seminar: Civic Engagement in America (July 12, 2012), p. 3.

28. Ibid., p. 19.

29. According to one estimate, among the fifty people who comprised a list of the richest person in every state, 80 percent built their fortunes from scratch or significantly grew a company that was inherited, while the remaining 20 percent were described as "largely do nothing heirs." Abram Brown, "The Richest Person in Every State," *Forbes* (April 29, 2015), http://www.forbes.com/sites/abrambrown/2015/04/29/richest-in-each-state/, accessed April 3, 2015.

30. Michael Hurwitz, "The Impact of Legacy Status on Undergraduate Admissions at Elite Colleges and Universities," *Economics of Education Review* 30, no. 3 (2011): 480–492.

31. Joseph Schumpeter, *Capitalism, Socialism, and Democracy*, 3rd ed. (New York: Harper and Row, 1950; originally published in 1942), pp. 156–163. For a discussion of why his prediction about the link between the erosion of family and the decline of capitalism was inaccurate, see Neil Gilbert, *A Mother's Work: How Feminism, the Market and Policy Shape Family Life* (New Haven, CT: Yale University Press, 2008), pp. 52–59.

32. Karl Marx and Friedrich Engels, "The Communist Manifesto," in Lewis Feuer, ed., *Marx and Engels: Basic Writings on Politics and Philosophy* (New York: Anchor Books, 1959), p. 25.

33. Mayo notes that the campaign against family life was a temporary episode. H. B. Mayo, *Democracy and Marxism* (New York: Oxford University Press, 1955), p. 234.

34. Jing Guo and Neil Gilbert, "Welfare State Regimes and Family Policy: A Longitudinal Analysis," *International Journal of Social Welfare* (October 2007): 307–313; Neil Gilbert, op. cit.

35. Gosta Esping-Andersen, *Social Foundations of Postindustrial Economies* (Oxford: Oxford University Press, 1999).

36. Gregory Clark, *The Son Also Rises: Surnames and the History of Social Mobility* (Princeton, NJ: Princeton University Press, 2014 [Kindle edition]), p. 43. Clark notes that Sweden's formal guild of noble families—the Riddarhurset—became a private institution in 2003, which lobbies on behalf of its members. Only men vote in the Riddarhurset, and titles are passed down through their sons.

37. The Names Adoption Act of 1901 prohibited anyone else from adopting the surnames of the families enrolled in the House of Nobility.

38. Clark, op. cit., p. 36.

39. Clark, op. cit., p. 135.

40. He contrasts the luck of endowment with the more transient "market luck." Gary Becker, *A Treatise on the Family* (Cambridge, MA: Harvard University Press, 1981).

41. Clark, op. cit., p. 15.

42. Francis Galton, "Regression Towards Mediocrity in Hereditary Stature," *The Journal of the Anthropological Institute of Great Britain and Ireland* 15 (1886), p. 253.

43. A number of works reflect this favorable reading of the Perry Preschool experience, including David Kirp, *The Sandbox Investment* (Cambridge, MA: Harvard University Press, 2007); James J. Heckman, Seong Hyeok Moon, Rodrigo Pinto, Peter A. Savelyev, and Adam Yavitz, "The Rate of Return to the High/Scope Perry Preschool Program," *IZA Discussion Paper No. 4533*, Bonn, Germany (October 2009); Lawrence Schweinhart, Helen Barnes, and David Weikart, *Significant Benefits: The High-Scope Perry Preschool Study Through Age 27* (Ypsilanti, MI: High/Scope Press, 1993); Lawrence Schweinhart, Jeanne Montie, Zongping Xiang, W. Steven Barnett, Clive Belfield, and Milagros Nores, *Lifetime Effects: The High/Scope Perry Preschool Study Through Age 40* (Ypsilanti, MI: High/Scope Press, 2005).

44. For a critical reading of the evidence, see Edward Zigler, "Formal Schooling for Four-Year-Olds? No." *American Psychologist* 42, no. 3 (1987): 254–260; Bruce Fuller, *Standardized Childhood: The Political and Cultural Struggle over Early Education* (Stanford, CA: Stanford University Press, 2007); Robinson G. Hollister, "The Role of Random Assignment in Social Policy Research," *Journal of Policy Analysis and Management* 27, no. 2 (2008): 402–409; Herman H. Spitz, "Were Children Randomly Assigned in the Perry Preschool Project?" *American Psychologist* 48, no. 8 (August 1993): 915; Lynn A. Karoly, Peter W. Greenwood, Susan S. Everingham, Jill Hoube, M. Rebecca Kilburn, C. Peter Rydell, Matthew Sanders, and James Chisea, *Investing in Our Children: What We Know and Don't Know About the Costs and Benefits of Early Childhood Interventions* (Santa Monica, CA: RAND, 1998), pp. 97–98; Douglas J. Besharov, Peter Germanis, Caeli A. Higney, and Douglas M. Call, *Assessing the Evaluations of Early Childhood Education Programs*, University of Maryland, School of Public Policy, Welfare Reform Academy (September 2011), http://www.welfareacademy.org/pubs/early_education/

45. Lawrence Schweinhart, Helen Barnes, and David Weikart, *Significant Benefits: The High-Scope Perry Preschool Study Through Age 27* (Ypsilanti, MI: High/Scope Press, 1993). This causal model was later revised to include differences in commitment to schooling and

educational achievement at age 14. The latter is based on reading, arithmetic, and language tests administered from ages 7 to 14. In the twenty tests taken between ages 7 and 11, a significant difference between the groups appeared only one time. At age 14, however, significant differences appeared on all three tests, despite no differences in the measures of IQ.

46. Although the discrepancy between working and stay-at-home mothers was the only statistically significant difference in the demographic characteristics of the experimental and control group, it is not a trivial matter.

47. Edward Zigler and Victoria Seitz, "Invited Comments on Significant Benefits of the High/Scope Perry PreSchool Study Through Age 27," in Lawrence Schweinhart, Helen Barnes, and David Weikart, *Significant Benefits: The High-Scope Perry Preschool Study Through Age 27* (Ypsilanti, MI: High/Scope Press, 1993), p. 248. For those who may not be familiar with his work, Zigler is an internationally renowned authority on child development and the founding director of the Edward Zigler Center in Child Development and Social Policy at the Yale University School of Medicine.

48. The program and its results are described in various materials on the Abecedarian Project website, http://abc.fpg.unc.edu/, accessed May 9, 2015.

49. The program group was also more likely to attend a four-year college. Significant differences did not appear on other outcomes such as self-reported criminal behavior and employment rates. Frances A. Campbell, Elizabeth P. Pungello, Shari Miller-Johnson, Margaret Burchinal, and Craig T. Ramey, "The Development of Cognitive and Academic Abilities: Growth Curves from an Early Childhood Educational Experiment," *Developmental Psychology* 37, no. 2 (March 2001), p. 234; Craig T. Ramey, Frances A. Campbell, Margaret Burchinal, Martie L. Skinner, David M. Gardner, and Sharon L. Ramey, "Persistent Effects of Early Childhood Education on High-Risk Children and Their Mothers," *Applied Developmental Science* 4, no. 1 (January 2000); Francis Campbell, Craig T. Ramey, Elizabeth Pungello, Joseph Sparling, and Shari Miller-Johnson, "Early Childhood Education: Young Adult Outcomes from the Abecedarian Project," *Applied Developmental Science* 6, no. 1 (2002): 42–57. Douglas J. Besharov, Peter Germanis, Caeli A. Higney, and Douglas M. Call, op. cit.

50. The Perry Preschool program showed no significant difference in earnings between the program and nonprogram group at age 40. Schweinhart, Montie, Xiang, Barnett, Belfield, and Nores, op. cit., p. 163.

51. According to Becker, an efficient marriage market is characterized by positive assortative mating wherein "high quality men are matched with high quality women and low quality men with low quality women." Gary Becker, op. cit., p. 108.

52. Charles Murray, *Coming Apart: The State of White America, 1960–2000* (New York: Crown Forum, 2012).

53. Douglas Almond and Janet Currie, "Killing Me Softly: The Fetal Origins Hypothesis," *Journal of Economic Perspectives* 25, no. 3 (2011): 153–172.

Chapter 7

1. Gregory Clark, *The Son Also Rises: Surnames and the History of Social Mobility* (Princeton, NJ: Princeton University Press, 2014 [Kindle edition]).

2. Michael Young, *The Rise of Meritocracy 1870–2033: An Essay on Education and Equality* (New York: Penguin Books, 1961), p. 181.

3. As protests erupt amid rising hostility led by feminists, the final footnote informs the reader that our fictional narrator was killed during one of the demonstrations. Ibid.

4. Joesph Stiglitz, *The Price of Inequality* (New York: Penguin Books, 2012), p. 22. A similar position is expressed by John Roemer, "Equal Opportunity and Intergenerational Mobility: Going Beyond Intergenerational Transition Matrices," in Miles Corak, ed., *Generational Income Mobility in North America and Europe* (Cambridge: Cambridge University Press, 2004), p. 49.

5. Irwin Garfinkel, Lee Rainwater, and Timothy Smeeding, *Wealth and Welfare States: Is America A Laggard or Leader?* (New York: Oxford University Press, 2010), p. 87.

6. Short of genetic engineering in the womb, perhaps the most extreme form of equal opportunity would involve taking all infants from their parents at birth and randomly assigning them to be raised in publicly operated facilities that provided roughly equivalent care and education. But even measures this radical would not cancel all inherited characteristics.

7. Jeremy Greenwood, Nezih Guner, Georgi Kocharkov, and Cezar Santos, "Marry Your Like: Assortative Mating and Income Inequality," *American Economic Review* 104, no. 5 (May 2014): 348–353.

8. Thomas Luke Spreen, "Recent College Graduates in the U.S. Labor Force: Data from the Current Population Survey," *Monthly Labor Review* (February 2013):3–13.

9. Charles Murray, *Coming Apart: The State of White America: 1960–2010* (New York: Crown Forum, 2012), p. 64.

10. Diana B. Elliott, Kristy Krivickas, Matthew W. Brault, and Rose M. Kreider, "Historical Marriage Trends from 1890–2010: A Focus on Race Differences." Presented at the annual meetings of the Population Association of America, San Francisco, CA, May 3–5, 2012. https://www.census.gov/hhes/socdemo/marriage/data/acs/ElliottetalPAA2012presentation.pdf, accessed May 23, 2015.

11. OECD, *Divided We Stand: Why Inequality Keeps Rising* (Paris: OECD, 2011), p. 33.

12. Richard Hofstadter, *Social Darwinism in American Thought* (Boston: Beacon Press, 1962), p. 167.

13. Daniel J. Benjamin, David Cesarini, Christopher F. Chabris, Edward L. Glaeser, David I. Laibson, Vilmundur Guðnason, Tamara B. Harris, Lenore J. Launer, Shaun Purcell, Albert Vernon Smith, Magnus Johannesson, Patrik K. E. Magnusson, Jonathan P. Beauchamp, Nicholas A. Christakis, Craig S. Atwood, Benjamin Hebert, Jeremy Freese, Robert M. Hauser, Taissa S. Hauser, Alexander Grankvist, Christina M. Hultman, and Paul Lichtenstein, "The Promises and Pitfalls of Genoeconomics," *Annual Review of Economics* 4 (September 2012): 627–662. http://www.annualreviews.org/doi/full/10.1146/annurev-economics-080511-110939, accessed May 25, 2015, Ibid., p. 628.

14. Steven Pinker, *The Blank Slate: The Modern Denial of Human Nature* (New York: Penguin Books, 2003), p. 3.

15. The .626 correlation in the study of Swedish twins, for example, is a moderate relationship, which explains 39 percent of variability in incomes between identical twins, leaving 61 percent due to influences other than genetic endowment.

16. Dan Froomkin, "Social Immobility: Climbing The Economic Ladder Is Harder in the U.S. Than in Most European Countries," *Huffington Post*, http://www.huffingtonpost.com/2010/03/17/social-immobility-climbin_n_501788.html, September 21, 2010;

Timothy Noah, "Sorry Conservatives—America's Mobility Problem Is Real," *MSNBC Online* http://www.msnbc.com/msnbc/us-social-mobility-problem, April 29, 2014; Jason DeParle, "Harder for Americans to Rise from Economy's Lower Rungs," *The New York Times*, January 5, 2012, A1; President Obama, "Remarks by the President on Economic Mobility," December 4, 2013, The White House, Office of the Press Secretary, https://www.whitehouse.gov/the-press-office/2013/12/04/remarks-president-economic-mobility, accessed March 17, 2015; Rana Foroohar, "What Ever Happened to Upward Mobility," *Time Magazine* 34, no. 3 (November 14, 2011); Alan B. Krueger, "The Rise and Consequences of Inequality in the United States," presented at the Center for American Progress (January 12, 2012).

17. OECD, *Economic Policy Reforms: Going for Growth* (Paris: OECD, 2010), p. 182; Garfinkel, Rainwater, and Smeeding, op. cit.

18. For example, the analysis of intergenerational elasticity usually involves the logarithmic transformation of positively skewed income data, which restores the symmetry of a more normal distribution. However, this transformation omits cases with zero income, which tends to overstate mobility because children with zero income are more likely to have come from low-income families. An alternative to the logarithmic transformation, which also compresses the skewed distribution, involves a rank-rank specification. This approach compares the percentile rank of parents based on the distribution of parental incomes for a cohort of children with the percentile rank of their children's income relative to the other children in their cohort. Raj Chetty, Nathaniel Hendren, Patrick Kline, and Emmanuel Saez, "Where Is the Land of Opportunity? The Geography of Intergenerational Mobility in the United States," National Bureau of Economic Research Working Paper No. 19843 (January 2014); Miles Corak, "Do Poor Children Become Poor Adults? Lessons from a Cross Country Comparison of Generational Earnings Mobility," IZA Discussion Paper No. 1993 (March 2006).

19. Corak, op. cit. The mean for the US studies was .37.

20. Nathan D. Grawe, "Life Cycle Bias in the Estimation of Intergenerational Earnings Persistence," Family and Labour Studies, Analytic Studies Branch Research Paper No. 207 (Ottawa: Statistics Canada, 2003).

21. Ibid. p. 11.

22. Using the National Longitudinal Survey to analyze the relation between parent–child incomes in the United States, Jantti and his colleagues found a correlation of .50, denoting a very low rate of mobility that was in sharp contrast to the .154 correlation reported in Grawe's analysis of the National Longitudinal Survey data. See Markus Jantti, Knut Roed, Robin Naylor, Anders Bjorklund, Bernt Bratsberg, Oddbjorn Raaum, Eva Osterbacka, and Tor Eriksson, "American Exceptionalism in a New Light: A Comparison of Intergenerational Earnings Mobility in the Nordic Countries, the United Kingdom, and the United States," IZA Discussion Paper No. 1938 (January 2006).

23. The additional calculations involved a multiple regression analysis estimating the extent to which the elasticity coefficients in twenty-two studies were related to three independent variables: the father's age, the number of years used to average incomes, and whether the study method involved ordinary least squares or instrumental variable regression. Specifying several reasonable values for each of the independent variables, the findings predicted elasticity rates that were in the range of .47. With a sample of only twenty-two cases, however, the ratio of sample size to the number of independent

variables in this analysis did not meet the conventional standard recommended to obtain a reliable equation. For a discussion of recommended sample sizes, see J. Stevens, *Applied Multivariate Statistics for the Social Sciences* (Hillsdale, NJ: Lawrence Erlbaum Associates, 1992); B. Tabachnick and L. Fidell, *Using Multivariate Statistics* (Boston: Allyn and Bacon, 2001).

24. Corak, op. cit., p. 8.

25. Markus Jäntti and Stephen P. Jenkins, "Income Mobility," IZA Discussion Paper No. 7730, November 2013, p. 189 (forthcoming in A. B. Atkinson and F. Bourguignon, *Handbook of Income Distribution*, Elsevier-North Holland).

26. Dan Froomkin, op. cit.; Timothy Noah, op. cit.; Jason DeParle, op. cit.; President Obama, op. cit; Rana Foroohar, op. cit.; Krueger, op. cit.; Stiglitz, op. cit.; Garfinkel, Rainwater, and Smeeding, op. cit.

27. According to the Harvard-Berkeley findings, the intergenerational income elasticity for the United States was .217 compared to the rate of .47 reported in Corak's comparative study. (Recall that the correlation between father's and son's incomes is inversely related to the degree of mobility; i.e., lower correlations signify higher mobility.) Raj Chetty, Nathaniel Hendren, Patrick Kline, Emmanuel Saez, and Nicholas Turner, "Is the United States Still a Land of Opportunity? Recent Trends in Intergenerational Mobility," National Bureau of Economic Research Working Paper No. 19844 (January 2014).Chetty and Saez were each recipients of the prestigious John Bates Clark Medal and the MacArthur fellowship.

28. Miles Corak, "Social Mobility and Social Institutions in Comparison: Australia, Canada, the United Kingdom, the United States," Sutton Trust/ Carnegie Foundation Seminar on Social Mobility, London May 21/22, 2012. https://milescorak.files.wordpress. com/2012/05/social_mobility_summit_v3.pdf

29. Neil Gilbert and Harry Specht, *Dimensions of Social Welfare Policy* (Englewood Cliffs, NJ: Prentice Hall, 1974), p.71, p.82.

30. Putting academic culture in his crosshairs, Joseph Epstein nails the putdown of "popularizers" as pure envy. But that was a decade ago, before the explosion of blogs, tweets, and Facebook. Joseph Epstein, *Envy* (New York: Oxford University Press, 2003), p. 33.

31. Noam Scheiber, "Academics Seek a Big Splash," *The New York Times*, May 31, 2015.

32. Christopher Jencks and Laura Tach, "Would Equal Opportunity Mean More Mobility?" KSG Working Paper No. RWP05-037 (May 2005), p. 2. http://papers.ssrn.com/ sol3/papers.cfm?abstract_id=779507

33. Gosta Esping-Andersen, "Unequal Opportunities and Social Inheritance." A slightly revised version of a chapter, authored by Esping-Andersen, in Corak, M., ed., *The Dynamics of Intergenerational Income Mobility* (Cambridge: Cambridge University Press, forthcoming) http://www.policy-network.net/article_documents/41.DOC, accessed June 3, 2015.

34. Messaoud Hammouya, "Statistics on Public Sector Employment: Methodology, Structure and Trends," Working Paper, International Labour Organization, Geneva, 1999. http://www.ilo.org/public/english/bureau/stat/download/wp_pse_e.pdf

35. Chetty, Hendren, Kline, Saez and Turner, op.cit. For the US cohort born in 1985 they found the rate of intergenerational mobility was .265 calculated according to the rank-based measure and .217 according to the log of income measure. Both of these rates

represent a higher degree of mobility than Corak's .27 estimate for Sweden. Corak, "Do Poor Children Become Poor Adults?" op.cit.

36. Julia Isaacs, *Economic Mobility of Families Across Generations* (Washington, D.C.: The Brookings Institution, 2007). These were conservative estimates because the measure of income did not include the value of fringe benefits, food stamps, and subsidized housing. The author reports that some of the increase in family income was related to more working wives in the current generation. http://www.brookings.edu/~/media/research/files/papers/2007/11/generations%20isaacs/11_generations_isaacs.pdf, accessed June 4, 2015.

37. Chetty, Hendren, Kline, Saez, and Turner, op. cit. This study reports a higher probability of moving from the bottom to the top quintile than the Brookings study, which relies on data from a sample of 2,367 individuals in the Panel Study of Income Dynamics. The Chetty et al. study is based on a sample of about 50 million people and is more recent.

38. Pew Research Center, *Second-Generation Americans: A Portrait of the Adult Children of Immigrants* (Washington, D.C.: Pew Research Center, 2013). http://www.pew-socialtrends.org/files/2013/02/FINAL_immigrant_generations_report_2-7-13.pdf

39. Ibid. Both regions include more than a dozen countries, injecting a considerable degree of cultural diversity into these groups. And second-generation immigrants have an intermarriage rate of 17 percent, further enriching the ethnic-cultural mix.

40. Rakesh Kochhar, "A Global Middle Class Is More Promise Than Reality" (Washington, D.C: Pew Research Center, 2105). http://www.pewglobal.org/2015/07/08/a-global-middle-class-is-more-promise-than-reality/

Chapter 8

1. See, for example, Irwin Garfinkel, "Economic Security for Children: From Means Testing and Bifurcation to Universality," in Irwin Garfinkel et al. (eds.), *Social Policies for Children* (Washington, D.C.: The Brookings Institution, 1996), pp. 33–82; Sheila B. Kamerman and Alfred J. Kahn, "Universalism and Income Testing in Family Policy," *Social Work* (July–August 1987): 277–280; Mike Reddin, "Universality versus Selectivity," *The Political Quarterly* (January/March 1969): 13–20.

2. Neil Gilbert and Paul Terrell, *Dimensions of Social Welfare Policy*, 8th ed. (Boston: Pearson, 2013).

3. John Micklethwait and Adrian Wooldridge, "The State of the State: Global Contest for the Future of Government," *Foreign Affairs* 93, no. 3 (July/August 2014): 118–132.

4. World Bank, *World Development Report 1990: Poverty* (Washington, D.C.: World Bank, 1990), p. 3; OECD, *Divided We Stand. Why Inequality Is Rising* (Paris: OECD, 2011).

5. Sune Sunesson, Staffan Blomberg, Per Gunnar Edebalk, Lars Harrysson, Jan Magnusson, Anna Meeuwisse, Jan Petersson, and Tapio Salonen, "The Flight from Universalism," *European Journal of Social Work* 1, no. 1 (1998): 19–29; Neil Gilbert, *Transformation of the Welfare State: The Silent Surrender of Public Responsibility* (New York: Oxford University Press, 2002); Sven Hort, "From a Generous to a Stingy Welfare State? Sweden's Approach to Targeting," in Neil Gilbert, ed., *Targeting Social Benefits* (New Brunswick, NJ: Transaction Publishers, 2001); Andreas Bergh,

"The Universal Welfare State: Theory and the Case of Sweden," *Political Studies* 25 (2004): 745–766.

6. Robert Goodin and Julian LeGrand, *Not Only the Poor: The Middle Classes and the Welfare State* (London: Unwin Hyman, 1987), p. 215.

7. Bo Rothstein, "The Universal Welfare State as a Social Dilemma," manuscript prepared for Mark Van Vugt, Mark Snyder, Tom Tyler, and Anders Biel, *Collective Problems in Modern Societies: Dilemmas and Solutions* (Routledge, forthcoming), p. 8.

8. This is one way that universal provisions can be designed to disproportionately benefit the poor, an approach sometimes referred to as "targeting within universalism." See, for example, Theda Skocpol, "Targeting Within Universalism: Politically Viable Policies to Combat Poverty in the United States," in Christopher Jencks and Paul Peterson, eds., *The Urban Underclass* (Washington, D.C.: The Brookings Institution, 1991), pp. 411–436.

9. Rothstein, op. cit., p. 9.

10. According to a popular typology of welfare state regimes, the principle of universalism is strongly represented in the Scandinavian countries. See Gosta Esping-Andersen, *Three Worlds of Welfare Capitalism* (Princeton, NJ: Princeton University Press, 1990).

11. Irving Kristol, "Taxes, Poverty and Equality," *The Public Interest* 37 (Fall 1974), p. 27.

12. Harold Wilensky, *The Welfare State and Equality* (Berkeley: University of California Press, 1975).

13. Wilensky described the United States as "moving toward the welfare state with ill grace, carping and complaining all the way." Ibid., p. 32.

14. Many comparative welfare state studies in the 1990s and early 2000s at some point in the analysis ranked countries according to their direct social expenditures as percent of GDP, which invariably placed the United States on the bottom of the list. For example, see Anton Hemerijck, "The Self-Transformation of European Social Model(s)," in Gosta Esping-Andersen, Duncan Gallie, Anton Hemerijck, and John Myles, *Why We Need a New Welfare State* (New York: Oxford University Press, 2002); Robert Goodin, Bruce Headey, Ruud Muffels, and Henk-Jan Drive, *The Real Worlds of Welfare Capitalism* (Cambridge: Cambridge University Press, 1999); A. Hicks and D. Swank, " Politics, Institutions, and Welfare Spending in Industrialized Countries," *American Political Science Review* 86 (1992): 658–674; Robert Moroney, *Social Policy and Social Work: Critical Essays on the Welfare State* (New York: Aldine de Gruyter, 1991); Pete Alcock, "The Comparative Context," in Pete Alcock and Gary Craig, eds., *International Social Policy* (Houndmills, Basingstoke: Palgrave, 2001); Jon Olaskoaga, Ricardo Alaez-Aller and Pablo Diaz-De-Basurto-Uraga, "Beyond Welfare Effort in the Measuring of Welfare States," *Journal of Comparative Policy Analysis* (2013): 1–14.

15. Spencer Rich, "How Much for Social Welfare, Health?" *The Washington Post*, February 19, 1990. https://www.washingtonpost.com/archive/politics/1990/02/19/how-much-for-social-welfare-health/c28d4bb4-f718-4bc1-b3bf-8df6d84ce1cc/

16. *The New York Times*, "The Less-Than-Generous State," August 16, 2007, A20.

17. Ive Marx, Brian Nolan, and Javier Olivera, "The Welfare State and Anti-Poverty Policy in Rich Countries," Institute for the Study of Labor (IZA) Discussion Paper No. 8154 April 2014 (Bonn, Germany: IZA, 2014).

18. Neil Gilbert, "The Least Generous Welfare State? A Case of Blind Empiricism," *Journal of Comparative Policy Analysis* 11, no. 3 (2009): 355–376.

19. Neil Gilbert and Ailee Moon, "Analyzing Welfare Effort: An Appraisal of Comparative Methods," *Journal of Policy Analysis and Management* 7, no. 2 (1988): 326–340. For other calculations of social spending see, Richard Clayton and Jonas Pontusson, "Welfare State Retrenchment Revisited: Entitlement Cuts, Public Sector Restructuring and Inegalitarian Trends in Advanced Capitalist Societies," *World Politics* 51 (1998): 67–98 and Francis Castles, *The Future of the Welfare State: Crisis and Myths* (New York: Oxford University Press, 2004).

20. Neil Gilbert and Barbara Gilbert, *The Enabling State: Modern Welfare Capitalism in America* (New York: Oxford University Press, 1989). This is a conservative estimate based on the $163 billion in tax preferences most directly related to social welfare.

21. Arthur Pigou, *Economics of Welfare* (London: MacMillan, 1920).

22. Irving Kristol, *Two Cheers for Capitalism* (New York: Basic Books, 1978), p. 194.

23. Richard Goode, "The Economic Definition of Income," in Joseph Pechman, ed., *Comprehensive Income Taxation* (Washington, D.C.: The Brookings Institution, 1977), pp. 1–36. Tax expenditures first gained formal recognition in the Congressional Budget Act of 1974.

24. Willem Adema, "Net Social Expenditure." Labour Market and Social Policy—Occasional Papers No. 39 (Paris: OECD, 1999).

25. Willem Adema, Marcel Einerhand, Bengt Eklind, Jorgen Lotz, and Mark Pearson, "Net Public Social Expenditure," Labour Market and Social Policy Occasional Papers No. 19 (Paris: OECD, 1996).

26. Thus, for example, Australia, Ireland, the United Kingdom, and the United States tax public transfers lightly compared to Denmark, Finland, the Netherlands, and Sweden, where tax levies exceed 5 percent of GDP. Willem Adema, "Revisiting Real Social Spending Across Countries: A Brief Note," *OECD Economic Studies No. 30, 2000/I* (Paris: OECD, 2000).

27. Willem Adema, "Net Social Expenditure," OECD Labour Market and Social Policy Occasional Papers, No. 39 (Paris: OECD, 1999). http://dx.doi.org/10.1787/446511258155

28. Bagehot, "George Osborne's sad triumph," *The Economist* (July 11, 2015), p. 52.

29. Gilbert, "The Least Generous Welfare State," op. cit.

30. Richard Freeman, *America Works: Critical Thoughts on the Exceptional U.S. Labor Market* (New York: Russell Sage Foundation, 2007).

31. OECD, *Economic Surveys: The Netherlands* (Paris: OECD, 1991).

32. David Armor and Sonia Sousa, "Restoring a True Safety Net," *National Affairs* 13 (Fall 2012): 3–28.

33. Allocating social welfare benefits according to financial need includes means testing, which takes the applicant's income and wealth into consideration, and income testing, a milder form that only counts income. In the discussion of selectivity, these terms are used interchangeably.

34. Richard Titmuss, *Commitment to Welfare* (New York: Pantheon Books, 1968), p. 129.

35. Wim Van Oorschot, "Targeting Welfare: On the Functions and Dysfunctions of Meanstesting in Social Policy," in *World Poverty: New Policies to Defeat an Old Enemy*, edited by P. Townsend and D. Gordo (Bristol, UK: The Policy Press 2002); Howard Karger and David Stoesz, *American Social Welfare Policy* (Boston: Allyn and Bacon, 2010); Rothstein, op. cit.

36. Joe Handler and Ellen Hollingsworth, "How Obnoxious Is the 'Obnoxious Means Test'? The View of AFDC Recipients," Institute for Research on Poverty Discussion Paper (University of Wisconsin, Madison), January 1969; Richard Pomeroy and Harold Yahr, in collaboration with Lawrence Podell, *Studies in Public Welfare: Effects of Eligibility Investigation on Welfare Clients* (New York: Center for the Study of Urban Problems, City University of New York, 1968); Martha Ozawa, "Impact of SSI on the Aged and Disabled Poor," *Social Work Research and Abstracts* 14 (Fall 1978): 3–10.

37. Ben Baumberg, Kate Bell, and Declan Gaffney, *Benefits Stigma in Britain* (London: Elizabeth Finn Care/Turn2us, 2012). https://www.turn2us.org.uk/T2UWebsite/media/Documents/Benefits-Stigma-in-Britain.pdf

38. For a detailed analysis of the expansion of eligibility into the middle class, see David Armor and Sonia Sousa, "Restoring a True Safety Net," *National Affairs* 13 (Fall 2012): 3–28.

39. Robert A. Moffitt, "The Temporary Assistance for Needy Families Program," in Robert Moffitt, ed., *Means-Tested Transfer Programs in the United States* (Chicago: University of Chicago Press, 2003), pp. 291–306. By 1997, he notes that forty states had increased the amount of income disregards.

40. Marx, Nola, and Olivera, op. cit.

41. Gilbert, *Transformation of the Welfare State*, op. cit., p. 67.

42. Robert Sherwood, *Roosevelt and Hopkins: An Intimate History* (New York: Grosset and Dunlap 1948), p. 102.

43. David Kirp, *The Sandbox Investment* (Cambridge, MA: Harvard University Press, 2007), p. 88.

44. Richard Titmuss, *Commitment to Welfare* (New York: Pantheon Books, 1968), p. 196.

45. Richard Titmuss, *Social Policy*, Brian Abel-Smith and Kay Titmuss, eds. (London: Allen and Unwin, 1974), p. 151.

46. Walter Korpi and Joakim Palme, "The Paradox of Redistribution and Strategies of Equality: Welfare State Institutions, Inequality and Poverty in the Western Countries," *American Sociological Review* 63 (October 1998): 661–687.

47. Lane Kenworthy, *Progress for the Poor* (New York: Oxford University Press, 2011), p. 62. From the 1980–2005 period, comparable data were available for only ten of the eleven countries in the Korpi and Palme study.

48. Christopher Howard, *The Welfare State Nobody Knows* (Princeton, NJ: Princeton University Press, 2007).

49. Martin Gilens, *Affluence and Influence: Economic Inequality and Political Power in America* (Princeton, NJ: Princeton University Press [Kindle edition], 2012).

50. Ive Marx, Lina Salanauskaite, and Gerlinde Verbist, "The Paradox of Redistribution Revisited: And That It May Rest in Peace?" IZA Discussion Paper No. 7414 (Bonn, Germany: Institute for the Study of Labor, 2013), p. 34. They suggest that the significant difference between their findings and those of the 1985 study reflect in part changes that had occurred over the last two decades as well as the benefits of additional data from the larger sample of countries in their study.

51. Contrary to the paradox of redistribution, a study of thirty-seven countries, including twenty rich democracies, reports a significant negative relationship between poverty and low-income targeting. That is, the more a country concentrates transfer on

low-income household, the lower its level of poverty. This study distinguishes among low-income targeting, high-income targeting, and universalism. David Brady and Amie Bostic, "Paradoxes of Social Policy: Welfare Transfers, Relative Poverty, and Redistribution Preferences," *American Sociological Review* 80, no. 2 (2015): 268–298.

52. Axel Pedersen, "The Welfare State and Inequality: Still No Answers to the Big Questions," Luxembourg Income Study Working Paper Series Working Paper No. 109 (June 1994).

53. Peter Ferrara, "Transforming Social Security," *National Affairs* 23 (Summer 2015): 85–99. This estimate is based on them having invested in an indexed portfolio of 90 percent large cap and 10 percent small cap stocks, earning the returns reported since 1965.

54. Peter Whiteford, "Transfer Issues and Directions for Reform: Australian Transfer Policy in Comparative Perspective," Chapter 3, Melbourne Institute, ed., *Australia's Future Tax and Transfer Policy Conference, Proceedings*, Melbourne, Australia.

55. Peter Whiteford, "What Difference Does Government Make? Measuring Redistribution in a Comparative Perspective" in Andrew Podger and Dennis Trewin, eds., *Measuring and Promoting Wellbeing: How Important Is Economic Growth?* (Canberra: Australian National University Press, 2014), p. 512.

56. Pedersen, op. cit. Another approach that has been suggested involves reclassifying public pensions as a delayed drawdown on private savings, which are represented by the Social Security contributions. The calculations here involve a number of issues, including the fact that unlike private insurance, public pension benefits are often progressive and do not match the tax contributions. See, for example, David Jesuit and Vincent Mahler, "Comparing Government Distribution Across Countries: The Problem of Second-Order Effects," Luxembourg Income Study Working Paper No. 546 (August 2010).

Chapter 9

1. Edward Bellamy, *Looking Backward* (New York: New American Library of World Literature, 1960, originally published 1888), p. 73. ". . . for the nation guarantees the nurture, education and comfortable maintenance of every citizen from the cradle to the grave."

2. Ross Douthat, "The Party of Julia," *The New York Times*, May 5, 2012.

3. In talking about two-earner families with children, I am referring here to heterosexual couples where the mother is the secondary earner, which is usually the case. However, about one-third of wives in two-earner households earned more than their husbands in 2004, in which cases the limited financial benefits of the secondary earner would refer to the fathers' employment. With the legalization of gay marriage, the number of two-earner homosexual couples with children is increasing and, needless to say, faces the same trade-offs regarding care and household production as heterosexual couples.

4. Managing the imposition of this discipline is not always pleasant, as suggested in the title of the popular work by Robert Sutton, *The No Asshole Rule: How to Build a Civilized Workplace and Surviving One That Isn't* (New York: Warner Business Books, 2007).

5. US Census Bureau, Annual Retail Trade Survey—2013: Sales (1992–2013). http://www.census.gov/retail/index.html, accessed January 28, 2015.

6. Gary Becker, *A Treatise on the Family* (Cambridge, MA: Harvard University Press, 1981), p. 303; Stein Ringen, *What Is Democracy For? On Freedom and Moral Government* (Princeton, NJ: Princeton University Press, 2007).

7. Salary.Com, " What Is a Mom's Work Worth?" http://www.salary.com/mom-paycheck/ accessed January 10, 2015.

8. Arlie Hoschild with Anne Machung, *The Second Shift: Working Parents and the Revolution at Home* (New York: Viking, 1989).

9. Liana Sayer, Philip Cohen, and Lynne Casper, *Men, Women and Work* (New York: Russell Sage Foundation, 2004).

10. US Department of Labor, Bureau of Labor Statistics, *Women's Earnings in California 2013*, http://www.bls.gov/regions/west/news-release/womensearnings_california.htm, accessed April 14, 2014.

11. The Child Welfare League of America recommends staff–child ratios of 1:3 for children under the age of three. Child Welfare League of America, *Standards for Day Care Service* (New York: Child Welfare League of America, 1984). The National Association for the Education of Young Children criteria for accreditation of child care centers specify adult–child ratios of 1:3 or 1:4 for children under the age of two and 1:4 through 1:6 for children between the ages of two and three. See Suzanne Helbrum and Carollee Howes, "Child Care Cost and Quality," *The Future of Children* 6, no. 2 (Summer–Fall 1996): 62–81.

12. Voting with their feet, the average of retirement for men in most OECD countries has declined considerably since the 1970s. Between 1970 and 2012, for example, it fell from 67.8 to 59.7 years of age in France, from 64.1 to 59.6 in Belgium, and from 66.8 to 61.9 in Austria. http://www.oecd.org/els/public-pensions/ageingandemploymentpolicies-statisticsonaverageeffectiveageofretirement.htm, accessed October 8, 2015.

13. Jorma Sipila, Katja Repo, and Tapio Rissanen, eds., *Cash for Childcare: The Consequences for Caring Mothers* (Cheltenham, UK: Edgar Elgar 2010); Jorma Sipila and Johanna Korpinin, "Cash versus Child Care Services in Finland," *Social Policy and Administration* 32, no. 3 (September 1998): 263–277.

14. The prevalent progressive view on this matter is expressed by the Organization for Economic Cooperation and Development's recommendation that social benefits should be arranged so that they "carry the same incentives for both sexes with regard to the division of time between paid employment, domestic duties and leisure." OECD, *The Integration of Women into the Economy* (Paris: OECD, 1985), 141.

15. Gosta Esping-Andersen, "Unequal Opportunities and Social Inheritance." A slightly revised version of a chapter, authored by Esping-Andersen, in Corak, M., ed., *The Dynamics of Intergenerational Income Mobility* (Cambridge: Cambridge University Press, forthcoming). The "cognitive" Gini coefficient was calculated from the International Adult Literacy Survey test scores. His explanation for the differences in this measure of cognitive equality did not consider other factors such as the higher level of cultural homogeneity and lower proportions of first- and second-generation immigrants in the Nordic countries, which might well impact the literacy scores. http://www.policy-network.net/article_documents/41.DOC, accessed June 3, 2015.

16. Sipila, Repo, and Rissanen, op. cit.

17. According to the 2014 Gallop Poll, nearly two-thirds of Americans believe that 50 percent or fewer public school students in this country are receiving a high-quality

education. PDK/Gallop Poll of the Public's Attitudes Towards the Public Schools, *The 2015 PDK/Gallop Poll Report*, http://pdkpoll2015.pdkintl.org/212, accessed October 9, 2015.

18. OECD, Programme For International Student Assessment (PISA), *Results from PISA 2012*. http://www.oecd.org/pisa/keyfindings/PISA-2012-results-US.pdf, accessed October 5, 2015.

19. The "does no harm" refrain is explicitly expressed in three independent reviews of the early research literature on child care: Kriste Moore and Sandra Hofferth, "Women and Their Children," in Ralph Smith, ed., *The Subtle Revolution* (Washington, D.C.: Urban Institute, 1979), pp. 125–158; Barbara Heyns, "The Influence of Parents' Work on Children's School Achievement," in Edward Zigler and Edmund Gordon, eds., *Day Care: Scientific and Social Policy Issues* (Boston: Auburn House, 1982); Jacqueline Lerner and Nancy Galambos, "Child Development and Family Change: The Influences of Maternal Employment on Infants and Toddlers," in Lewis Lipisitt and Carolyn Rovee-Collier, eds., *Advances in Infancy Research*, vol. 4 (Hillsdale, NJ: Ablex, 1986).

20. This research project was the National Institute of Child Health and Human Development's (NICHD) Study of Early Child Care. The following sample of the project publications were all prepared by the NICHD Early Child Care Research Network, "Nonmaternal Care and Family Factors in Early Development: An Overview of the NICHD Study of Early Child Care," *Applied Developmental Psychology* 22 (2001): 457–492; "Early Child Care and Children's Development Prior to School Entry: Results from the NICHD Study of Early Child Care," *American Educational Research Journal* 39, no. 1 (Spring 2002): 133–164; "Does Quality of Care Affect Child Outcomes at Age 4 1/2?" *Developmental Psychology* 39, no. 3 (2003): 451–469; "Child Care Structure, Process, Outcome: Direct and Indirect Effects of Child-Care Quality on Young Children's Development," *Psychological Sciences* 13, no. 3 (May 2002): 199–206; "Does the Amount of Time Spent in Child Care Predict Socioemotional Adjustment during the Transition to Kindergarten?" *Child Development* 74, no. 4 (July–August 2003): 976–994. Also see Jeanne Brooks-Gunn, Wen-Jui Han, and Jane Waldfogel, "Maternal Employment and Child Cognitive Outcomes in the First Three Years of Life: The NICHD Study of Early Child Care," *Child Development* 73, no. 4 (July–August 2002): 1052–1072; Deborah Lowe Vandell, "Early Child Care: The Known and the Unknown," *Merrill-Palmer Quarterly* 50, no. 3 (July 2004): 387–414.

21. Children in regularly scheduled day care more than thirty hours per week during the first four and a half years of life were almost three times more likely to behave aggressively toward other children than children who had been in care less than ten hours per week. NICHD Early Child Care Research Network, "Overview of Early Child Care Effects at 4.5 Years," paper presented at the Early Child Care and Children's Development Prior to School Entry symposium, conducted at the Biennial Meeting of the Society for Research in Child Development, Minneapolis, Minn., April 2001; NICHD Early Child Care Research Network, "Further Exploration of the Detected Effects of Quantity of Early Child Care on Socio-Emotional Adjustment," paper presented at the Early Child Care and Children's Development Prior to School Entry symposium, conducted at the Biennial Meeting of the Society for Research in Child Development, Minneapolis, Minn., April 2001; NICHD Early Child Care Research Network, "Does the Amount of Time Spent in Child Care Predict Socioemotional Adjustment during the Transition to Kindergarten?" *Child Development* 74, no. 4 (July–August 2003): 976–994; for an insightful discussion of

how these findings were interpreted in the media, see Statistical Assessment Service, "The Good News and the Bad News on Daycare: Perspective Matters," *Vital STATS: Newsletter of the Statistical Assessment Service*, June 2001, p. 1.

22. NICHD Early Child Care Research Network, "Early Child Care and Children's Development in the Primary Grades: Follow-Up Results from the NICHD Study of Early Child Care," *American Educational Research Journal* 45 (2005): 537–570.

23. Susanna Loeb, Margaret Bridges, Daphna Bassok, Bruce Fuller, and Russ Rumberger "How Much Is Too Much: The Influence of Preschool Centers on Children's Development Nationwide: Summary," paper presented at the Association for Policy Analysis and Management Meeting, Washington, D.C., November 4, 2005. They report overall gains in academic skills that amounted to an "effect size" of .10 standard deviation (SD) and about .20 SD for the poorest children. For a sense of this magnitude, on a standard IQ scale with a mean of 100 and a standard deviation of 15 points, an effect size of .20 SD would be equivalent to a three-point increase.

24. Although these differences were statistically significant, in both cases the effect sizes (.11) were weak. See Mike Puma, Stephen Bell, Ronna Cook, Camilla Heid, Pam Broene, Frank Jenkins, Andrew Mashburn, and Jason Downer, *Third Grade Follow-up to the Head Start Impact Study Final Report*, OPRE Report No. 2012-45 (Washington, DC: US Department of Health and Human Services, 2012); the first-grade results are examined in detail in US Department of Health and Human Services, Administration for Children and Families, *Head Start Impact Study. Final Report* (January 2010).

25. For example, dual-language learners with the low pretest scores showed a lasting gain in math skills. Howard Bloom and Christina Weiland, "Quantifying Variation in Head Start Effects on Young Children's Cognitive and Socio-Emotional Skills Using Data from the National Head Start Impact Study," Washington D.C.: MDRC, March 2015. http://www.mdrc.org/publication/quantifying-variation-head-start-effects-young-children-s-cognitive-and-socio-emotional, accessed October 10, 2015.

26. David Kirp, "The Benefits of Mixing Rich and Poor," *The New York Times*, May 10, 2014. http://opinionator.blogs.nytimes.com/2014/05/10/the-benefits-of-mixing-rich-and-poor/?_r=0, accessed October 8, 2015.

27. Douglas J. Besharov and Jeffrey S. Morrow, "Nonpoor Children in Head Start: Explanations and Implications," *Journal of Policy Analysis and Management* 26, no. 3 (October 2007): 613–631.

28. National Center for Health Statistics. *Health, United States, 2014: With Special Feature on Adults Aged 55–64*. Hyattsville, MD. 2015. http://www.cdc.gov/nchs/hus.htm, accessed January 28, 2016.

29. C. Eugene Steuerle and Jon M. Bakija, *Retooling Social Security for the 21st Century: Right and Wrong Approaches to Reform* (Washington, D.C. Urban Institute Press, 1994). These figures are based on projections in Table 3.1, p. 41.

30. OASDI Trustees Report, *The 2015 Annual Report of the Board of Trustees of the Federal Old-Age and Survivors Insurance and Federal Disability Insurance Trust Funds* (Washington, D.C.: US Government Printing Office, 2012). Under the Trustees' intermediate assumptions, the ratio will continue falling to 2.1 workers for each beneficiary by 2035. https://www.ssa.gov/OACT/TR//2012/index.html, accessed January 30, 2016.

31. The dependents' allowance for spouses creates serous inequities among two-earner couples with different patterns of income, between two-earner couples and one-earner

couples, and between one-earner married couples and single workers that have the same average lifetime incomes. For details see Neil Gilbert, *Welfare Justice: Restoring Social Equity* (New Haven, CT: Yale University Press, 1995).

32. Benefits are subject to taxation when the adjusted gross income plus half the Social Security benefit exceeds $25,000 for single and $32,000 for married people. For a discussion of these reforms, see C. Eugene Steuerle and Jon Bakija, op. cit.

33. OASDI Trustees Report, op. cit. This figure refers only to old-age pensions; there is also a huge deficit associated with disability benefits.

34. OASDI Trustees Report, op. cit. These are the amounts needed to achieve solvency. They do not include the additional cost of accumulating a target trust fund equal to 100 percent of annual program costs—a buffer that is considered necessary to eliminate the actuarial deficit. To do this would require increasing the payroll tax from 12.40 to 15.18 percent or reducing scheduled benefits by 17.2 percent.

35. Congressional Budget Office, Social Security Policy Options, 2015. https://www.cbo.gov/sites/default/files/114th-congress-2015-2016/reports/51011-SocSecOptions.pdf, accessed February 1, 2016.

36. Andrew Biggs and Sylvester Schieber, "Is There a Retirement Crisis?" *National Affairs* 20 (Summer 2014): 55–75. Biggs was principal deputy commissioner of the Social Security Administration and Schieber former chairman of the Social Security Advisory Board.

37. Treasury Inspector for Tax Administration, *Statistical Trends in Retirement Plans*, August 9, 2010. Although the average value of assets per participant was only $63,000, contributions have been increasing. The overall value of assets in the defined contribution plans increased from $91 billion in 1977 to $3.4 trillion in 2007. https://www.treasury.gov/tigta/auditreports/2010reports/201010097fr.pdf, accessed January 28, 2016.

38. National Research Council. *Assessing the Impact of Severe Economic Recession on the Elderly: Summary of a Workshop.* M. Majmundar, Rapporteur. Steering Committee on the Challenges of Assessing the Impact of Severe Economic Recession on the Elderly. Committee on Population, Division of Behavioral and Social Sciences and Education (Washington, D.C.: The National Academies Press, 2011). This rate of home ownership is up from 68 percent in 1950. US Census Bureau, Historical Census of Housing Tables. https://www.census.gov/hhes/www/housing/census/historic/ownerchar.html, accessed February 3, 2016.

39. The median net worth of those 65 years and older was $170,494 in 2009. Richard Fry, D'Vera Cohn, Gretchen Livingston, and Paul Taylor, *The Rising Age Gap in Economic Well-being* (Washington, D.C.: PEW Research Center), November 7, 2011.

40. Annika Sunden, "The Swedish NDC Pension Reform," *Annuals of Public and Cooperative Economics* 69, no. 4 (December 1998): 571–583.

41. Runo Axelsson, Eskil Wadensjö, and Elisa Baroni, *Annual National Report 2010 Pensions, Health and Long-term Care*, Sweden (May 2010). On behalf of the European Commission DG Employment, Social Affairs and Equal Opportunities http://socialprotection.eu/files_db/1145/asisp_ANR10_Sweden.pdf, accessed February 1, 2016.

42. Bo Könberg, "The New Swedish Pension System—A Fair and Sustainable Model," *Scandinavian Insurance Quarterly* (January 2004), http://nft.nu/en/new-swedish-pension-system-fair-and-sustainable-model, accessed February 1, 2016.

43. K.-G. Scherman, "The Swedish Pension Reform: A Good Model for Other Countries?" *Scandinavian Insurance Quarterly* (2003): 304–318.

44. Jan Hagberg "Shifting the Burden of Risk with NDC: The Swedish Example," paper presented at the 28th Congress of Actuaries, May 28–June 2, 2006, Paris, France. Hagberg is the chief actuary for the insurance organization serving Sweden's labor market parties. http://www.actuaries.org/CTTEES_SOCSEC/Documents/Hagberg.pdf, accessed February 5, 2016.

45. For a review of these various proposals, see Rebecca A. Van Voorhis, "A Socio-Economic Analysis of Three Paths to Social Security Reform," *Journal of Sociology and Social Welfare* XXVI, no. 2 (June 1999): 127–149; William A. Galston, "Why President Bush's 2005 Social Security Initiative Failed, and What It Means for the Future of the Program," NYU John Brademas Center (September, 2007).https://www.nyu.edu/brademas/pdf/publications-legislating-future-galston.pdf, accessed February 1, 2016.

46. Social Security Administration, *Social Security Programs Throughout the World: Europe 2014.* SSA Publication 1311801 (September 2014), https://www.ssa.gov/policy/docs/progdesc/ssptw/2014-2015/europe/sweden.html accessed January 13, 2016.

47. Runo Axelsson, Eskil Wadensjö, and Elisa Baroni, op. cit.

Chapter 10

1. Progressives tend to look for increased spending to expand the Great Society, whereas, as Yuval Levin comments, "conservatives have focused on the size and scope of government, but not on its proper purpose—on yelling stop, but not on where to go instead." Yuval Levin, "Beyond the Welfare State," *National Affairs* (Spring 2011): 7.

2. Douglas Besharov and Neil Gilbert, "Marriage Penaltiers in the Modern Social-Welfare State, *R Street Policy Studies No. 40* (September 2015). The Affordable Care Act provides subsidies for health insurance premiums to households with incomes between 133 and 400 percent of the poverty line.

3. For example, the income eligibility level for the Weatherization Assistance program is 200 percent the federal poverty guideline; the Children's Health Insurance program goes as high as 350 percent of the federal line, Section 8 Housing Choice Vouchers may go to household with income up to 80 percent of the median in their area. See, Karen Spar, *Federal Benefits and Services for People with Low Income: Programs Policy and Spending FY2008–FY2009* (February 15, 2011), Congressional Research Office Report R41625, January 31, 2011.

4. US Census Bureau, *Current Population Survey, Annual Social and Economic Supplement, 1967 to present*, http://www.census.gov/hhes/families/data/adults.html, accessed October 17, 2015.

5. Besharov and Gilbert, op. cit. In five states the eligibility calculation under the Temporary Assistance for Needy Families (TANF) program includes the income of the cohabiter who is not a biological parent.

6. Supplemental data to Congressional Budget Office, *Trends in the Distribution of Household Income Between 1979 and 2007* (October 2011). https://www.cbo.gov/sites/default/files/112th-congress-2011-2012/reports/10-25-HouseholdIncome_0.pdf, accessed October 13, 2015.

7. Neil Gilbert and Barbara Gilbert, *The Enabling State: Modern Welfare Capitalism in America* (New York: Oxford University Press, 1989); Christopher Howard, *The Hidden Welfare State: Social Expenditures and Social Policy in the United States* (Princeton, NJ: Princeton University Press, 1997).

8. Eli Lehrer and Lori Sanders suggest the possibility of replacing almost all existing welfare programs with a single grant. Eli Lehrer and Lori Sanders, "Moving to Work," *National Affairs* 18 (Winter 2014): 21–35.

9. Implementation of the Universal Credit began in October 2013 and is set for completion by 2015. Various issues have been raised in the course of implementation. See, for example, Sam Royston, "Understanding Universal Credit," *Journal of Poverty and Social Justice* 20, no. 1 (February 2012): 69–86; M. Brewer, J. Browne, and W. Jin, "Universal Credit: A Preliminary Analysis of Its Impact on Incomes and Work Incentives," *Fiscal Studies* 33 (2012): 39–71; United Kingdom, Department for Work & Pensions Policy paper: *2010 to 2015 Government Policy: Welfare Reform*, https://www.gov.uk/government/publications/2010-to-2015-government-policy-welfare-reform/2010-to-2015-government-policy-welfare-reform, accessed October 27, 2015.

10. In 2013 the fertility rate in Germany and Italy was 1.39; Spain's rate was 1.27. Eurostat, File: "Total Fertility Rate, 1960–2013 (live births per woman)," http://ec.europa.eu/eurostat/statistics explained/index.php/File:Total_fertility_rate,_1960%E2%80%932013_(live_births_per_woman)_YB15.png

11. Mitch Pearlstein, *Broken Bonds: What Family Fragmentation Means for America's Future* (New York: Rowman & Littlefield, 2014); Besharov and Gilbert, op. cit.

12. Daniel Patrick Moynihan, "How the Great Society 'Destroyed the American Family'" *The Public Interest* 108 (Summer 1992): 56.

13. Mitch Pearlstein, op. cit., p. 127.

14. Justin R. Garcia, Chris Reiber, Sean G. Massey, and Ann M. Merriwether, "Sexual Hookup Culture: A Review," *Review of General Psychology* 16, no. 2 (June 1, 2012): 161–176, http://www.ncbi.nlm.nih.gov/pmc/articles/PMC3613286/, accessed October 24, 2015.

15. Stephanie Coontz, *Marriage, a History: How Love Conquered Marriage* (New York: Penguin Books, 2005), p. 313.

16. Neil Gilbert, *A Mother's Work: How Feminism, the Market and Policy Shape Family Life* (New Haven, CT: Yale University Press, 2008).

17. Two summaries of the evidence are given by David Olds, Testimony Before the Subcommittee on Income Security and Family Support of the House Ways and Means Committee, July 19, 2007; and Deborah Daro, "Home Visitation: The Cornerstone of Effective Early Intervention," Written Testimony on the Early Support for Families Act to the U.S. House of Representatives Ways and Means Committee, June 9, 2009; also see David L. Olds, Charles R. Henderson, Jr, Robert Tatelbaum, and Robert Chamberlin, "Improving the Delivery of Prenatal Care and Outcomes of Pregnancy: A Randomized Trial of Nurse Home Visitation," *Pediatrics* 77 (1986): 16–28; David L. Olds, Charles R. Henderson Jr, and Harriet Kitzman, "Does Prenatal and Infancy Nurse Home Visitation Have Enduring Effects on Qualities of Parental Caregiving and Child Health at 25 to 50 Months of Life?" *Pediatrics* 93, no. 1 (1994): 89–98; David L. Olds, John Eckenrode, Charles R. Henderson Jr., Harriet Kitzman, Jane Powers, Robert Cole, Kimberly Sidora, Pamela Morris, Lisa M. Pettitt, and Dennis Luckey, "Long-Term Effects of Home Visitation on Maternal Life Course and Child Abuse and Neglect: Fifteen-year Follow-up

of a Randomized Trial," *Journal of the American Medical Association* 278, no. 8 (1997): 637–643; David Olds, Charles R. Henderson Jr., Robert Cole, John Eckenrode, Harriet Kitzman, Dennis Luckey, Lisa Pettitt, Kimberly Sidora, Pamela Morris, and Jane Powers, "Long-Term Effects of Nurse Home Visitation on Children's Criminal and Antisocial Behavior: Fifteen-Year Follow-up of a Randomized Controlled Trial," *Journal of the American Medical Association* 280 (1998): 1238–1244; John Eckenrode, Mary Campa, Dennis W. Luckey, Charles R. Henderson Jr., Robert Cole, Harriet Kitzman, Elizabeth Anson, Kimberly Sidora-Arcoleo, Jane Powers, and David L. Olds, "Long-term Effects of Prenatal and Infancy Nurse Home Visitation on the Life Course of Youths 19-Year Follow-up of a Randomized Trial," *Archives of Pediatrics and Adolescent Medicine* 164, no. 1 (2010): 9–15; Harriet J. Kitzman, David L. Olds, Robert E. Cole, Carole A. Hanks, Elizabeth A. Anson, Kimberly J. Arcoleo, Dennis W. Luckey, Michael D. Knudtson, Charles R. Henderson Jr, and John R. Holmberg, "Enduring Effects of Prenatal and Infancy Home Visiting by Nurses on Children," *Archives of Pediatrics and Adolescent Medicine* 164, no. 5 (2010): 412–418.

18. Ross McKay suggests that the reverse can be argued; the means test creates social cohesion in that it represents a social compact between the fortunate and unfortunate members of society, which asserts that the former are bound by the obligation to assist the latter. And that this is seen as just because it excludes those who are able to pay for themselves from claiming an unfair share of public benefits. Ross McKay, "The New Zealand Model: Targeting in an Income Tested System," in Neil Gilbert, ed., *Targeting Social Benefits: International Perspectives and Trends* (New Brunswick, NJ: Transaction Publishers, 2001).

19. Corporation for National and Community Service, http://www.nationalservice.gov/programs/americorps, accessed October 25, 2015.

20. Jeff Zeleny, "Obama Issues Call for Public Service," The Politics and Government blog of *The New York Times* (December 5, 2007). http://thecaucus.blogs.nytimes.com/2007/12/05/obama-issues-call-for-public-service/?_r=0, accessed December 24, 2015.

21. John McCain, "Putting the 'National' in National Service," *Washington Monthly* (October 2001).

22. Robert Nisbet, *The Quest for Community* (Oxford: Oxford University Press, 1953).

AUTHOR INDEX

Aaronson, Daniel, 182n8
Abebe, Daniel, 180n76
Abel-Smith, Brian, 193n45
Ackerman, Bruce, 157n30
Adema, Willem, 123, 155n7, 156n17, 192nn24–27
Aguiar, Mark, 170nn25–26, 170nn31–32
Alaez-Aller, Ricardo, 191n14
Alcock, Pete, 191n14
Alderman, Liz, 167n62
Alesina, Alberto, 179n58
Alger, Horatio, 91, 94
Allen, Jodie T. 156n16, 166n50
Alm, Richard, 170n31
Almond, Douglas, 186n53
Alstott, Anne, 157n30
Alvaredo, Facundo, 173n59
American Political Science Association
    Task Force on Inequality and American
    Democracy, 179n53
Andersen, Torben M. 157n25
Anderson, R. J. 162n66
Andrews, Dan, 180n70, 180n72
Anson, Elizabeth, 200n17
Arcoleo, Kimberly J. 200n17
Argyle, Michael, 181n77
Aristotle, 47, 168n5
Armor, David, 192n32, 193n38
Armour, Philip, 57t, 171n36, 171n43, 171n45,
    172n49, 172n52
Arnold, 181n79
Arnold, James, 176n15
Ashok, Vivekinan, 166n51
Atkinson, Anthony, 157n23, 173n59, 189n25
Atwood, Craig S. 187n13
Axelsson, Runo, 198n41, 199n47

Bagehot, 192n28
Bakija, Jon M. 197n29, 198n32
Banerjee, Abhijit V. 174n74
Banerjee, Sudipto, 161n50
Barnes, Helen, 185n43, 185n45, 186n47
Barnett, W. Steven, 185n43, 186n50
Baroni, Elisa, 198n41, 199n47
Barr, Nicholas, 169n15
Bassok, Daphna, 197n23
Baumberg, Ben, 193n37

Beauchamp, Jonathan P. 187n13
Becker, Gary, 99, 170n25, 185n40, 186n51, 195n6
Belfield, Clive, 185n43, 186n50
Bell, Daniel, 4, 5, 10, 155n4, 157n34, 168n3
Bell, Kate, 193n37
Bell, Stephen, 197n24
Bellamy, Edward, 46–47, 69, 133, 194n1
Benjamin, Daniel J. 187n13
Bentham, Jeremy, 8, 156n21
Benton, Gregor, 180n73
Benzeval, Michaela, 177n29, 178n34
Bergh, Andreas, 190n5
Besharov, Douglas, 33, 159n18, 160n36, 162n2,
    165n29, 165n33, 165n37, 185n44, 186n49,
    197n27, 199n2, 199n5, 200n11
Best, Joel, 165n31
Bhattacharya, Joydeep, 157n25
Biel, Anders, 191n7
Biggs, Andrew, 198n36
Bildt, Carl, 5
Bishaw, Alemayehu, 161n60
Bjorklund, Anders, 188n22
Blank, Rebecca, 19, 20, 33, 159n26,
    159n30, 165n28
Blomberg, Staffan, 190n5
Bloome, Deirdre, 94, 183n14, 184n21
Blow, Charles, 159n22
Boarini, Romina, 164n22
Bok, Derek, 166n45
Booth, Charles, 15, 157n1
Bostic, Amie, 193n51
Bourguignon, F. 189n25
Bowring, John, 156n21
Bradshaw, Jonathon, 161n48
Brady, David, 193n51
Brandon, Peter D. 184n23
Brandt, Richard, 171n40
Brannon, Ike, 174n73
Bratsberg, Bernt, 188n22
Brault, Matthew W. 187n10
Brewer, M. 200n9
Bridges, Margaret, 197n23
Brinton, Mary, 179n62
Broene, Pam, 197n24
Brooks, David, 181n89
Brooks-Gunn, Jeanne, 196n20

203

Santos, Cezar, 187n7
Saunders, Peter, 73, 176n23, 177n24
Savchuk, Katia, 178n42
Savelyev, Peter A. 185n43
Sawangfa, O. 166n45
Sayer, Liana, 195n9
Sayer, Suzanne, 195n11
Scheiber, Noam, 189n31
Scherman, K.-G. 142, 199n43
Schieber, Sylvester, 198n36
Schlesinger, Arthur, Jr., 16
Schoenberg, Nara, 165n27
Schor, Juliet, 170n27
Schumpeter, Joseph, 8, 10, 86–87, 97, 155n9, 156n19, 181n81, 184n31
Schwartz, Barry, 175n78
Schwarz, Norbert, 181n77
Schweinhart, Lawrence, 185n43, 185n45, 186n47, 186n50
Scott, Robert, III, 160n38
Searcey, Dionne, 173n67
Seitz, Victoria, 102, 186n47
Sendi, Pedram, 170n34
Sensenbrenner, Julia, 179n62
Shapiro, Jeremy, 176n19
Sheffield, Rachel, 161n56
Shelton, Kathryn, 172n54, 179n52, 182n4
Sherwood, Robert, 193n42
Shollenberger, Tracey, 180n64
Short, K. 160n37
Short, Kathleen, 159n32
Sidora, Kimberly, 200n17
Simey, M. B. 157n1
Simey, T. 157n1
Simon, Bill, 77
Simon, Kosali, 168n11, 171n45
Simpson, George, 179n59
Sinozich, Sofi, 165n25
Sipila, Jorma, 195n13, 195n16
Skinner, Martie L. 186n49
Skocpol, Theda, 191n8
Slavov, Sita, 174n76
Smeeding, Timothy M. 76, 168n11, 171n36, 177n31, 178n35, 187n5, 189n26
Smith, Adam, 8, 23–24, 39, 161n58
Smith, Albert Vernon, 187n13
Smith, G. D. 177n30, 177n32
Smith, Jessica, 162n2, 162n67
Smith, Ralph, 196n19
Smith, Steven Rathgeb, 155n9
Snellman, Kaisa, 184n27
Snow, C. P. 17
Snyder, Mark, 191n7
Solberg, Erna, 6
Solnick, Sara, 84, 180n74

Solon, Gary, 182n8, 183n13
Soros, George, 77
Sousa, Sonia, 192n32, 193n38
Spar, Karen, 160n42, 193nn9–10, 199n3
Sparling, Joseph, 186n49
Specht, Harry, 189n29
Spitz, Herman H. 185n44
Spreen, Thomas Luke, 187n8
Squires, Becky, 159n33
Stefanov, Stoyan, 170n28
Steinbeck, John, 68
Steuerle, Eugene, 82, 180n65, 197n29, 198n32
Stevens, J. 188n23
Stevenson, Richard, 156n14
Steyer, Tom, 77, 178n42
Stiglitz, Joseph, 65–66, 67, 106, 175n2, 175n79, 178n36, 187n4, 189n26
Stoesz, David, 192n35
Strachey, James, 157n32
Strack, Fritz, 181n77
Strain, Michael, 174n76
Struening, Elmer L. 162n1
Sturm, Roland, 164n15
Sullivan, James, 158n16, 160n41, 160nn44–45, 161n52
Sunden, Annika, 198n40
Sunesson, Sune, 190n5
Surrey, Stanley, 174n70
Susser, Ezra, 162n1
Sutton, Robert, 194n4
Svetlik, Ivan, 155n9
Swank, D. 191n14
Switek, M. 166n45

Tabachnick, B. 188n23
Tach, Laura, 113, 189n32
Tait, William, 156n21
Tanenhaus, Sam, 167n54
Tatelbaum, Robert, 200n17
Tavernise, Sabrina, 159n20
Taylor, Paul, 159n34, 160n35, 198n39
Terrell, Paul, 190n2
Theobald, Robert, 157n30
Thomas, Gail, 165n26
Thompson, Jeffrey P. 171n36
Titmuss, Kay, 193n45
Titmuss, Richard, 126, 127, 128–29, 174n70, 192n34, 193nn44–45
Tomasky, Michael, 178n40
Torfing, Jacob, 155n9
Townsend, P. 192n35
Townsend, Reanne, 165n26
Treasury Department, US, 172n53
Treasury Inspector for Tax Administration, 198n37

SUBJECT INDEX

AARP. *See* American Association of Retired Persons
Abecedarian Project, 102–3
absolute monetary gains, 113–14
abundance. *See also* wealth
　challenge of having too much, 36–41
　Keynes on, 40–41
Additional Child Care Tax Credit, 148
Adema, Willem, 123
advertising, 16–17
The Affluent Society (Galbraith), 16, 17, 29–30
age
　inequality and, 58–59
　poverty and, 20–21
alternative progressive agenda, 40
American Association of Retired Persons (AARP), 77–78, 159n33, 178nn45–46
American Recovery and Reinvestment Act, 30, 163n10
anarchy, 8
aristocracy, 91
Aristotle, 47
assortative mating, 107
athletes, 60, 85–86

basic necessities, 23–24
Becker, Gary, 99, 170n25
Bell, Daniel
　on capitalism, 10
　on credit, 10
　on end of ideology, 4
　on progressive agenda, 4
Bellamy, Edward, 46–47
Bentham, Jeremy, 8
birth control, 177n26
Blank, Rebecca
　on malnutrition, 33
　on poverty, 19, 20
Booth, Charles, 15
Brookings Institution study, 114
Brown, Jerry, 53
Brown, Willie, 77
Buchanan, James, 79
Buffet rule, 38–39, 48
Buffett, Warren, 82

Bureau of Labor Statistics Consumer Expenditure Survey, 21
Burkhauser, Richard, 56

capital gains tax, 56–58, 172n49
capitalism
　Bell on, 10
　creative destruction in, 8
　credit under, 10
　on family, 97
　globalization and, 82
　Hirschman on, 10
　intellectual class and, 86–88
　progressives on, 10, 11–12
　religion and, 10
　Schumpeter on, 10, 86–87
　Soviet Union and hostility toward, 10
　Weber on, 10
　welfare state relating to, 6
Carlyle, Thomas, 8
cash transfers, 71, 171n45, 176n19
CBO. *See* Congressional Budget Office
Census Bureau, 19–21
CEOs. *See* chief executive officers
Chicago School of Economics, 8
chief executive officers (CEOs), 60
child care research, 137–39, 196nn20–21. *See also* daycare
Child Welfare League of America, 195n11
China, 82
chronic poverty, 25, 148, 162n2
Clark, Gregory, 98–100, 105
classical liberalism, 7, 8
Clinton, Bill, 18, 33
college attendance rates, 94, 183n10
college campus rape, 32–33, 164n23, 165nn26–27
Columbia University Population Research Center, 162n69
Congressional Budget Office (CBO), 56–58, 59
conservatives
　on inequality, 65–66
　liberals compared to, 156n18
　on universalism, 119
Consumer Price Index Research Series (CPI-U-RS), 158n16

211